WHOSE IS THE KINGDOM?

John Arden was born in Barnsley, Yorkshire, in 1930. While studying architecture at Cambridge and Edinburgh universities, he began to write plays, four of which have been produced at the Royal Court Theatre: *The Waters of Babylon, Live Like Pigs, Serjeant Musgrave's Dance* and *The Happy Haven;* while a fifth, *The Workhouse Donkey,* was produced at the Festival Theatre, Chichester. For a year he held an Annual Fellowship in Playwriting at Bristol University, and Bristol Old Vic produced *Ironhand*, his free adaptation of Goethe's *Goetz von Berlichingen. Armstrong's Last Goodnight* was first produced at the Glasgow Citizens' Theatre and later at the National Theatre. *Left-Handed Liberty* was specially commissioned by the Corporation of London to commemorate the 750th Anniversary of Magna Carta and was produced at the Mermaid Theatre. He is married to Margaretta D'Arcy with whom he has collaborated on several plays. Arden's first novel, *Silence Among the Weapons* (1982), was short-listed for the Booker Prize. A collection of essays written with Margaretta D'Arcy entitled *Awkward Corners* was published in 1988.

Margaretta D'Arcy is Irish and has worked with improvisational and theatre techniques since the fifties. Her work with Arden includes *The Business of Good Government* (1960), *The Happy Haven* (1960), *Ars Longa, Vita Brevis* (1963), *Friday's Hiding* (1965), *The Royal Pardon* (1966), *Muggins is a Martyr* (1968), *The Hero Rises Up* (1968), *The Ballygombeen Bequest* (1972), *The Island of the Mighty* (1972), *Keep the People Moving* (for radio, 1972), *The Non-Stop Connolly Show* (1975), *Vandaleur's Folly* (1978) and *The Little Gray Home in the West* (1978). Her play *A Pinprick of History* was performed at the Almost Free Theatre, London in 1977. *Tell Them Everything* (1981) is an account of her imprisonment in Armagh Gaol. She is a member of Aosdána, the Irish artists' association, and receives from it a grant to explore alternatives to Judaeo–Christian patriarchal culture; in pursuit of which she has organised an autonomous women's group, the Galway Women's Entertainment.

WHOSE IS THE KINGDOM?

JOHN ARDEN &
MARGARETTA D'ARCY

A METHUEN PAPERBACK

ACKNOWLEDGEMENTS

Books quoted or consulted include:
ALLEGRO, J.M. *The Dead Sea scrolls* Penguin, 2nd edn., 1964. ARDEN, J. and D'ARCY, M. *Awkward corners* Methuen, 1988. ARMSTRONG, K. *The gospel according to woman* Pan, new edn., pbk., 1987. BOWDER, D. *The age of Constantine and Julian* Elek, 1978. CHADWICK, H. *The early church* Penguin, pbk., 1968. CROSS, F.L. ed. *The Oxford dictionary of the Christian church* OUP, 1957. EUSEBIUS. *Ecclesiastical history* Penguin, pbk., 1965. EUSEBIUS. *Life of Constantine* Bagster, 1845. GIBBON, E. *Decline and fall of the Roman Empire* Penguin, pbk., 1982. JONES, A.H.M. *Constantine and the conversion of Europe* University of Toronto Press, new edn., pbk., 1979. LEWIS, N. and REINHOLD, M. *Roman civilization: a sourcebook. Vol. 2: the Empire* Harper & Row, new edn., pbk., 1966. *The new Encyclopaedia Britannica* Encyclopaedia Britannica Inc., 15th edn., 1985. PAGELS, E. *The Gnostic gospels* Penguin, new edn., pbk., 1982. STEVENSON, J. ed *The new Eusebius: documents illustrating the history of the church to AD 337* SPCK, pbk., 1987.

With thanks to Dr Cathy King. Ashmolean Museum: BBC Reference Library: Picture Publicity. BBC programme material compiled and edited by Penny Leicester. Designed by Eve White. Illustrations, Pip Moon.

A METHUEN PAPERBACK

First published in Great Britain as a paperback original in 1988 by Methuen London Ltd, 11 New Fetter Lane, London EC4P 4EE and in the United States of America by Methuen Inc, 29 West 35th Street, New York, NY 10001

Printed in Great Britain by Redwood Burn Ltd, Trowbridge, Wilts

British Library Cataloguing in Publication Data

Arden, John
  Whose is the kingdom?
  I. Title   II. D'Arcy, Margaretta
  822'.914   PR6051.R3

  ISBN 0-413-18710-1

Copyright © 1988 by John Arden & Margaretta D'Arcy
Programme material copyright © BBC January 1988

CONTENTS

NICENE CREED·AD325

We believe in one God, the Father, Almighty, Maker of all things visible and invisible; and in one Lord Jesus Christ, the Son of God, begotten of the Father, only-begotten, that is to say from the essence (ousia) of the Father; God from God, Light from Light, true God from true God, begotten not made, of-the-same-essence (homo-ousios) as the Father; by whom all things were made, both in heaven and in earth; who, for us men and for our salvation, came down, and was incarnate; was made man; suffered and rose again the third day; ascended into heaven; and is coming to judge the living and the dead; and in the Holy Spirit.

And those who say "There was when he was not," and "before his generation he was not," and "he came into being out of nothing," or those who claim that the Son of God is of other substance or essence, or created, or alterable, or mutable; the Catholic and Apostolic Church anathematizes.

GENERAL CONCEPTS

These nine plays cover some twenty-five years of the reign of the Emperor Constantine, during which Christianity changed from an illegal – and often persecuted – series of revolutionary cults into an institutionalised and dominant religion of Empire. The journeys and adventures of the characters in the story wind through an ideolgical landscape of religions, philosophies and superstitions-Greco-Roman polytheism, sceptical rationalism, Judaism, goddess-worship, druidism, Zoroastrianism, sun-worship and Mithraism; and all the sub-divisions of these which were co-opted to make up the various aspects of Christianity, a sort of cultural asset-stripping whose effects are still with us today. Spirituality, materialism, magic, and power-politics combine to use and abuse the religious yearnings of people inside and outside the Empire, for the preservation of a threatened regime. The story is seen through the eyes of a rational Greek, Kybele, who tells it to the druids of Ireland: a nation unconquered by Rome but soon to develop and disseminate its own brand of missionary Christianity in a collapsing Roman world where the concept of 'one church, one culture, one power-bloc' seemed about to disappear for ever.

John Arden. Margaretta D'Arcy.

THE BIRTH OF AN IDEA

It was in 1981 that I first approached John Arden with the proposition that he and Margaretta D'Arcy might like to consider writing a serial based on the Christian story. I was prompted by the fact that 1981 marked the 40th anniversary of the first broadcast of "The Man Born to be King", that remarkable sequence of plays by Dorothy L Sayers about the life of Christ which had survived initial uncertainties, some hostility and even outrage (it happened at a time when the portrayal of Christ in vision on the stage was strictly forbidden) to become one of the best loved, and most frequently requested, items in the radio drama repertoire.

A number of developments in recent years seemed to me to make the anniversary of more than academic interest. "The Man Born to be King" was written and broadcast in the middle of the Second World War, with Dorothy L Sayers referring frequently in her correspondence with the BBC to the activities of Hitler which coincided with her work on the scripts. It was a time when the world was going through great travail, when the House of Commons could consider a motion to set aside a whole day for the nation to be called to prayer, and when the idea of presenting the life of Christ in dramatic form was frankly revolutionary.

Since then, of course, attitudes and customs had changed a great deal. Churchgoing had certainly declined. The nature of belief had become the subject of debate within the Church itself. Such discoveries as that of the Gnostic gospels, only relatively recently translated and discussed, gave us cause to look afresh at the early history of Christianity. Reason and belief had perhaps never been so hard pressed to find reconciliation.

It was with these things in mind that we held our first discussions about a potential serial. We parted and thought further and did some reading. We were agreed that it would not be appropriate simply to re-tell the life of Christ from a different angle. That had already been done many times in books and films, plays and television serials over the past forty years, exploring almost all legitimate areas of speculation. It was not so much the events of Christ's life but the way in which they had subsequently been interpreted that had become the centre of enquiry.

The writers returned, bearing Constantine. Under his rule, the Roman Empire adopted Christianity. Under his rule, the Council of Nicaea had opted for the Pauline orthodoxy. His investigation of the nature of Christianity surely paralleled our own? Besides, he had succeeded to the imperial purple while in York; might that not be an appropriate place to begin?

It was, I think, an inspired choice of period, though at that stage none of us realised precisely where it would lead us. Six years were to pass before the scripts reached studio and production, and in that time the process of writing and research, discussion and revision had pursued the trail through countries, and the lives of characters, not envisaged in the original broad synopsis.

The result is a sequence of plays; not documentaries, still less an academic argument for any single truth. Like all good plays they involve one emotionally: they are passionate and partisan and they stimulate thought. In concentrating on the politics of a historical period in which Christianity emerged for the first time in the centre of world affairs, they should appeal to believers and non-believers with comparable force. It was a central part of the authors' concept that they should be accompanied by structured debate amongst contemporary figures – and that is how, on radio, they have been first presented. As a contribution to an even wider discussion of eternal issues, I think they do all that we hoped for in 1981.

Richard Imison, Deputy Head of Drama, BBC Radio

'Three hundred and five A.D. The Empire of Rome:
So vast it had become
So unwieldy from shore to shore
They decided to divide it,
By agreement, into four.
Four great men over four huge regions,
Bound by their marriage, bound by religion
Each with his tax-gatherers, each with his legions,
Above all, to hold safe the border,
Above all, to maintain good order,
Above all, to drive down dissent.
All new notions, bright ideas,
By word-of-mouth or pen-and-ink,
Are subject now to punishment.
Obedience, loyalty, the sole requirement.
But nowhere does the Empire now lament
The loss of loyalty more than among these four great men
Themselves, as they crouch and cast their envious eyes
The width of the world. One of them dies:
In the north-west corner. He has a son, to carry the line:
A strong young man called Constantine.
Young Constantine in the city of York
Surveys the Empire, prepares his work.'

WEST	EAST	THE CHRISTIANS
		298 Expelled from army
		303 Diocletian's great persecution
		305 Persecution ceases
306 Constantine (Caesar)		306 Galerius and Maximin Daza persecute
Maxentius (usurper)		
307 Return of Herculius (Maximian). Alliance with Constantine (m. Fausta)		
308 Constantine Augustus		
Licinius Augustus ⎱ The 6	Galerius Augustus	
Maxentius Augustus ⎰ Emperors	Maximin Daza Augustus	
Herculius (Maximian) Augustus		
310 Death of Herculius (Maximian)	311 Death of Galerius	311 Galerius recants. Maximin Daza Persecutes
311 Alliance of Licinius and Constantine	313 Licinius defeats	
312 ✕ Milvian Bridge: Constantine defeats and kills Maxentius	Maximin Daza	

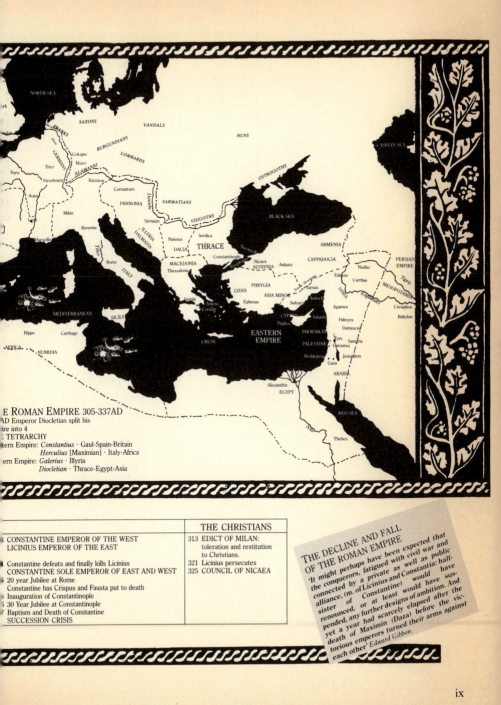

THE ROMAN EMPIRE 305-337AD

305 AD Emperor Diocletian split his
Empire into 4
: TETRARCHY
Western Empire: *Constantius* · Gaul-Spain-Britain
Herculius [Maximian] · Italy-Africa
Eastern Empire: *Galerius* · Illyria
Diocletian · Thrace-Egypt-Asia

Map labels (north to south, west to east):
NORTH SEA · SAXONS · VANDALS · HUNS · CASPIAN SEA · FRANKS · BURGUNDIANS · LOMBARDS · Cologne · GERMANY · Mainz · OSTROGOTHS · Paris · Trier · ALAMANNI · Strasbourg · Ratisbon · Carnuntum · Autun · Milan · PANNONIA · SARMATIANS · BLACK SEA · Ravenna · Sirmium · VISIGOTHS · ARMENIA · Marseille · ILLYRIA · DALMATIA · Naissus · Serdica · DACIA · THRACE · CAPPADOCIA · PERSIAN EMPIRE · Rome · ITALY · MACEDONIA · Constantinople · Nicaea · Ankara · Nisibis · Edessa · Carrhae · MESOPOTAMIA · Thessalonica · BITHYNIA · Tarsus · SYRIA · Tigris · Delphi · PHRYGIA · Antioch · Apamea · Ctesiphon · Athens · LYDIA · ASIA MINOR · Seleucia · Babylon · Corinth · Ephesus · CYPRUS · Salamis · Palmyra · MEDITERRANEAN · SICILY · Paphos · Damascus · PHOENICIA · Tyre · Samaria · Hippo · Carthage · CRETE · EASTERN EMPIRE · PALESTINE · Caesarea · AFRICA · NUMIDIA · Bethlehem · Jerusalem · Gaza · ARABIA · Alexandria · EGYPT · RED SEA · Thebes

---

	THE CHRISTIANS
CONSTANTINE EMPEROR OF THE WEST LICINIUS EMPEROR OF THE EAST	313 EDICT OF MILAN: toleration and restitution to Christians.
Constantine defeats and finally kills Licinius CONSTANTINE SOLE EMPEROR OF EAST AND WEST	321 Licinius persecutes 325 COUNCIL OF NICAEA
20 year Jubilee at Rome Constantine has Crispus and Fausta put to death Inauguration of Constantinople 30 Year Jubilee at Constantinople Baptism and Death of Constantine SUCCESSION CRISIS	

THE DECLINE AND FALL
OF THE ROMAN EMPIRE

'It might perhaps have been expected that
the conquerors, fatigued with civil war and
connected by a private as well as public
alliance, (m. of Licinius and Constantia: half-
sister of Constantine) would have
renounced, or at least would have sus-
pended, any further designs of ambition. And
yet a year had scarcely elapsed after the
death of Maximin (Daza) before the vic-
torious emperors turned their arms against
each other' *Edward Gibbon.*

ix

4TH CENTURY TRANSITIONS. . . An Empire reeling in shock.

3rd century AD: The Roman Empire almost foundered in prolonged convulsions of barbarian invasions, incessant civil wars, and a worsening economic crisis. In this critical situation survival lay in military strength. From the reign of Septimus Severus (AD 193-211) imperial power was openly based on the armed forces. The State was increasingly militarised while the soldiery, enriched by legal donatives and illegal extortions, became the new privileged and powerful class supplanting the civilian propertied ruling class.

Under the Severan dynasty (193-235) a degree of stability was maintained in the Empire. This was shattered, however, by the rebellion of Maximinus in AD 235. Half a century of internal chaos followed, accompanied by devastating epidemics, depopulation, and runaway inflation.

Armies became a law unto themselves, elevating and liquidising emperors at will. From AD 235 to the accession of Diocletian in AD 284, twenty six 'soldier Emperors' were proclaimed. All but one met a voilent death. Unity of the State cracked; Gaul was temporarily detached from the Empire as its defences slipped. Barbarian hoards penetrated at numerous points, even into Italy: one German tribe advancing to the very gates of Rome.

Where military solutions failed, the emperors resorted to the expensive and ineffective policy of 'buying off' attackers: making regular payments to peoples beyond the frontiers. In an attempt to meet these military and administrative costs a reckless debasement of the Imperial coinage was undertaken. The new currency, however, was considered so worthless that the government refused to accept its own coinage, insisting instead on payment of tax in kind. The shortfalls in fiscal resources led to numerous abuses of authority by civil and military officials – confiscations, tax increases, requisitions, and looting by the soldiery which further shook the economy.

Imperial government began to interfere increasingly in municipal government, believing that social immobility was the answer to economic crisis. Hereditary 'castes' were created eg. the *curiales* of the propertied classes who were now compelled to discharge the once coveted duties of municipal councils.

The functions of the merchant and artisan guilds (originally of privileged status) also became obligatory and hereditary.

If the Roman Empire was to be saved, a saviour was needed. In AD 284 "By the decision of the generals and tribunes, Valerius Diocletian, commander of the Palace Guards, was chosen as Emperor because of his wisdom" – Aurelius Victor, *Lives of the Emperors*.

Diocletian's accession was not without its share of suspicion and bloodshed. A man of humble origin, Diocletian was educated in the militarist world of the late 3rd century. But he was no reckless or foolish commander. Even from his detractors, such as Lactantius, arises the image of a determined, hard-working, clear-headed man. But any new emperor's position was precarious. To secure against usurpers Diocletian surrounded himself with successors and colleagues. In AD285 Diocletian raised his long standing friend and colleague Maximian (Herculius) to the status of Caesar, a year later to that of Augustus. Together, as joint rulers, they waged unceasing and successful war against barbarians, rebellious provinces, and usurpers in all parts of the Empire. Although they worked in separate spheres of influence there was no question of a division of Empire between East and West; their mutual objective was to restore unity and security to the whole Roman State. They still saw themselves emphatically as Romans and guardians of Roman traditions.

Nevertheless, in AD 290/1, after a major victory in the East, when Diocletian planned a joint celebration with Maximian, they chose Milan, not Rome, to host their triumph. This event officially recognised an unspoken truth of the late 3rd century that the City on the Tiber need not be the centre of the Roman Empire. The real 'Rome' was wherever the Emperor was. This fact was increasingly realised after AD 293 when Imperial power was multiplied again. Constantius Chlorus (father of Constantine 'The Great') and Gaius Galerius were chosen as two more co-Caesars. Trier, Milan, Salonica and Nicomedia all achieved new status as favoured Imperial residences. But these rulers were constantly travelling, and when the Emperor moved, the centre of government moved with him.

Under Diocletian's guiding influence this united tetrarchy, backed by military strength, set about restoring order to a post anarchic Empire.

The separation of military and civil lines of authority was of primary importance. As a result of this, however, the Imperial bureaucracy, already huge and lumbering, was enlarged still further.

Diocletian divided the whole Empire into 12 dioceses (6 in the East and 6 in the West), subdivided into a total of about 100 provinces. To diffuse power further Vice Prefects were appointed; an extra tier of authority between the Emperor and his Provincial Governors.

Diocletian issued new coinage – but the cost of on-going wars, major building programmes, and the ever growing bureaucracy set inflation soaring once more. New poll and land taxes were introduced covering all provinces (previously Italy had been exempt from such impositions) In support of this tax system and in answer to depopulation (resulting in a critical man-power shortage) the policy of social immobility was enforced with increasing rigidity.

Although these reforms and others made progress towards the restoration of order, the tetrarchy system did not survive Diocletian's illness and subsequent abdication in AD 305.

Bloody and complex rivalry ensued involving Maxentius, Licinius, Galerius, Constantine and others. In AD 313 Constantine and Licinius emerged as joint rulers, but from AD 324-337 Constantine was sole Emperor.

With the Imperial administration Constantine extended and completed many of Diocletian's reforms. Military changes were also made. The Praetorian Guard, which had fought for Maxentius against Constantine in 312, were disbanded and their camp pulled down. On the frontiers Constantine reduced the strength of his forces, concentrating resources on mobile troops, centrally positioned and under his direct control. Constantine also continued a trend initiated in the 3rd century of making cavalry, not infantry, the basic military arm of the Empire. The traditional military supremacy of the Roman infantryman was gone. Now the Empire employed highly barbarianised armies, weaponry and tactics.

It had long been realised that Rome was no longer the true centre of the Empire. Thus, in AD 330 when Constantine dedicated his new Imperial capital, Constantinople (on the site of Byzantium), the transition was not difficult to achieve. This movement marks the beginning of the split between the Western and Eastern arms of the Roman Empire. The first official division of Imperial power was in AD 335. This developing separation was matched by a division of language. The Byzantine court and Eastern Empire used Greek, while Latin was retained in the West. The old bilingual tradition of a once united Roman Empire was gradually extinguished.

In religious matters Diocletian had leaned emphatically on Rome's traditional gods, but he also asserted a more definite doctrine of their relationship to the Emperor. Also, as imperial rule moved increasingly towards absolutism, making closer contact with the East and its traditions of ruler worship, the imperial house took on the attributes of a divine right monarchy.

Under Diocletian obeisance in the presence of the Emperor became fashionable and the address 'Dominus noster' replaced the earlier concept of the Emperor as 'first among equals'. Emperors adopted the radiate crown and the use of rich clothing. Aurelius Victor wrote of Diocletian: '. . . he was the first to wear a cloak embroidered in gold and to covet shoes of silk and purple decorated with a great number of gems.'

Colossal imperial statues, regal palaces and ritualised court protocol are all typical of the age – devices and props used by Diocletian, Constantine and colleagues to elevate their apparent stature to that of godlike monarchs. But Diocletian and Constantine were not merely revelling egocentrically in these public displays of magnificence; they *used* them to 'hypnotise' subjects and obtain loyalty. The army's traditional oath of allegiance to the Emperor had long since lost its credibility and Diocletian and Constantine realised that if the soldiers were allowed to recall their recent power to make and break emperors, their own fates could be as short as those of their predecessors. Therefore the Emperor raised himself above his subjects, isolating his position with the intention of appearing sacrosanct. It was psychological not legal authority which was represented by these visual displays. It was also longstanding Eastern tradition for rulers to demonstrate their power by blatant shows of wealth. Eusebius in his Life of Constantine, describes the Emperor's entrance to a general synod in AD 325: . . . "dazzling the eyes of all with the splendour of his purple robe and sparkling with firey rays as it were, adorned for the occasion as he was with an extraordinary splendour of gold and jewels.'

Diocletian, like several other Roman rulers, believed that suppression of the Christians was necessary for the unity and security of the Empire. In contrast Constantine (whether genuinely inspired or politically motivated) decided that for success in military and secular affairs adoption of the Christian faith was the answer.

For the sake of unity however Constantine accepted the continuation of paganism and advocated a balance between the two faiths. The Emperor's new capital, Constantinople, both spiritually and architecturally, displayed a contrasting combination of a receding pagan religion side by side with rising Christianity.

J. K. Wortley

THE ROAD TO NICAEA

There is a tradition, more ancient than the oldest church building, that John the son of Zebedee, the disciple whom Jesus loved, alone of all the apostles achieved old age. Later Jerome, the feisty scholar hermit of Bethlehem, built on that belief describing how in the feebleness of old age John would have to be carried to religious services. At the very end of his life the last apostle preached with brevity and extreme simplicity and his sermon was always the same. All he would say was, "My little children, love one another, that is enough." The practicality of the fisherman had won over the mysticism of the evangelist. He did not ask the impossible – he did not ask them to agree with one another.

In the years between the death of a carpenter from Nazareth on a hill called Calvary and the elaborate politicking of the Council of Nicaea, that command of love had been honoured as much in the breach as in the observance. Just as the summers of childhood brighten with the acquisition of years, in the same way the early years of the Christian story have been burnished into a golden age of selfless idealism and faithful accord.

That golden age of harmony never existed. Every religious controversy troubling mitred and non-mitred heads today can be found in the first three hundred years of Christian history – only written larger and with a more vituperative hand. Problems of misunderstanding (exactly *how* often do I have to forgive, Lord?), jockeying for position (grant, Lord, that we may sit one on your right hand and one on your left when you come into your glory) and a feeling that faith was only for the righteous elite (see, he eats with publicans and sinners) bedevilled even Jesus' ministry.

And after his death, the disagreements would intensify. All the twentieth century's religious questions were forged in the three hundred years between Christ and Constantine – the role of women, the need for church discipline and uniformity, the regulation of sexual behaviour, the nature of belief and of God's purpose and the enigma of Jesus himself, man-god, God or man. Above all these debates there loomed one issue which may sound more secular than sacred but which remains the single most important point dividing Christian factions today – the question of the magisterium – or teaching authority – does any single Christian have a claim to it, do all Christians have an obligation to seek it? Is the claim of authority over the mustard seed kingdom blasphemous, or just ridiculous, or is it an authentic search for divine inspiration – the greatest necessity for the survival of truth?

Because we look back on the early days of Christianity through centuries of faith in the man-god of Galilee, who healed on the Sabbath, blessed lepers, and healed the unclean woman, it is easy to overlook the picture which allegiance to "The Way", as Christianity was first known, would have presented to the non-Judaic pagan world. In Jewish eyes, Jesus was a taboo breaking blasphemer who left few religious sensibilities uncrushed and who went beyond what was permissible even for the most eccentric wonder-working rabbi. He had freed men from their sins on his *own* authority. He had claimed to be the son of the God of Abraham, Isaac, and Jacob. This had been done without any cloak of an esoteric philosophy. Yeshua bar Joseph spoke to a God he called "Abba" – not Lord or master but "Dad" – this was an unbearable outrage.

A non-Jewish audience would find Jesus' claims less appalling. In many ways Christianity fitted in well with the religious ideas of a world caught between the waning of Hellenism and the early years of imperial Rome. For years there had been a reawakening of personal and emotional religious awareness. In Rome itself eastern mystery cults became popular – devotion to Isis and Osiris, Dionysios and Ariadne, Demeter and Triptolemus and worship of the Magna Mater, Phrygian Cybele and her castrated shepherd consort, Attis.

To the agnostic observer, the early Christians were first seen as off-beat Jews. Later, as "The Way" ventured more into the Gentile world, it would have seemed yet another one of the near eastern saviour cults. But there were important differences. The followers of the Way, whether Jewish, Greek, or Roman, had inherited the jealousy of the Hebrew God. No compromise was possible. Dual religious nationality was out of the question – a prohibition which would cost many lives. Also Christianity was emphatically not for an elite – spiritual or social. Slave and freeman learned that the truth only remained hidden from men because they did not open their ears. There were no secrets. All you needed, said Jesus, were ears with which to hear.

Added to all of this there was a conviction stronger than logic, held from Rome to Babylon in those years we think of as the last of the old age and the first of the new, that the future held the promise of an age of peace and justice.

Christianity could answer many of these hopes. One of its weaker points was its simplicity – not only were there no arcane formulae – it was a faith with remarkably few abstract ideas. Its largest teachings have been expressed in domestic parables. God was a father prodigal in his love waiting for, not demanding, the return of a miscreant child; good teaching cannot come from evil men any more than good fruit can come from a rotten tree. The Nicaean debates about homoousios – of one nature, or homoiousios – of like nature, are as far removed as we are from the Galilean who rode in triumph on a donkey and predicted his own death.

But the abstractions were not long in coming. Paul's experience of conversion on the Damascus road was more than personally traumatic. It transformed Christianity and launched its ideas into the non-Jewish world. *His* convictions, held with all the single-mindedness of a convert, ensured that Christianity would exist independently of Judaism. Even today there is no Christian unaffected by Pauline thought – the prejudices as well as the insights.

Paul was at one remove from the life which had ended and started on a cross. He never met Jesus and very possibly this is why his letters are so different from the Gospels. He believed in, rather than personally mourned Jesus. He was more concerned with the Jesus who stood beyond time and death, fulfilling the promises of Hebrew scripture and opening them out to the whole world.

In the years before Nicaea, Paul's writings – two thirds of the New Testament letters are his – were used by both sides in many theological debates, both as a storehouse of ideas and as a final court of orthodox appeal. Those like the Donatists and Ebionites, who believed that Jesus was God not man and only appeared to undergo the ignominy and agony of crucifixion, point to Paul's lack of emphasis on Jesus' humanity. The Arians, who would so agitate Constantine by their divisive insistence that Jesus was man only, not God, and was awarded sonship for his goodness, could also claim Paul. Nowhere, they pointed out, does Paul categorically state that Jesus was God. The years which followed Paul's death saw a ferment of Christian dispute – fuelled by enthusiasm, curiosity, insight, and ignorance.

But there was another more brutal element which formed the Christian mind. No one knows exactly when Paul died, but there is a tradition that he was beheaded and Peter crucified in the persecution which followed the great fire of Rome. More persecutions would follow. Christians refused to go through the pantomime of offering incense to successive emperors. Their refusal branded them as fifth columnists unworthy of the protection of the rulers they refused to deify. Those who put their beliefs before civic duty deserved death.

There were many such persecutions – the major persecutions were those of the emperor Decius in 250 AD and Diocletian fifty years later. Both persecutions created martyrs who are still revered today. The church's survival over two imperial antagonisms foreshadowed what would have to happen. The state could not beat the Christians. Sooner or later it would have to join them.

Christianity was moulded by internal conflict as well. Inevitably, as soon as the faith spread geographically, it came to have leading

PEOPLE	BOOKS	EVENTS
618-541 BC. Zoroaster		
469-399 BC. Socrates		
429-347 BC. Plato		
342-270 BC. Epicurus		
7 BC-29 AD. John The Baptist		26/30 AD John the Baptist baptises Jesus
		Jesus' ministry begins
6/4 BC-29/33 AD. Jesus of Nazareth		29/33 AD Jesus crucified
27 BC-14 AD Augustus emperor		
14 AD-37 AD Tiberius emperor		45 AD Paul begins missionary journeys.
	50 AD following. Paul's letters	49 AD Council of Jerusalem.
54 AD-68 AD Nero emperor		c62 AD Death of Paul.
		64 AD Great fire of Rome, and subsequent
		persecution of Christians. Death of Peter.
—	75-100 AD Gospels and rest of books	70 AD Fall of Jerusalem.
	known as the New	
	Testament	
81 AD-96 AD Domitian emperor		
	140 AD Marcion's canon	
	150 AD Approx. Gnostic Gospel of Truth	
	written, perhaps, by Valentinus	
	155 AD following. Justin Martyr's	
	First and second Apologies, and	
	Dialogue with Trypho.	
	196 AD following. Tertullian's Apology,	
	Against Marcion, Against Praxeas	
	230 AD following. Origen's Hexapla,	
	De Principiis, and Against Celsus	250 AD Decian Persecution
306 AD-337 AD Constantine emperor		303 AD Diocletian anti-Christian edicts,
		and persecution.
	325 AD Eusebius' Ecclesiastical History.	325 AD Council of Nicaea

exponents from different cultural backgrounds. Even the most enthusiastic convert, or most rigorous cradle Christian, would have some non-Christian philosophical language. Orthodoxy was influenced by heresy and alternative beliefs.

Stoicism, Platonism, Pythagoreanism, Fatalism, and Zoroastrianism all contributed to the turmoil of debate. Many of the movements which came to be labelled as Christian heresies had in fact begun centuries before Jesus was born. Gnosticism has its roots in a dualism which can be traced back as far as the sixth century BC. Christian gnosticism came to the fore in the second century AD. The world-denying teaching of the old gnostics, who held that the material creation was the work of an anti-God, became intertwined with some of the more ascetic trends in Christianity. Marcion, the shipowning Donatist, identified the creating anti-god of the gnostic thought with the God of the Hebrew Bible who was – he claimed – different from the God of Love of the Gospels.

Ideas were in flux. The ultra orthodox Tertullian, the first important Christian author to write Latin, penned *Against Marcion* and *On the Exclusion of Heretics* and yet died a Montanist attracted by the rigour of that particular school's heretical teaching. Heretics even disagreed among themselves. The Monarchianists, who stressed the oneness of God, were split into two schools – the Adoptionists who held that Jesus was only divine in so far as God's power rested on him, and the Patripassians who held that the Father and Son were so bound together that both felt the pain of crucifixion.

And then there was schism as well as heresy. The Donatists in North Africa could not accept the bishop of Carthage because he had surrendered scripture during Diocletian's persecutions. Earlier the priest Novatian, author of an orthodox work on the Trinity, was disappointed in a papal power bid in 251. He threw his lot in with the hardliners who refused to forgive the Christians who had lapsed during the Decian persecution. His following, orthodox but schismatic, lasted for two hundred years.

Novatian's reaction to his failure to become the bishop of Rome points to another facet of Christian life and belief potentially more dangerous than any heresy. In the kingdom of heaven the first might be last and the last first, but inescapably in the temporal world the waxing of Christianity brought with it the temptation of power. The office of bishop of Rome was the most alluring. Irenaeus, the 2nd century bishop of Lyons, cites the reasons for Rome's importance – the Christian community there was founded by the first among the apostles – Peter, and the apostle of the Gentiles, Paul. The Roman church, says Irenaeus, was both ancient and justly famous for its faith. But there were less spiritual reasons as well. The Fall of Jerusalem in AD 70 meant that the city of David was a spent force. Rome was the centre of the political and commercial world. It stood at the hub of a complex wheel of communication. Rome's claims were apostolically persuasive and administratively uncontestable.

By the time Constantine issued the edict of Milan in 313 promulgating religious toleration towards Christians, the church was the only organisation which could not be contained and controlled within the imperial system. Constantine, despite his vision before the battle of the Milvian Bridge, was to delay his baptism until just before death. He retained the pagan title pontifex maximus which had belonged to the old cult of Neptune. He even permitted a temple to himself to be built. Imperial hands get dirty very easily. Constantine was pragmatic enough to realise that Christianity was an ideal which he could only succumb to personally at the end of life.

He was no theologian, but he was an organiser. He wanted a unified church so he summoned the first ecumenical council. Some 230 bishops attended – more from the East than from the West. The Arian creed of Eusebius of Nicomedia was rejected and that of Eusebius of Caesarea accepted with crucial amendments.

The Council of Nicaea whatever its shortcomings was remarkable as more than an ecclesiastical event. At that time bishops were elected from their communities. Therefore, it was arguably not only the first ecumenical council but also the first democratic international forum the world had known.

The Council gave the orthodox church the Nicene creed, to the Arians it gave little mercy, and to the state it gave both a challenge and dangerous precedent. It is a legacy which will last as long as those with temporal power voice a claim over the beliefs of others. It is a legacy which will last as long as the Christian churches hold that the beliefs of individual teachers, however gifted, are only valid if they conform to a truth which outshines brilliance. And whose is the authority to decide on that truth? That kingdom is still in dispute.

Frances Gumley.

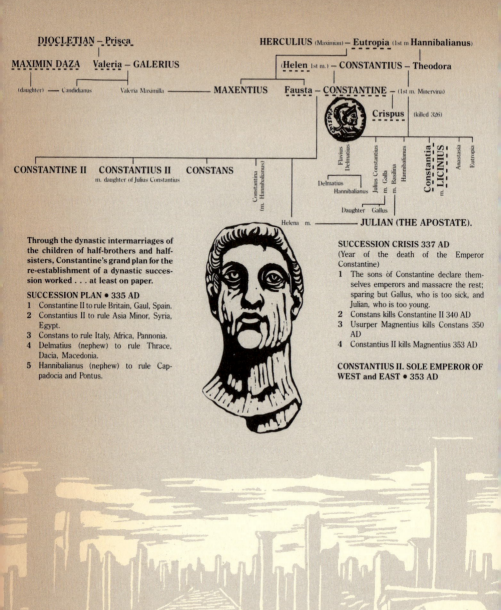

DIOCLETIAN – Prisca

HERCULIUS (Maximian) – **Eutropia** (1st m **Hannibalianus**)

MAXIMIN DAZA   **Valeria** – **GALERIUS**

(**Helen** 1st m.) – **CONSTANTIUS** – Theodora

(daughter) — Candidianus   Valeria Maximilla ————— **MAXENTIUS**   **Fausta** – **CONSTANTINE** – (1st m. Minervina)

Crispus (killed 326)

CONSTANTINE II   **CONSTANTIUS II**   **CONSTANS**
m. daughter of Julius Constantius

Constantina
(m. Hannibalianus)

Flavius
Delmatius

Delmatius
Hannibalianus

Julius Constantius
m. Galla
m. Basilina
Hannibalianus

Constantia
m. **LICINIUS**

Anastasia
Eutropia

Daughter   Gallus

Helena   m. ————— **JULIAN (THE APOSTATE)**.

Through the dynastic intermarriages of the children of half-brothers and half-sisters, Constantine's grand plan for the re-establishment of a dynastic succession worked . . . at least on paper.

SUCCESSION PLAN • 335 AD
1   Constantine II to rule Britain, Gaul, Spain.
2   Constantius II to rule Asia Minor, Syria, Egypt.
3   Constans to rule Italy, Africa, Pannonia.
4   Delmatius (nephew) to rule Thrace, Dacia, Macedonia.
5   Hannibalianus (nephew) to rule Cappadocia and Pontus.

SUCCESSION CRISIS 337 AD
(Year of the death of the Emperor Constantine)
1   The sons of Constantine declare themselves emperors and massacre the rest; sparing but Gallus, who is too sick, and Julian, who is too young.
2   Constans kills Constantine II 340 AD
3   Usurper Magnentius kills Constans 350 AD
4   Constantius II kills Magnentius 353 AD

CONSTANTIUS II. SOLE EMPEROR OF WEST and EAST • 353 AD

"THERE IS NO RELIABLE RECORD OF 4TH CENTURY MUSIC".

My first clues to the task of writing the music for 'WHOSE IS THE KINGDOM?' were to be found in a Galway kitchen. Our director and two authors spent many hours round a kitchen table discussing the work as a whole and, for one afternoon, the music in particular; all of which was faithfully recorded on video for later reference. It was a fitting location for what was to become a mixture of musical styles – a sort of musical casserole begun in a kitchen.

The general idea was to borrow from history, place, and religion, and to combine these sources with musical metaphors which, though anachronistic, would be dramatically appropriate. The Hebraic, the Pauline, the Muslim, the Byzantine, the Persian, and the Western could be augmented by gospel song, the ringing harmonies of a Welsh choir, or even the triumphant burst of Hollywood trumpets as the conquering army marched into Rome. After all, this was a drama not an historical documentary.

My familiarity with the music of the Middle East was limited. Fundamentally an aural tradition, the music spread across the generations so that although change must have taken place, perhaps some germ of the original exists in the music one hears today. This is particularly the case with some Ethiopian and Yemenite tribal songs and chants. Such vocal traditions are strange to Western ears; the singers subtly split tones into fractions that we barely perceive at first hearing, and they improvise as a matter of course – strange demands to make on our choir of trained singers. They had to emulate the vibrant quality of Hebrew or Coptic chant where spontaneity, improvisation, and a certain roughness would have been more authentic than the measured tones of a Western choir. They had to ululate wildly through Antioch to the accompaniment of shawms and cymbals – with Frank Olegario's rich bass voice to thicken the gospel and work songs.

As regards instruments, visual evidence tells us that many have remained the same or similar and were modified by the West to provide the basis for our orchestral ensemble. The REBŌB (pronounced kebab with as rich and raw a flavour) is the precursor of the medieval rebec and, later, the violin. The QANUN is an evocative zither-like instrument. The SHAWM is a primitive oboe still much used; and flutes and reed pipes (transverse and end-blown) are common to all musical traditions.

Our flute player, Adrian Brett, produced a treasure chest of instruments (actually a suit-case) containing over eighty flutes from the DIDDUK of Turkey, a decorated wooden flute (half of it cut square) to the more Oriental membrane flute which produces a fragile but penetrating note by means of a thin vibrating membrane (rather in the way a kazoo does).

This was not out of place in our drama since there was considerable traffic of trade and people between the Middle and Far Easts in the 4th century.

Brass instruments of the time, more identified with Rome, would have been the CORNU – a straight horn like a hunting horn – and the BUCCINA, wound into a circular tube which was rested on the shoulder. But many horns used in the battle scenes needed a more primitive sound – as produced by animal horns – like the SHOFAR, a ram's horn used in Hebrew

Stephen Boxer

worship, with little range but an unmistakeable quality.

The harp in various guises embraces cultures from Mesopotamia to Ireland and it seemed appropriate to use both a Celtic and conventional harp to accompany anything from the banquet scenes of Maximin Daza to Kybele's exile in Hibernia. The organ was for me too evocative an instrument to exclude from a play dealing with the roots of our religion. There was an historical precedent for this: an invention of the Greeks refined by the Romans – a primitive hydraulic system emitting a deep watery tone. Some experiment with a synthesiser resulted in a compromise which would give us prescient echoes of cathedrals to come.

It was easier to surmise on the percussive sounds of the period. Drums come in infinite varieties but the basic principle has remained the same. Most percussive instruments have an ancient pedigree: sticks, rattles, the sistrum (a prong with a tambourine-like rattle but no skin) and bells. Bells have always played a significant role in the religious rite – not only calling the faithful to prayer, or announcing events of great moment, but also in the ceremony itself. The ritual chants of the Coptic church are filled with the strange harmonies of young boys and with the insistent ringing of small bells which hang both from the garments of priests and from their parchment scriptures. Some licence was taken here as we found that the caps to a well-known brand of mineral water made exactly the right sound.

For cymbals and gongs we tended to favour those that were bent or dented, as they had a less pure but more authentic sound. Our most used drum was one with a split in it producing a dull but definite thud, which Constantine's army might have marched to, or, which might have been played (if not split) in an ecstatic frenzy at the orgy outside Nicaea.

My favourite percussive instruments were the mortar-and-pestle and copper bowls, inspired by a record I had heard of Moroccan market-traders rythmically selling ground grain and water. It seemed a fitting background for the religious zealots chanting the Beatitudes in a Nicaean market-place; and of course neither instrument would be out of place in a kitchen.

Stephen Boxer

GLOSSARY

ARIUS/ARIANISM Arius: born c. 250 AD. Pupil of Lucian of Antioch (cf. Lucian; Origen): Priest of Alexandria, champion of the theory of subordination of the Son to the Father: that Christ is not a divine but a created being. The first great controversy within the Church, leading to the condemnation of Arianism at the Council of Nicaea (325 AD): the Emperor's hope for a compromise solution defeated by the intricacies of theological speculation and instransigence of the participants, Arian and Orthodox. Arianism later found Imperial favour: its chief defender, Bishop of Nicomedia.

ATHANASIUS born c. 296 AD. Chief defender of Christian orthodoxy in the battle against Arianism. Uncompromising Bishop of Alexandria (328): dominating personality and leader of Nicene party.

CLEMENT OF ALEXANDRIA died c. 215. Christian Apologist with mission to render simple style of scriptures into language acceptable to educated Greek; whilst (it being the age of the gnostics) reassuring the local uneducated orthodox that the enquiring mind of the intellectual Christian does no harm to faith itself. During the persecutions of the emperor Severus, he left Alexandria; his catechetical school he left to his student, Origen.

COPTIC CHURCH Christian church in Egypt which become monophysite in the 5th century (acknowledging only one nature in Christ, the divine, as opposed to orthodox teaching of double nature – divine and human: the Incarnation). Church isolated 451 following condemnation of the Patriarch of Alexandria.

COUNCIL OF NICAEA First ecumenical council convoked AD 325 to refute heresy and safeguard orthodoxy. Orthodoxy's champions – Athanasius and Hosius – versus Arius and the Bishop of Nicomedia. Constantine, prompted by Hosius, proposed the word homo ousios, to define the relationship of the Son to the Father ... of one substance with the Father. With this word in their Creed, the orthodox had their oath of loyalty. But whose was the victory? Some bishops had signed with reluctance enabling the debate and personal rivalries still to rage; imperial intrusion had failed to unite.

EBIONITES Jewish Christian sect rejecting Pauline Epistles. Not mainstream Christianity: Christ is human son given powers by Holy Spirit in the form of a dove, at baptism.

EUSEBIUS OF CAESAREA d. c 340. Constantine's biographer and pioneer writer of Christian Church history. (Caesarea – centre of Christian scholarship following Origen of Alexandria's residence in the 3rd century). Eusebius inclined to Arianism, if not to Arius. Trained in the traditions of Origen, his hatred of Sabellianism prevented him giving full support to orthodox champion, Athanasius.

BISHOP OF NICOMEDIA (also called Eusebius) d. 371. Eastern church statesman-bishop, born in Syria; fellow student with Arius in Antioch, under Lucian. Chief defender of Arianism and opponent of Homoousians at the Council of Nicaea. His friendship with the emperor's half-sister, Constantia, helped tip imperial favour towards Arianism. The Bishop of Nicomedia baptised Constantine in the year of the emperor's death, 337.

EPICURUS Greek philosopher and founder of the Epicurean School. Virtue, simple living, and freedom from pain (= pleasure) will bring harmony to mind and body (= serenity) ... thus are you freed from fear of death and superstition. A philosophy that became unpopular after the death of Epicurus when some claimed to be Epicureans as an excuse for sensualism and apathy.

GNOSTICISM Pre-Christian: form of theosophy owing much to the dualism of Zoroaster. Gnosticism taught that the created world was the world of an anti-God. Its tendency to ascetic rejection of the material world made it attractive to the Christians. Schools of *Christian* gnosticism flourished in the 2nd century AD. They identified the pre-Christian anti-God as the creating demiurge who was the god of the Hebrew Bible – a being lower than the New Testament's God of Love. They rejected the uniformity of orthodoxy, preferring independence; they rejected hierarchical authority, preferring freedom to look and to seek the secret knowledge essential for salvation.

HOSIUS OF CORDOVA Died c. 358. Spanish bishop and ecclesiastical advisor to Constantine from 312 AD. Defender of orthodoxy in the West. (cf Council of Nicaea). After the death of Constantine, Hosius defended Athanasius from the pro-Arian Constantius II. Hosius himself was detained in 356 and broke under physical pressure to sign the Arian formula; retracting before his death in 358.

IMPERIAL CULT It became accepted – particularly in the provinces of the East – that making the imperial family a cult was one way of impressing state power on the minds of the ruled. Private individuals allowed religious freedom provided they took part in the imperial cult: less a religious act than a paying of respect to the emperor and his family.

ISIS The Egyptian form of the great mother.

KYBELE Great Mother Goddess, the Phrygian Magna Mater, Sumerian Inanna, Assyrian Ishtar and Cappadocian Ma. She was regarded as the giver of life to gods, human beings and beasts alike. Orgiastic nature of her worship. Attis myth-jealous of his love for a nymph, Kybele drove him to madness in which he castrated himself, and died – this was ritually re-enacted with Attis represented by the pine trunk (see Catullus 63).

LACTANTIUS Born N. Africa 240 AD. Christian theologian/apologist. Diocletian appointee as teacher of rhetoric in Nicomedia. Conversion to Christianity: 300, Lactantius resigned when the Persecutions began. Later, summoned by Constantine to tutor his son, Crispus, at Trier. Died 320.

LUCIAN OF ANTIOCH born Syria c. 240 AD. Christian theologian martyred in 312 during the persecution of Maximin Daza. Lucian's analytic approach influenced students (Arius and the Bishop of Nicomedia). Lucian followed the rationalist's path, looking for the literal sense as opposed to the Alexandrian (Egyptian) symbolical interpretation. His subordinationist teaching led Arius to question the nature of Christ and the Trinity.

MANICHAEISM Hellenistic, dualistic religion of the Iranian prophet, Mani (born c. 216) who claimed to be the last and greatest apostle of Jesus. His teachings, influenced by Gnostic ideas, attempted to unite the doctrines of Jesus with those of Zoroaster. Initially favoured by Persian kings, Mani was later executed and Persia purged of his religion by the priests of the Zoroastrian church.

MITHRAISM Mithra ... Indo/Iranian god of light whose cult spread through Persia and throughout the Hellenic world following the defeat of the Persians by Alexander the Great. Its emphasis on loyalty to the king made it attractive to the Roman Empire, which assimilated the god to create a men-only religion especially favoured by the military. Imperial favour ceased AD 312 X Milvian Bridge.

MONARCHIANISM Christian heresy of 2nd and 3rd century which held to an extreme monotheistic view: there is only one God. Either Christ was a mere man filled with divine wisdom (Unitarian church of today) or Christ is God the Father as he appears to humanity (see Sabellians.)

MONOPHYSITE A Christian professing one nature in Christ rather than the two (divine and human). The one nature is primarily divine, with human attributes.

MONTANISTS Christian heresy of Asia Minor and N. Africa. Its founder, Montanus, was a priest of the oriental cult of Kybele before conversion. The ecstatic state of the cult, by redefinition became evidence of oracles from the Holy Spirit. This, with neglect of the bishop's role, offended orthodoxy. Montanists downed tools in their conviction that the end of the world was at hand ... not a socially useful group for an Empire low on manpower. It lasted in Phrygia until the fifth century.

NOVATIONISTS Rigorist breakaway group who saw themselves as true champions of orthodoxy. Their total condemnation of apostates led to their leader, Novation, declaring himself a rival pope.

ORIGEN Born c. 185 AD: pupil of Clement of Alexandria, Origen interpreted Christianity in terms derived from Greek philosophy. A theologian and biblical scholar whose emphasis – all knowledge comes from God – led to accusations of subordinationism (the Son is inferior to the Father). Origen thus considered precursor of Arianism.

PALMYRA Syrian caravan city: an empire in miniature under its queen, Zenobia. She was defeated by the Romans in 272 AD, when her use to the empire of Rome had outlived its strategic importance as buffer state (between Rome and Persia). A city of slaves.

PELAGIUS British/Irish monk whose system of belief was thought to minimise the role of Divine Grace in man's salvation. Considered anti-Roman Empire: Pelagians concentrated on social duties of Christ's message. Pelagius denounced by Augustine for minimising concept of Original Sin, and importance of the Bishops

PORPHYRY 234-305: Neoplatonist Greek philosopher disciple of Plotinus, who became a fierce critic of the new religion. His treatise against Christianity was destroyed by order of Theodosius.

SABELLIANISTS Christian heresy named after Sabellius (died c. 220). A development from Monarchianism, teaching that God is a monad (the one) manifested in 3 modes: Father, Son, Holy Spirit. (Arius accused those accepting the Nicene Creed of falling into the error of Sabellianism.)

SIMON MAGUS A sorcerer of Samaria who converted to Christianity and tried to purchase Apostolic power. Further conflict with St. Peter at Rome led to his dramatic fall from the top of the Roman Forum; a demonstration of occult power that failed. Middle Ages called him the arch-heretic and credited him with having founded Gnosticism. Some claim he said a woman was the Saviour, not Christ.

ZOROASTRIANISM Pre-Islamic religion of Iran (Persia) that influenced both Judaism and Christianity. Zoroaster wanted to unite polytheistic religions under the one supreme God. It was a dualisic religion: entities of his God battle against evil. After Alexander the Great conquered Persia, these entities were demoted to the deities of Greek and Persian name (e.g. Apollo Mithra, the sun god). Central also to its belief was the doctrine of the coming of a Saviour. A moralistic theology whose founder nevertheless became known as the arch heretic because of his associations with astrology and magic. The Parsis are the descendants of the Zoroastrians.

Pious Founders by John Arden

'You shall pray,' the headmaster used to pronounce in our school chapel twice a Sunday during the 1940s, 'for the memory of our pious founders . . .' and then followed a long list of English gentlemen from the sixteenth century onward who had given portions of their incomes (however earned, and *that* was not gone into) toward building, equipping, and staffing the establishment in which we were fostered. The same headmaster had a nice line in indoctrinating school-leavers: 'Always remember, you have been trained here, not to lead but to *serve*.' And then he would hand out booklets giving details of possible careers in the Palestine Police, the Indian Civil Service, or the East African Rifles. When, in his classrooms, I learned Roman History, it fell easily into this pattern. We understood that the 'good emperors' ran an empire very much on the model of the one that Queen Victoria's great men had left to us, and the 'bad emperors' did their best to sabotage it by wanton self-indulgence (although the *tradition of service* in the Roman army and civil administration was usually strong enough to prevent too much damage being done).

Constantine, for example, was obviously a 'good emperor'. He had to be: he was a sort of 'pious founder' himself, being the first one to adopt Christianity, whereas the persecution of Christians had been a notorious feature of the reign of the most notorious of the 'bad emperors', Nero. Roman History, however, was not a very important subject in my particular course of study, and my lessons in it terminated just at the point where a few contradictions and ambiguities were becoming apparent. Politically-speaking, it seemed that Diocletian, who was emperor at the end of the 3rd century just before Constantine, had been 'good'. He was not personally debauched, he put his army and civil servants under very proper control (tradition of service or not, they *had* been getting debauched), and his reforms in general made it possible for Constantine to exert a 'moderate and humane' rule. But Diocletian had also been the most deadly de-termined persecutor of Christianity. This particular period of the Roman Empire was therefore rather difficult, and indeed the school curriculum tended to shy away from it. Everything after the end of the first century AD was treated in a perfunctory fashion, and the emperors who followed Constantine were briefly summarized as symptomatic of 'Decline and Fall', which we were not encouraged to worry about – 1946 and 1947 were not good years for either the Palestine Police or the Indian Service, even though East Africa was still going strong: and morale had to be kept up.

Later on, I discovered that Constantine was held responsible (by such as Dante) for all manner of things that went wrong with the Church in the Middle Ages, and also that during the English Reformation there were calls upon Henry VIII and his son Edward VI to become 'new Constantines' and place England, under their leadership, in the forefront of revived European Christendom. Some of my old school's 'pious founders' might probably have contributed to these calls.

So a series of plays for the BBC on the rise of the religion from a persecuted underground cult to the official faith of a great empire seemed, at first glance, to be inevitably a series of plays about Constantine. If credit was to be taken, he had already grabbed it all: if blame was to be allotted (and by 1981 I had read Gibbon who thought that the main cause of 'Decline and Fall' was in fact Christianity), then he would be taking the lion's share. Most modern historians seemed to agree. The character of the emperor, they said, was murkily enigmatic, superstitious, power-hungry, often cruel, always efficiently pragmatic: his personality was crucial to the events of his reign. He had seen a vision, or had thought he had seen a vision, or let it be put about that he saw a vision: a cross in the sky with an order-of-the-day in letters of fire, 'Win with this battle-flag!' And from then on he did it more or less all by himself, just as Diocletian, all by himself, had tried to annihilate the Christians. On his arch in Rome, Constantine's inscription still stands to inform us of his personal responsibility: 'with the guidance of divinity and the loftiness of his own mind, he freed . . . the republic . . .' *etc*. Of course, at other times, he also let it be inferred that he was a *servant* rather than a *leader*, although such protestations are not necessarily worth any more than those of British headmasters laying their charge upon cadets of the old imperial officer-caste.

We read in the *Concise Oxford Dictionary of the Christian Church* that '*Constantine's* policy was to unite the Church to the secular State by the closest possible ties.' Paul Johnson in his *History of Christianity* asks, 'How could the Christian Church, apparently quite willingly, accommodate *this weird megalomaniac* in its theocratic system?' Fr. Ricciotti, author of *The Age of the Martyrs*, describes the enormous changes that took place under Constantine's rule, states that no one at the time could know how they would finish or when equilibrium could be expected to be restored, and then adds: 'No one was able to answer such questions, perhaps not even the *main cause of the changes, Constantine himself.*' (My emphases in these quotations.)

So it looked, when Margaretta D'Arcy and I began to read all the books we could get together on this period, that as we would be dealing with one main historical character – a Napoleon or a Queen Elizabeth I (whose lives we had already seen serialized on TV), or a James Connolly (about whose involvements in revolutionary struggles we had already written a series of six stage-plays), our dramatic form would be quite a simple one: Youth, Maturity, Old Age, with a crowd of subordinate personages floating in and out of the events as they went along. Our commissioned theme – the development of a religion rather than of a man – would be automatically reflected in his words, actions, and internal meditations. He would, of course, be partnered, and at times opposed, by a 'second lead', a figure – or figures – representing 'the Church', just as he represented 'the State'. The assumption was that Christianity had at that time a fundamentally unified voice, with certain disruptions from 'heretics', and that when Church and State entered into debate they would do so in scenes like that in Shaw's *Saint Joan* between the Earl of Warwick and Bishop Cauchon. We started our preliminary reading at least three years before we were sufficiently on top of the material to begin writing. By the time our first words were on paper, all the preconceptions had completely changed.

It had, for instance, become apparent that Constantine was by no means the great decision-maker: nearly everything he did came upon him out of the blue, he spent his whole life trying desperately to keep up with the forces that were swaying his empire, and he died without having anywhere secured any form of equilibrium. When he tried to handle this strange phenomenon called Christianity he was even more at a loss than are modern Western governments trying to 'stop communism': and just as the word 'communism' can be used to cover all varieties of dissidence from liberal American film-scriptwriters to black nationalists in South Africa, to Trotskyite red-brigades in Europe, to British coal-miners on strike, to the IRA, to post-Maoist

China, Sandinist Nicaragua, or post-Stalinist Russia, including by the way, the Women's Movement, CND, Greenpeace, and Polish Solidarity, so the Christian community at the beginning of the fourth century contained so many different schools of thought that to talk of 'the Church' and 'the heresies' totally begs the question. Moreover, all these variations claimed to derive directly from Jesus of Nazareth, and most of them had books to prove it. Even so apparently simple a statement as 'toleration and imperial favour were given (by Constantine) to the Church' – from the *Oxford Dictionary of the Christian Church* again – became almost meaningless. What Church? And what was to be tolerated? And how did he – or anyone else in the empire – understand any of these terms?

By the time Constantine made his bid for empire, his world had filled up, without his being aware of it, with an enormous number of drifting individuals and groups, all of them believing themselves to be Christians, and very few of them in any unity with each other. They all represented what Diocletian's government had termed 'subversion', and had frantically, unwillingly, attempted to suppress. Constantine made one big decision: not to suppress but to encourage. And then, after that, he was as it were at their mercy. The very nature of his decision is historically in doubt. A vision? Perhaps. Or perhaps such a description was no more than a convenient shorthand for a state-of-affairs to which he had come without really understanding how. At all events, his centrality in any dramatic setting-out of the events began to be less and less important. Our plays took on an entirely different shape. A number of stories about the interweaving lives and ideas of these individual 'Christians' took over the narrative structure, and the figure of the emperor was almost lost in their ebbing and flowing. One central point in the overall story remained: the Council of Nicaea, a formal meeting-place between the old State and the new Church, a little over half-way between Constantine's vision and his baptism and death. In our episode dealing with the Council there are two long conversations, duologues of the Emperor and the Bishop of Cordova, which approach nearest to the Shavian model. The second of these, although at first sight it seems to promise a regular debate between Church and State, turned out to be more of an exposition of how decisions of great weight are often made almost by accident before they are actually decided upon. The first conversation also emerged on

the page as rather an odd one: it ought to have been an explication by
Bishop Hosius of the basic difference between Christianity and
Judaism, but it ended up as a confrontation between two different
ideas of history.

The more our work on the plays progressed, the more I became
aware that these two ideas of history were the very root of the problem
of this period. The history of Rome, by which Romans understood
'the history of civilization', commenced with myth and legend –
Aeneas on his travels, Romulus and Remus fed by the wolf, gods and
goddesses overseeing the foundation of the City which was to master
the world. Livy, who wrote the 'definitive' account of all this, was not
unduly credulous: he told the old stories in the full knowledge that
they were a kind of fairy tale, and he introduced a commonsense
political and sociological comment into them from his earliest
chapters. In this, he followed the Greek tradition of Herodotus. Later
writers, such as Tacitus, were sceptical critical observers of the political
facts of life: when we read them today we are aware that they lived in a
society run on much the same principles as our own – power of money
and armed force, party-intrigue, class-rivalries, concretely determining
the people's destinies. Again, the Greek tradition: Thucydides,
Xenophon. The nearer to their own day they approach in their
narrative, the less reliance they place on paranormal phenomena. Of
course, they describe portents: Romans believed in the scientific
validity of extra-terrestial signs and did not see how government could
be carried on without taking them into account. But there is a great
deal of difference between, say, ghosts walking in the streets just
before the Ides of March (which notably did *not* deter Julius Caesar
from going to meet the Senate), and the miraculous ascension-into-
heaven of Romulus (even though Livy does hint that he may actually
have been secretly murdered). 'The Gods', in short, issued warnings
and encouragements: but in general they did not physically intervene.
Humanity was responsible for its own successes and failures, and
rational history is the reporting of them.

But according to Christianity (of whatever sect or tendency) a vital
and unprecedented divine intervention *had* taken place, only three
hundred years before Constantine became emperor. Which meant, of
course, between seven and eight hundred years *after* the divinely-
blessed Foundation of the City. If the Nazareth Carpenter was what
the Christians said he was, instead of being merely an obscure rural

philosopher who fell foul of the colonial police, then mythological
magic was much more up-to-date and decisive in its operations than
any educated Roman of the early Empire would have cared to
acknowledge. And moreover the Christians were able to produce an
entire corpus of hitherto unknown history-books to show this to have
been the case.

Once you accepted the divinity of Jesus Christ, then you had to
accept the truth of the Jewish scriptures (and their sequels – not only
our 'New Testament', but a bewildering array of other gospels,
epistles, apocalypses, and apocryphas, not at all reduced to a canon)
wherein God's intervention had been constant in human affairs since
the creation of the world. To read Livy alongside the *Book of Judges*,
or Tacitus alongside the *Acts of the Apostles*, must have been a disturbing experience. To start with, the authors of Holy Writ were not
really its 'authors': they took dictation, as it were, from the Almighty;
and such a source could not be doubted. If it said in the *Book of Kings*
that Elijah was caught up into heaven in a fiery chariot, there was
absolutely no room for any cynical alternative version (such as Elisha
privately knifing him and disposing of the corpse in order to obtain
leadership of the prophetic cabal). And yet it was clear that these books
did contain real history, not necessarily more erroneous than
Herodotus (and everyone knew Herodotus had made certain mistakes). And if Elijah and Ahab were basically 'true', as they certainly
seemed to be, then what of Herod, and Caiaphas; what of Jesus
himself, whose miraculous resurrection and ascension had somehow
slipped out of the regular imperial records? The arguments fed each
other, both forward and back . . . It was as though modern history had
been retouched by Homer, with Jerusalem and Galilee as his narrative
centres instead of Troy and Ithaca. Pontius Pilate was a real Roman
who could be looked up in the archives: and he had signed the death-
warrant for the Immeasurable Infinite . . .?

Did this therefore invalidate the whole of Livy and his colleagues?
How could it? Rome existed, still in charge, still civilizing the world.

Two possible explanations. One: that God's Adversary rather than
the old gods had made Rome great, reaching its height of power just in
time to damn itself by presiding over the Crucifixion. And, two: that
the Christians' One True God had been disguisedly fostering the
greatness of Rome throughout those previous seven-and-a-half
centuries, expressly for the purpose of providing an imperial system

that could most adequately receive the New Gospel (after, of course, a certain time-lag of hostility and misunderstanding).

The first explanation was obviously impossible, except to thoroughly subversive elements who would have opposed imperial power in any case. The second one was in fact adopted almost as soon as Constantine's government began to accept rather than repel Christianity. Eusebius, Bishop of Caesarea, wrote his *History of the Church* as an immediate ideological justification of the new policy and a guide to its fulfilment. He made it clear that he was compiling the definitive sequel to Holy Writ, taking up the story from the end of the *Acts of the Apostles*, and fitting it carefully into both traditions of history, Greco-Roman rationality and Hebraic credulity. His book was taken by Constantine's government as an official expression of its historical philosophy: and it led to certain consequences.

1. Faith rather than reason became essential to political technique.
2. Eusebius's view of the Church (i.e., that St Paul had been correct, with his acceptance of the right of Empire to rule the material world while the Church disposed of humanity's eternal destinies) prevailed over all alternative schools of thought (e.g., that the Kingdom of God meant social revolution here-and-now, casting the mighty from their seats, exalting the humble and meek). From which followed, that the Pauline strand of Christianity was correct in other ways too: the hierarchy of bishops and clergy, the subordination of women, the deprecation of individual prophetic voices, and so forth.
3. All those who did not agree with the Pauline view could officially be described as 'heretics', a word which previously had been meaningless to those, outside the Christian community, who saw all sorts of Christians denouncing each other but had no standard by which to assess the merits of the disputes.
4. Hostility to Jews by Christians was assured for ages to come. If the Roman Empire had been pre-ordained as the worldly receptacle for Christ's Spiritual Kingdom, then the guilt of the Crucifixion could hardly be Roman, and those parts of Holy Writ putting all the blame on the Jews must be absolutely true.

But Eusebius's book alone could not have supported these huge alterations in the imperial way of looking upon the world. The theory it put forward had to be confirmed by administrative action. So Constantine and the Pauline bishops found themselves arranging the Council of Nicaea in what appears to be the very year Eusebius finished writing. The Council was intended to clear the decks of all ideological and legal and historical confusion by establishing the main aspects of Eusebius's argument as an official part of Empire: and it did this, finally, through repression and censorship. Dissident Christians were banished by government edict, and their books were burnt. Constantine himself was accorded the title of 'Thirteenth Apostle' and his 'vision' became part of history. Within little more than half a century, indeed, the Emperor Theodosius was to take Nicaea to its logical conclusion: and *all* canonically-authorized Holy Writ became a mandatory part of history, all imperial servants were compelled to be 'correct' Christians.

Myth and legend had been brought in to surround the person of a living emperor, and to shore up his groping policies. Constantine's invocation of the miraculous was not at all comparable to the formalistic deification of dead emperors that had been happening for generations: it was much more akin to the hysterical assertions of Caligula or Elagabalus, who identified their own persons with various pagan gods and so incurred the scorn and hatred of their better- informed subjects. The only difference was: those 'bad emperors' failed, while Constantine – at least partly – succeeded. Nearly everything else decided at Nicaea was very soon evaded: heresies did not disappear, bishops did not remain invariably closely associated with, and approving of, secular state policies, and the authority of the 'Thirteenth Apostle' gave way (in the West) to the authority of the Bishop of Rome as Pope. But even today the idea of immediate divine intervention is still surprisingly strong in Christian parts of the world. Only recently, for example, I read that the President of the United States is impressed by prophecies of 'Armageddon', and may well be conducting his Middle-East affairs on that basis. If he doesn't really believe this himself, at least he finds it useful to have many of his voters believe that he believes it . . .

If heretics were censored and repressed, so, too, was official history. It is remarkable how hard it is to discover what really went on in the years covered by *Whose Is The Kingdom*? When Acts of State are presented as a religious revelation to be accepted by an act of faith, the world is given one big lie and must learn to make the best of it. For dramatists living and working some 1,650 years later, there is only one course: to invent. By and large, we have invented the areas of dissidence which church-and-state 'magic' endeavoured to 'wish away'.

The Moon of The Dispossessed
by Margaretta D'Arcy

I came to explore the wreck.
The words are purposes.
The words are maps.
I came to see the damage that was done
and the treasures that prevail.

Adrienne Rich

Patriarchy is a religion of the entire planet and whether it takes the
form of Hinduism or Buddhism or Christianity or Judaism or
Freudianism or Marxism or Maoism, it is a religion of male
worship . . . (women should therefore leave patriarchal religion entirely, not just because its laws and rules are unfair but because) its
whole symbol system and mythic system is utterly gynocidal.

Mary Daly

I put these and other cuttings (from daily papers) on the wall of my
workroom to prepare me for *Whose Is The Kingdom*?

Scholars Defend Liberation Theology.
A group of leading Catholic theologians sharply criticized Vatican
officials yesterday for attacks on liberation theologians whose
followers are linked to Third World political struggles (and) on
feminists. 'Within the Church we have also seen people defamed,
forbidden to teach theology, rendered suspect of infidelity to the
Christian message . . .'

Irish Times

If a man murders his wife, it is only natural to ask why? My
starting-point for these plays was to find out why Fausta, wife of
Constantine, was murdered by her husband. I could not find an
answer in any of the history books written by men shaped within the

Judaeo-Christian culture. They skipped rapidly over the murder, implying a kind of regrettable accident . . . 'This dark and unaccountable occurrence would seem to detract from the greatness of Constantine's blah blah blah . . .' It had never been fully documented in the minutes of the efficient Roman administration, so, therefore, it could not have been 'important', so, therefore, it is not necessary for us to know . . .

Unexplained gaps in history cause historians to pass them by and carry on: if they were to stop and really explore they would discover that most of history in fact consists of gaps. To fill them in would be to divert the flow of interpretation from a comfortable 'mainstream' into a series of eddies representing the so-called 'losing' side in one historical conflict after another. 'Mainstream' is winners' history: eddies and backwaters are where the losers still survive, refusing to be entirely written-out. I have never accepted that ideological conquests have ever been complete, or indeed that it is possible for them to be complete until the root cause of the conflicts are understood and dealt with.

I believe that all conflicts are at root one conflict: the rivalry between *we* and *I*, between co-operation and domination; and the constant refusal of the human race to recognize this. A little story: recently, at the Celtic Film Festival in Inverness, where I was showing my polemical video *Circus Exposé of the New Cultural Church*, I was engaged in an ancient argy-bargy – 'why were there no women on any of the public discussion-platforms?' – with a very 'important' media-executive, a sort of ITV Constantine. I asked him did he resent having been born from his mother's womb? His reply was: 'When I was in the womb, we were *we*, I was a dependant. When I was born, I became *I*, an independent.' *I* am the Lord thy God. Thou shalt have no other gods before *me* . . .

In 1981, John Arden and I accepted the task proposed by Richard Imison of the BBC radio-drama department, to write a series of plays about the beginnings of Christianity. We decided that we should focus our story upon the consolidation of Christianity in Constantine's reign at the Council of Nicaea. Richard's own interest in Constantine was that he, like the emperor, had had a vision, at the age of nine . . . The last big series of broadcast plays on the Christian theme was Dorothy L. Sayers' *The Man Born To Be King*. She was a committed anglican Christian: in the middle of World War II the plays were her statement against Nazism and neo-paganism. She also wrote a stage-play in 1951,

The Emperor Constantine: this coincided with the onset of the Cold War and the beginnings of the McCarthyite persecution in the USA, circumstances reflected in her evident approval of the orthodoxy of Nicaea. To me, Nicaea represented a triumphalism of conformity which has led directly to the triumphalism of those who would sacrifice the whole world to nuclear destruction for the sake of Christianity. And it was a male triumphalism: in the early church women had often held positions of high authority – even bishoprics, we now discover from certain feminist historians. But after the Council, never again . . . and also, never again, the free circulation of the 'gnostic' gospels alongside the four 'canonical' ones. In some of these works there are texts stating outright that the 'giver of life' is the female principle. I began to ask myself if the murder of Fausta (which happened immediately after Nicaea) was not part and parcel of the same process: the bishops killed Woman as a threat to 'their' religion, the emperor killed 'his' woman as an interference with *his* god-given rule . . .?

It was said to me, in joke, that I was 'writing a play, not making a revolution'. I doubt if anyone said that to Dorothy L. Sayers. The reason for the joke was that I had asserted it was impossible to understand the history of Nicaea without first experiencing the various shifts and debates in modern feminism: and also the liberation theology in the Third World, which has revitalized so much of what Nicaea had declared 'heretical' – Christ as human-being involved with the struggles of subject-peoples of empire, Christ as bodily healer, as provider of food, as 'subversive' challenger of both military and theocratic power. This meant travel, and of course the BBC drama department had no money for that type of research: we would have to make do with books, but to find the right books and buy them cost more money than we were able to afford at the time.

But the books did not answer my questions. How can plays be written with only questions and no answers? There has to be some *story*: after all, plays are just acted stories. And the radio-form we were using gave such great scope for story-telling: the imagination could roam without boundaries. Now it so happened at about the same time there was a dramatic change in my fortunes – the Irish government had set up a scheme called Aosdána to 'honour artists' and to help them financially with their work. And I was one of the lucky ones to receive a grant. I could now buy all the books I needed, I could carry out my own creative cultural experiments with other women, and I could travel.

1981 was a crossroads year for the dispossessed and the dissidents: the Irish prisoners' campaign for political status, the growth of Solidarity in Poland, the Women's Peace Camp at the USAF base on Greenham Common, the struggles in Central America.

And then, in 1983, I was invited to go to Nicaragua. Living in Galway in the west of Ireland I was able to make contact with the local bishop, Eamonn Casey. He had been in San Salvador at Archbishop Romero's funeral, when police opened fire on the crowd of mourners. He introduced me to Sally O'Neill of the Latin American Project in *Trocaire*, the Irish Christian Aid organization; and she gave me names of people to meet in Nicaragua, including an Irish priest from the Falls Road district of Belfast who was working in Managua with the Guatemalan Church-in-exile. Not long before, Sally herself had been deported from Honduras. Soon after my return from Nicaragua, in 1984, Ronald Reagan came to Ireland, visiting Galway as part of his tour. Demonstrations against him were notable for the participation of church-people as well as secular left-wing political groups, women's peace organizations, and the Chilean refugee community. On one of these I met Fr Pat O'Brien, a 'liberation-priest', lately serving in El Salvador, and now back again in a west of Ireland parish. *The Heroes & Martyrs of the North*, a Nicaraguan musical-group representing the rural-workers' trade union, then came on their own tour of Ireland. The enthusiastic welcome they received was an ironic contrast to that given the US President. In Galway they marched gaily and openly with their music through streets which Mr Reagan could only reach by helicopter and had had to traverse in a dark-windowed 'Al Capone' limousine with armed escorts.

As for my practical feminist work: I started a series of events called 'Galway Women's Entertainment'. On our first weekend we examined ancient Greek theatre, with particular reference to Euripides' *Hippolytus*. What we found in the play was rather surprising, because it actually contained *two* plays: one of them showed, with approval, a woman (Phaedra), in tune with her sexual instincts, contrasted with the man who denied his and used up his energy against nature by hunting and killing animals. The other one presented the woman as *destroyer*: she 'goes along' with the forces of nature and the forces of nature thus turn out to be 'unnatural'. Half-way through, the play seemed to come to a stop and change its tune completely between these two themes. Euripides had enjoyed himself, first of all, with an attack on male attitudes; and then suddenly became all pompous and heavy to keep in with the patriarchal Athenian drama-adjudicators . . .

An unexpected connection between this legend and the Fausta story. One of the books I had been reading, *The Age of Martyrs, Christianity from Diocletian to Constantine*, by Fr Guiseppe Ricciotti, referred to the fact that Constantine's son Crispus had been put to death at about the same time as Fausta (his stepmother), and noted that ancient commentators who had linked the two events in a speciously romantic scandal 'may very easily have been under the influence of the myth of the incestuous love of Phaedra and Hippolytus.' If, as I now believed, the Phaedra myth itself in Euripides' version was only a cover-up for a much deeper ideological confrontation, its employment to explain Constantine's crimes was a cover-up of a cover-up, and pointed the way at once to the crucial question behind all feminist dialectic – are we totally contained within nature, or is there a part of us 'outside nature' and belonging to an external superior being? In other words: the old conflict between the idea of a mother-goddess who is *all nature inclusive*, and a father-god who has *created* nature.

It was possible for me to unravel these historical riddles because the BBC in the end gave us a small sum of money for a researcher, the scholar Geoff O'Connell of Kinvara, who found texts and references for us in the National University Library that we would never have been able to ferret out for ourselves. He discovered several important classical documents, and a most particularly helpful dynastic analysis of the third and fourth-century emperors and all their families, arranged in tabular form, from which I could place the Constantine household as a dramatist needs to – their respective ages, and backgrounds, their complicated marital arrangements, made far clearer to the understanding than in any ordinary narrative history-books. Having at last established some real facts to support the assumptions, I now had to find some way of experiencing the spirit behind the facts.

Fortunately, in Ireland, the old matriarchal rituals can still be discerned hidden under the mantle of Roman-Catholic orthodoxy. I joined various Catholic pilgrimages, which are mainly supported by women. I went to Loch Derg, a very ancient ritual, and the strangest of them all, where one goes barefoot, fasting, without sleep, for three days on an island. A number of ceremonies have to be performed, circling round and round at various points in combinations of threes and nines, inducing hallucinations by the rapid inhaling of air to fill our lungs for the repetitive chanting. All the time the priests are there to keep an eye on us and stop us from lying down on the grass, with hints that if we were so to indulge ourselves there might very well be no stopping the orgiastic fervour. Another pilgrimage was to Ballinspittle, to see the phenomenon of the 'moving statue' of the Blessed Virgin. I found that by quickly moving my head and eyes at great speed it was possible to see *anything*. I saw the statue change from the Virgin, to Padre Pio, to the Sacred Heart, and finally to a giant white-and-black cat's face (which is of course a chief symbol of the ancient mother-goddess). The night I was there, there was no religious or sacred feeling – apart from a number of pious old men trying to get us all to say the Rosary – simply one of wonder. There was a chip-van to feed us, and in the coach on the way home the women sang modern pop-songs. I discovered also that several of these women were strongly influenced by home-viewing videos on occult themes which, they said, contained secret messages about the end of the world, and rumours indeed were spreading from Connemara that this event was to take place three days after our pilgrimage.

A group of us from the Galway Women's Entertainment made a point of visiting ancient sacred sites in our own area. One of these was Knock Ma – 'The Hill of Maeve', or of 'Queen Mab' – standing isolated in a vast flat fertile plain, looking out over three counties and the Atlantic Ocean. One of my neighbours, a very old woman, told me that she would never have the courage to go up Knock Ma, because the little-people would put her eyes out – as happened to someone she'd heard of, when he saw them there preparing themselves for a visit to the town of Tuam . . . On the very top of this mountain we saw the grave of General Kirwan – he had originally wanted to be buried standing up, but the ground proved too rocky. Maeve had been the mythical Queen of Connacht, but the General was the legal landlord, and owned every inch of her hill.

I do not think that military men and military bodies have moved very far forward from the days when the worship of Mithras, the male embodiment of the Unconquered Sun, was endemic throughout the Roman legions (its initiation open only to men). The Roman army fought only two truly religious wars – one against the intolerant male rival of their gods, Jahve of the Jews, and one against the British

Goddess as incarnate in Boudicca (who can easily be identified with her Irish neighbour and kinswoman, Maeve of Connacht). Sexual superstition and sexual humiliation are still weapons of war and of coercive law-and-order. Just as Boudicca was flogged by Roman soldiers and her daughters raped, so today women are forcibly strip-searched in our gaols ... And at the Women's Peace Camp on Greenham Common, the soldiers of the RAF Regiment and the US Air Force have been told that we are 'witches', that we 'cast spells' – their very cantonment is planted on the burial site of the last witch to be killed in that part of the world. She 'walked on water', to the horror of Oliver Cromwell's soldiers, and when they fired bullets at her she caught them in her hands and threw them back. She would not die until the troopers had tied her up and shot directly into her temple, and even the she kept on singing songs and laughing at them.

The witch's laughter and her un-masculine scorn for the bullets that make us remember her today, when the dispossessed women and the dissident women line the roads at midnight to witness the exercises of the cruise missiles going to Salisbury Plain (another sacred site): the Americans have their orders – 'Drive on, never stop, don't look, don't listen to the chants!' –

> We are the witness of your violence
> We are the victims of your violence
> And we will remember your face:
> Blood on your hands ...

What gaps in history are being skated-over in NATO's Judaeo-Christian internal analysis of the protest? Catholics, Protestants, Anglicans, Quakers, Methodists, Presbyterians, Jews – all women who choose peace rather than war, life rather than death, free choice rather than subservience to a clerical hierarchy – linking arms with women who are opposed to the very concept of the male god. Here the Mother is held and guarded. Do the military, aware of all this, choose the precise night when the moon is at her greatest strength to flaunt their rivalry and destructive power?

Out of such experiences I began to sense what must have lain behind the Fausta story, and what must have been the male-female tensions inside the belly of early Christianity. To quote Mary Daly again: 'If you can't remember, invent.'

But what about men's structures, and the tensions inside *them*? I had two experiences to help me understand these. The first was the Irish 'Artists' Parliament', Aosdána. This was meant to be open to all artists: but I saw its democratic principles being transformed and our communal decisions transferred into the hands of a clutch of misogynist malevolent goblins hunkered over their crock of knowledge. Secondly, the BBC itself, a glorious Byzantine labyrinth, where, at the very time I was working on the plays, a series of traumatic happenings that would have done credit to Constantine's court was being revealed in the daily press as State and Media clashed, just as though it were State and Church; police entered studios and seized film, resignations were accepted, heads rolled.

I now felt I was able to read history books without being prejudiced by their authors' concepts of vital mainstreams and irrelevant eddies. The plays themselves were begun in August 1984; the first drafts of all nine were completed by March 1986: and the final text was finished in the summer of 1987. The countries I visited, thanks to my grant, were Nicaragua, Germany, Italy, China, USSR, England, Wales, Scotland, Cornwall, and the North of Ireland.

I feel strongly that the totality of Christian and post-Christian culture belongs to everyone – that the whole world for good or ill has been affected by it – and that in principle everyone should have an equal right and opportunity to voice opinions and to raise and develop issues implicit in our interpretation of the story. It was agreed with Richard Imison that a format of radio seminars should accompany the presentation of the plays. This meant that John Arden and I were released from the burden of imposed objectivity, and that we were free while writing to come to grips with our own experience, our own individual views, and to allow the gaps in *our* narrative to be filled in by other voices.

WHOSE IS THE KINGDOM?

Whose is the Kingdom? was first broadcast by BBC Radio Three in February 1988. The cast was as follows:

CONSTANTINE ⎫	Michael N. Harbour
MAXIMIN DAZA ⎬ *Emperors*	Kenneth Cranham
LICINIUS ⎭	Laurence Payne
DIOCLETIAN, *Retired Emperor*	Willoughby Goddard
CRISPUS, *Constantine's Son and heir-apparent*	Nicholas Gecks
FAUSTA, *Constantine's Wife*	Samantha Bond
CONSTANTIA, *Constantine's Sister*	Karen Archer
HELEN, *Constantine's Mother*	Mary Wimbush
EUTROPIA, *Fausta's Mother*	Jill Bennett
PRISCA, *Diocletian's Wife*	Pauline Letts
VALERIA, *Diocletian's Daughter*	Julie Berry
HOSIUS, *Bishop of Cordova*	Timothy West
EUMOLPUS, *A Christian Scholar; later, Hosius's secretary*	Steve Hodson
BISHOP OF NICOMEDIA	Ronald Herdman
BISHOP OF ANTIOCH	John Rye
BISHOP OF LONDON	David Goodland
A CYPRIOT BISHOP	Joseph O'Conor
IRENE, *Daughter of the Cypriot Bishop*	Maggie Shevlin
JOACHIM, *A Christian Soldier*	Stephen Boxer
SEMIRAMIS, *Fausta's Slave-woman*	Souad Faress
MARY THE COMPANION, *An Evangelist*	Angela Pleasence
JOHN THE READER, *A Survivor of the Persecutions*	Geoffrey Matthews
DION, *A Christian scholar*	Stephen Thorne
OENOTHEA, *Priestess of the Great Goddess*	Anne Jameson
MELANTHO, *Oenothea's Daughter*	Cassie McFarlane
HELEN-FAUSTA, *Melantho's Daughter*	Jade Maravala
THEOTECNUS, *Priest of Zeus*	Peter Howell
PHYSCON, *A Baker*	David Buck
JAXARTES, *Director of the Secret Service*	Sam Dastor
'PAUL OF TARSUS', *A Voice in Constantine's Mind*	Roshan Seth
KYBELE, *An Epicurean Philosopher*	Elizabeth Spriggs

with

Michael Deacon, Michael Tudor Barnes, Jonathan Tafler, Zelah Clarke, Paul Sirr, Alan Dudley, Margaret Ward, Anthony Jackson, Sheila Grant, Victoria Carling, John Samson, Diana Olsson, Raad Rawi, Frank Olegario, Tony Wredden, Brian Hewlett, John Baddeley, Alix Refaie and Leonard Fenton,

The music was composed and conducted by *Stephen Boxer* and played by The Conchord Ensemble. Singers: London Voices *with members of the* Trinity Boys Choir, *and members of the cast.* Production Assistants *Josephine Clark and Jean Bower.* Technical Presentation *Carol McShane, Rosamund Mason, David Blount.* Music recorded by *Peter Harwood.* Executive Producer *Ronald Mason.* The plays were directed by *Ronald Mason and Penny Leicester.*

Authors' Note

Passages marked with square brackets [–] were cut, for reasons of length, from the recorded text. One or two additional small cuts may have been made in the broadcast recordings since this volume went to press.

There are always minor differences between a broadcast play and its written text, as the production is an organic process involving team-work between producer, actors, studio-staff and writers. We have not always indicated these on the page: but listeners following the broadcasts from the book will notice them here and there.

J.A. & M. D'A.

1

THE CROSS OF LIGHT

Scene One

KYBELE. (*as narrator: brisk and factual – a woman aged 60*).
305 AD. The Empire of Rome:
So vast it has become
So unwieldy from shore to shore
They decided to divide it,
By agreement, into four.
Four great men over four huge regions,
Bound by their marriage, bound by religion
Each with his tax-gatherers, each with his legions,
Above all, to hold safe the border,
Above all, to maintain good order,
Above all, to drive down dissent.
[All new notions, bright ideas,
By word-of-mouth or pen-and-ink,
Are subject now to punishment.]
Obedience, loyalty, the sole requirement.
[But nowhere does the Empire now lament
The loss of loyalty more than among these four great men
Themselves, as they crouch and cast their envious eyes
The width of the world.]

East, West, North and South: I was there when Diocletian ruled; [and I was there when he turned this world into a filing cabinet;] and I was there when he retired. 'Diocletian, great hater of Christianity'. And now I am here, in the year of the death of the Emperor Constantine, [337 AD – as the Galileans put it: they've got the cabinet now.]

I call myself Kybele of Thessalonika, philosopher in exile. I live outside the Empire, among the islanders of Hibernia, [who observe customs and practise ritual we no longer use.] I have been accused by the Chief Druid of Armagh. He has charged that I came here under false pretences, accepting hospitality as a refugee from Christian persecution, [using the noble calling of philosophy to gain a status in this land to which I am not entitled; and here I am to be judged according to custom.] It seems to me, there is no way I can refute this accusation, except [to satisfy *myself*, that it cannot be true . . .] to explain the whole process of history. . . from the beginning of the reign of Constantine. 305 AD.

Four great men who crouch and cast their envious eyes
The width of the world. One of them dies:
In the north-west corner. He has a son, to carry the line:
A strong young man called Constantine.
Young Constantine in the city of York
Surveys the Empire, prepares his work.

CONSTANTINE.
Outside the Empire: Germans and Persians,
Irish, Goths, Arabians,
The Slavs, the Caledonians,
Unable to wait for their prey any longer –
Inside: there's poverty, banditry, hunger,
Whole populations living on the dole,
Cut it short, they'll all rebel–
[The price of corn as high as a mountain,
The soldiers' wages pour out like a fountain –]

Four of us to make up one: and not one of the four
Able to cope with the chaos any more.
Do I have to wait until they're all three dead?

KYBELE. – Constantine said.

CONSTANTINE. No, I do not.

KYBELE. But, for the time being, he did.
In order to consolidate his control of the west, he married the sister of Co-Emperor Maxentius.

FAUSTA. Are we marching into Italy or aren't we?

KYBELE. That's Fausta, child-wife of Constantine, sister of Maxentius. And in order to consolidate his consolidated control, Constantine quarrelled with her father, and her father was killed.

CONSTANTINE. The old man killed himself.

KYBELE. Not everyone believed this and Maxentius swore revenge.

CONSTANTINE. Why should they not believe it?

KYBELE. Said Constantine.

CONSTANTINE.   It is noble and fine
To take one's own life
When all hope is gone.
My wife, the lady Fausta, will confirm that her father is dead.

KYBELE. – Constantine said.

CONSTANTINE (*winningly*).
– by his own act and deed.
Which is good enough for me,
Why can you not agree?

(*His voice expresses bottled-up rage:*)
Seven years already of treachery, diplomacy, assassination, war,
I am still no more than one among four:
Maxentius keeps me out of Rome,
In the whole of Gaul I have no room
But to jump like a hooked pike at the end of a line:
High time I did it and then it's done.

KYBELE. – said Constantine.

CONSTANTINE.   Until it is done, neither rest nor sleep
For the man who must do it, if I am to keep
My life and my throne
Maxentius must go down.

KYBELE.   Who cares that Constantine's wife will weep
If her husband should kill her brother stark dead?

CONSTANTINE. Already I murdered her dreadful old dad.

KYBELE. – Constantine said.
Year of Christ, 312: the Imperial Palace at Trier, in northern Gaul.

Scene Two

Interior: outside – military evolutions, SOLDIERS *marching, drum-taps, m.q.1.*
DRILL-INSTRUCTORS' *shouts; inside – cupboards and boxes being cleared out and/ or packed.*

FAUSTA. (*aged 14: between child and woman, and very tense with it*). Are we marching into Italy or aren't we?

SEMIRAMIS. (*from Persia: early twenties, cautious not to overstep the allowed liberties with her young mistress*). One, two, three, four full-bottomed wigs. Four blonde switches and the dark one.

FAUSTA. And if we are, when do we go? Semiramis, don't bother to pack the red: it's years out of fashion, I couldn't possibly be seen with it in Rome. I shall certainly need the wine-coloured Grecian style –

SEMIRAMIS. But, madam, if we don't go, you're going to need it here.

FAUSTA. I know, I know, but bring it with us. Don't put it in the trunks, keep it for the hand-baggage. Is he really going to fight my brother, or botch up another treaty with him? If we fight, we'll be living in a tent for God knows how long: our whole life will be bloody hand-baggage. *If* he makes up his mind.

SEMIRAMIS. The regiments *have* been placed upon instant readiness, madam –

FAUSTA. Don't I know it, girl, I haven't had a siesta all week for the stamping and shouting. In any case 'instant readiness' could just as well mean Germany. I suppose all he's doing is waiting for a portent. So am I. Perhaps I've had one and didn't recognise it for what it was . . .? (*A thought strikes her: she lowers her voice nervously.*) Shut the window. The gardener could overhear, I'm quite certain he's a secret policeman.

Window shuts

FAUSTA. Semiramis: who have you met among the cults who could interpret a text for me?

SEMIRAMIS. (*carefully*). If it is a Christ-text, madam?

FAUSTA. I suppose it must be. It's all about Adam and Eve. Surely no one has Adam and Eve except Christians and Jews? It's not at all the usual story. It goes – ah – (*She repeats the text from memory, like a child that has learnt a lesson:*) 'After the seventh day, the Lady of Wisdom sent her daughter who is called Eve as an instructor to raise up Adam. When Eve saw Adam cast down she pitied him, and told him: "Adam, live: rise up upon the earth". And her word became a deed. He saw her and said, "You will be called the Mother of the Living because you are the one who gave me life." ' Did you ever hear that before?

SEMIRAMIS. No, madam.

FAUSTA. Are you sure? You are a Christian?

SEMIRAMIS (*carefully*). I go to a meeting on the first day of every week, madam –

FAUSTA. A Christ-meeting.

SEMIRAMIS (*not incriminating herself*). We call it the House of the True Way. We all get together, mostly women, mostly like I am, slaves, foreigners. Last week, there was this woman, an ecstatic, from Spain. She called herself Mary the Companion: she read from the book, and spoke a few words afterwards –

FAUSTA. What about?

SEMIRAMIS. Love.

FAUSTA. How much money did you pay her?

SEMIRAMIS. She took nothing, not even food, except the bread of the love-feast, and then she scrubbed the meeting-room.

FAUSTA. Did she do any magic tricks?

SEMIRAMIS. All her magic was in the truth of her voice, madam.

FAUSTA. If she were a police agent she would have learned magic tricks. . . Child, you must get her for me, she will know what my text means, follow her up, find her out –

SEMIRAMIS. But she's already left the city –

FAUSTA. Go –:

SEMIRAMIS *hurries out, closing the door after her.*

FAUSTA. Oh yes, it is a portent. I read that text so long ago, last night in my dream
it came back. He said to her: 'You are the one who gave me life.' Did not *I* give
life to Constantine? But my father's life was taken, and now perhaps my brother's
life. But suppose it should be my brother kills my husband, what then? You will
have made the wrong choice, Fausta, Empress of this quarter-world, you will have
made it for ever and ever . . . amen.

Scene Three

KYBELE (*as narrator*). They were all making choices. [Military decisions inextricably
confused with religious ones.] For instance, what choice before soldiers converted to
Christ, the Prince of Peace? They ought not to serve at all, but Constantine
tolerates Christians, and all their enemies so far have been heathen. Now they hear,
Maxentius is no persecutor either: there are Christian men behind *his* banners as
well. In the Balkans, Co-Emperor Licinius permits Christian worship: but Co-
Emperor Maximin Daza of Egypt and Asia – where Christianity in fact is a majority
faith – is still furiously persecuting. [Decisions to be made: if Constantine allies
himself with Licinius, will Maximin Daza be compelled into friendship with
Maxentius? And if so, what difference will this make to the Christians?] A Christian
army will lead to a Christian empire. But it must be a *successful* army – Constantine
so far has always been successful. If he is not –

HOSIUS (*smooth and suggestive – to himself*). If he is not, the atavistic idolatry of
Maximin Daza could reassert itself over the whole world. Grant, O Lord Jesus, the
advice I give will lead neither to hot-headed zealotry nor yet to shameful apathy.

KYBELE. Bishop Hosius of Cordova, a Spanish nobleman converted to Christ, he
withstood outrageous torture for his faith, [but Constantine has accepted him as the
respectable representative of an irregular religion.] He is allowed to minister to
Christians in the army of Gaul. He is *not* perhaps allowed secret meetings at dead
of night with disaffected Christian officers – including the garrison purveyor.

PURVEYOR. Bishop, if our Emperor were to ally himself with Licinius against
Maximin Daza it might be a different matter. But marching alone into Italy against
Maxentius; why, I doubt if we can even win. Maxentius has an army twice the size
of ours.

Murmurs of worried agreement.

HOSIUS (*to himself*). Do I dare suggest to them that whichever side looks like losing,
the Christians in that army should change over to the other side and thereby
establish a single Christian Emperor over the whole of the west? Maximin Daza is
the greatest enemy, we must all unite somehow to conquer him. If *I* persuade the
officers, and they persuade the rank and file – Let me now play the strategist of
Christ, replacing from within the brutal strategies of Imperial power . . . (*Aloud*)
. . . and so my friends, we are to render unto Caesar that which is Caesar's,
however many Caesars there may be. And then, and only then, may the resulting
Caesar be induced to render unto God that which is ·

PURVEYOR (*gloomily*). It is not very glorious.

HOSIUS. Why Colonel, it is not supposed to be: we have had the glory, and we have
had the martyrdoms: now we need politics and very little money. Our Lord needs
from us now the wisdom of the serpent, it is written in His book. But do not tell
your soldiers, not just yet. There are arrangements to be made.

KYBELE. Hosius being in touch with the Bishop of Rome, and the Bishop of Rome
in touch with certain officers of Maxentius. [Had those two Christian networks been
able to combine with Constantine's military intelligence, many who fought to the
death might still be alive.]

Scene Four

Interior: conference room.

KYBELE. The following morning, Constantine's headquarters office, a council of war.

CONSTANTINE. We'll dispense with the protocol, gentlemen, up from your knees. Treasurer, please: sit down.

They seat themselves.

CONSTANTINE (*before they are all in place*). My secret service tells me Maxentius in Italy is about to invade Gaul. That's *this* report. But in *this* one: my secret service tells me he cannot raise enough taxes to keep his army in being. Well? General?

GENERAL (*a German*). Sir, I believe the second report. Civilian disaffection south of the Alps is already so widespread he cannot invade us. My opinion, it would be safe to resume the German war. I speak as a German myself. Our appeasement-subsidies to the hostile tribes are all but exhausted: as soon as we stop paying them, they will swarm upon us over the Rhine. Attack them first: it's the only strategy.

CONSTANTINE. Ah, but if we do, and if this *first* report should prove true: then we leave Gaul undefended for Maxentius to occupy. Treasurer, the appeasement-subsidies, can we prolong them just six more months?

TREASURER. Most Unutterable Refulgent Majesty, that would require –

CONSTANTINE. Didn't you hear me? No protocol: This is an *ad hoc* staff meeting.

TREASURER. Your pardon, sir. Sir: that would require a reassessment of taxes, which in turn would require the submission of estimates through the following departments – land-revenue, import-export, industrial production –

CONSTANTINE (*not letting him finish his list*). Make a guess: yes or no?

TREASURER (*with a gulp*). Sir: it – it could be done.

CONSTANTINE. Treasurer, prolong the appeasement-subsidies for another six months: I asked for a supply-schedule for a march as far as Turin. Purveyor, do you have it?

PURVEYOR. Here it is, sir.

CONSTANTINE (*briskly leafing through a document*). This won't do. [Too much reliance upon the wagon train. Cut the transport to a minimum, this is to be a *forced* march, and your numbers are incorrect.] Not sixty thousand soldiers but forty.

Clamour of complaint.

VOICES. Forty thousand – no more than forty –:

CONSTANTINE (*stilling the complaint*). Even though the Germans are paid, we must leave enough regiments to guard the Rhine against them: and the smaller the force against Italy the greater the chance of surprise.

GENERAL (*a last appeal*). Sir – sir – I beg you believe it: Maxentius' command falls already to pieces, you need only wait one year, all Italy will be anarchic, and *then* you can invade –

CONSTANTINE (*very solemnly*). I am Emperor Augustus and Italy is mine. If I wantonly allow that sacred land to collapse into anarchy, why, gentlemen, the great gods will have abandoned humankind. (*A change of tone: to a lighter sardonic manner.*) Some of them may have done so already. Which is why I dare to tell you that at first light this morning I inspected the entrails of sacrifice: and the results were not good.

More worried murmurs.

CONSTANTINE. I almost determined to forget about Italy. (*His voice takes on its weight again*.) But then, gentlemen, I looked up, and saw the Unconquered Sun, the Giver of Life, the only god that matters. I looked straight into his blazing face, I saw the face of my father: and *there* was my portent.

An awe-struck silence.

Imperial decision: we set forward our banners tomorrow.

Fade.

Scene Five

Exterior: army on the march; CENTURIONS, *up and down the column, exhorting the* TROOPS, *who sing most of the time.*

SOLDIERS' SONG.   One two where do we go?
Three four who do we know?
Jup-it-er Jup-it-er
Mars Mars rules the wars
Hercules went overseas
Nep-tune Nep-tune
Neptune changed his bloody tune
Ven-us Ven-us
Venus rules the penis
Mars Mars rules the wars
Where do we go one two?
Who do we know three four?
Jup-it-er Jup-it-er
Jupiter's Emperor wins the war
Call his name along the line
*Con*stan – *Con*stan –
Constan-bloody-Constantine –

Use as much as seems needful for any particular sequence.

CENTURION (*en passant*). Come on, keep it going, keep it going, forced march, backs up, chests out, keep up the chant – Mars Mars rules the wars – (*Etcetera.*)

Scene Six

Exterior: cross-fade to suggest passage of time. Marching and chanting continues.

3RD SOLDIER. Hey, what about this cavalry?

1ST SOLDIER. Maxentius' bloody cavalry. Steel plate, articulated, head-to-foot on horses and men. There's no way a regiment-in-square can stand up against that.

1ST SOLDIER (*resentfully*). Ent there? How long you been in *this* regiment, boy?

3RD SOLDIER (*after a few paces in silence*). I heard it said bloody Constantine's marching under unfavourable entrails. If *I* know that, Lord Mithras the Saviour knows it . . .

1ST SOLDIER (*correctively*). Lord Mithras can do without *your* voice. They weren't his entrails anyway. Mars. And Mithras in my book goes way ahead of bloody Mars.

CENTURION (*en passant*). One two, one two. Belgian bastards bellyaching in the middle rank? Come on, keep it going. One two, one two – (*Etc.*)

Cross-fade.

Scene Seven

Exterior: strong wind; marching and chanting in distance. A heavily laden wagon train: groaning and tumbling about of the passengers. Driver's whip and his yells at oxen. The women camp-followers are in the wagon; a woman cries out – she is in labour.

1st WOMAN (*put out*). What is it, what's happening at the back?

2nd WOMAN. Its that black girl with the bangles, another of 'em what says she's got a husband in the commissariat – I think she's due.

1st WOMAN. Aphrodite, she can't be, we won't catch up the column for at least another hour! And this one'll never stop his oxen on these slopes –

2nd WOMAN. Can't you manage another hour – just over the next ridge, they'll be bound to make camp there?

MELANTHO (*in pain and fear*). An hour? I can hold on an hour. I think – I think – oh – oh –:

1st WOMAN (*very ill-tempered*). She'll have to stay behind.

MELANTHO (*in a panic*). No no – you'll not leave me to die in these mountains. The child'll be born without regimental papers. Oh please, in the name of Isis, my child must be born under protection of Constantine's army!

The wagon comes to a halt.

DRIVER (*angrily, as the wind rises*). All right, that's it, too steep, everyone that can walk, out you get – walk!

Moaning and complaining as the women climb out.
Cross-fade . . .

Scene Eight

Exterior: Marching and chanting now very ragged: the wind blows strongly.

1st SOLDIER. Blood of the Bull, look at the state of that village! You wouldn't think these mountains had ever been civilised.

PEASANTS, WOMEN and CHILDREN (*running beside the column*). Love o' the Gods, soldiers, spare us some food, love o' the Lord Mithras – a handful of corn –!

2nd SOLDIER. It's through this valley a good few years ago that old Co-Emperor bastard Herculius brought his regiments down. Suppressing terrorism, wasn't he? Pacification . . . Left not one blade of corn nor a turnip alive behind him.

CENTURION (*en passant*). Keep the step up! One two, one two. Take no notice or they'll infect you with their own ill-luck. Come on. One two, one two.

Cross-fade.

Scene Nine

Exterior: marching and chanting. Wind. A succession of orders from up the column – 'Half-company, halt!' The units come to a stand. A horse approaches..

OFFICER (*on horse: a young man*). Centurion, take care the men wrap themselves up well – march 'em at the double over the ridge – would you believe it's blowing a snowstorm up there, so let's not have stragglers! Across the Alps and on to Rome!

He clatters off on his horse, calling the halt further back down the line.

CENTURION (*savagely*). You heard that? Snowstorm-order from now on, hoods and cloaks.

Confused noises as they pull their cloaks around them: before they are quite ready –

CENTURION. Half-company, by the right, double march!

They set off at the double.

CENTURION (*new speed*). One-two, one-two, one-two – (*Etc*).

Cross-fade to suggest passage of time.

Scene Ten

Exterior. Double-marching continues in the storm.

CENTURION (*in distance*). Keep it going, watch your footing, we're nearly at the top –!

4TH SOLDIER. Brother Joachim, some of the heathen soldiers believe that this march is doomed. There is talk, brother, about the entrails. You'd have thought, if that was true, Lord Jesus would have warned *us* before he'd let the false gods give warning to their own people?

JOACHIM (*a young soldier, very tense and taut in his expression*). It could be we have *had* warning but have not taken heed of it? There are Christian men in Maxentius' regiments, and we drive against them with the sword? And for what purpose?

4TH SOLDIER. Might it not be, there is a prophecy at hand – brother will slay brother . . . the end of the world is nigh and I come in all my glory –?

The chanting has broken up because of the MENS' weariness.

CENTURION (*his voice cracking with the strain*). Keep the chant up, keep it going there –

There is a pathetic attempt to keep it going, but the voices fade away into groans.

4TH SOLDIER (*while this is going on*). It's high time we came in with our own chanting – the song of our Lord when he danced with his lads in the garden, the night the crushers came to lift him – brother, give voice!

JOACHIM. Join me, brethren, join me in praise –! (*He starts to chant, rather than sing, in strong rhythm; singing strongly:*)

> The dance of God belongs to all the world
> A-men A-men dance with the Lord
> If you don't dance you cannot know the word
> A-men A-men dance with the Lord –

The chorus is picked up by others: and after a line or two nearly everyone is singing.

CENTURION (*as they sing: vastly pleased by the return of morale*). Hercules, Jesus, or Mars, I don't give a damn, just keep it going, that's all, or else we'll all freeze to death in the dark –

JOACHIM (*singing with added force*).

> Follow the dance and see yourself in Jesus
> A-men A-men Jesus is the Lord
> They'll hang him on the cross and you'll never know the
> reason
> A-men A-men Jesus is the Lord
> Until you join the dance and the dance is for you
> A-men A-men Jesus is for you!

The march continues vigorously, the men shouting out repeatedly 'A-men a-men JESUS is for you!' Fade.

Scene Eleven

Exterior: High wind. Confused shouting and noises of gear being unloaded etc. as the camp is established. Nearer noise: The lowing of oxen.

KYBELE (*as narrator*). They made camp upon an Alpine pass under forests of fir-trees and snowstorm. Fausta's maid, Semiramis, caught sight of a pale woman, crookbacked and lame, moving swiftly among the draught oxen in the wagon-park –

SEMIRAMIS. Hey – you – yes, you – stop a minute – I want you –!

MARY (*quiet, positive*). Yes? My name is Mary.

SEMIRAMIS. Mary the Companion! Oh this is a portent! Mary, you are needed, my mistress Fausta cries out for you every day, come, the headquarters-lines, come –

MARY (*not impressed*). I have no words for the wives of these Emperors. They are rich enough to speak with those who are far more learned than I am. At the corner of the camp there is a woman giving birth, alone, under the open sky – she is nobody, she joined this march upon pretence she had a husband here, she has no documents, nothing – in the morning she will be abandoned, she could die in the snow with her child: I am going to stay with her. Is it not written how our Lady was cast aside and likewise gave birth in a cave?

Cross-fade to suggest passage of time.

Scene Twelve

Exterior: as before. Howl of wind, A BABY crying.

KYBELE (*as narrator*).

> An Empress should command, but this little Empress obeyed.
> And found there in the hollow of the storm-driven wood
> Red torchlight upon the face of a new-born baby,
> Agony of weeping: blood.

MELANTHO (*sobbing*). Oh Gods, it is a girl-child . . .

MARY. Lady of heaven help me now, give me words I can comfort this woman, whose child in my arms is made in the likeness of you, the eternal mother – oh Lady you sent your Son to tell the meek to inherit the earth: who should be meeker than these forsaken fragments of your life?

FAUSTA. Woman, if I tell you a test, will you hear it, interpret it?

MARY (*abruptly*). What is it worth to you?

FAUSTA (*astonished*). Semiramis, what does she mean?

SEMIRAMIS (*sharply*). Are you asking my lady for money?

MARY. Not for myself: for the child. Because here is a great lady concerning whose husband it were better he be drowned with a millstone round his neck than he should offend any of these little ones.

FAUSTA (*genuinely puzzled*). Is that what is written? Or is she being insolent?

SEMIRAMIS. Oh yes, madam, it *is* written.

FAUSTA (*relieved*). Ah. So, tell her I'll give her something.

MARY (*simply*). The jewels you are wearing. They will be enough for this little one and for all the others who will be born and cast away upon the fringe of your cruel army, which goes to designate, they say, the ruler of this world – nothing to us: we are the meek: we will inherit.

FAUSTA (*anxious to get it over quickly*). Here, take the jewels and I'll tell you the text.

Cross-fade to suggest passage of time.

Scene Thirteen

Exterior: as before.

KYBELE (*narrating*). And when she has told it –

FAUSTA. It must have a meaning?

MARY. It means there is God. One God. And behind him, there is the female, the one who is always there, and before her there was no other.

FAUSTA. Is that – Christianity?

MARY. You can call it what you want. You either believe it or you don't.

FAUSTA. And if I do believe it, what must I do?

MARY. Remember it, when everyone else forgets: utter it, when it is needed: keep guard over it when they try to destroy it. Above all, bear in mind: Eve gave Adam life and for her reward he now treads upon her head.

A bugle blows mournfully in the camp, some distance away..

MARY. So there you are, child, back to your tent – keep the freezing cold wind from your beautiful face.

Scene Fourteen

KYBELE (*as narrator*). Constantine crossed the Alps. Not even he expected what he found: Maxentius' mounted vanguard in the northern plain, a faceless barricade of iron – invincible, invulnerable.

CONSTANTINE (*in high excitement*). Invincible? Invulnerable? Sensible improvisation – I took the swords away from the front-rank infantry and had them fight with sledge-hammers. My idea, no one else's – I put it to the troops, good idea? They said: yes –

Exterior: as he talks the sounds of battle come up behind him. A brief thunder of a cavalry charge, the clash of metal against metal, cries, collapsing horses, etc.

CONSTANTINE. So they did it: and the blood ran red.

KYBELE (*as narrator*). Constantine said.

And having said so, he marched upon Rome.

Fade out battle noises, fade in marching army.

KYBELE. He knew that Maxentius had made the city impregnable. Constantine could now have sought alliance with his Co-Emperor Licinius and brought in another army to reinforce his insane enterprise. But he would not trust Licinius.

CONSTANTINE.   So what *do* I trust?
Gods, demons, furies, the Unconquered Sun –?
I am possessed, I think –
The sun on fire above is mine, all mine –!

KYBELE (*as narrator*). – said Constantine.

The marching ceases.

KYBELE. Ten miles from Rome, he halts, his regiments take breath.

CONSTANTINE (*dreadfully disturbed in the sudden silence*).

> Helios-god, what have I done?
> If Maxentius stays behind his walls I cannot get at him,
> He must march out, or I must concede defeat.
> Tomorrow my men will murder me if I order their retreat.

Scene Fifteen

Exterior: A meeting of a large number of MEN, *clustering and shuffling their booted feet among the grass and small bushes of a field.*

KYBELE (*as narrator*). Those of his men that worshipped Christ came together under the moon to seek for divine guidance.

JOACHIM. Brethren, I, Joachim, with permission of Almighty God and of this meeting, will give out no text but present you with a question: is it the Lord's will that Christian should fight Christian here at the gates of Rome? If He grant us a clearness upon His ultimate purpose, we may then inform our officers as to how we perceive our duty. So let us therefore pray in silence.

A pause, broken by the odd catch in the throat or other pious evidence.

5TH SOLDIER (*an officious self-important voice*). There can be no clearness without an informed guide. There is a Christ-Bishop with this army, Hosius the Spaniard.

Some murmurs of agreement.

JOACHIM (*hotly*). Why, brother, you do not think, for want of a Bishop, we shall all fall about and flee, like Peter and his comrades in the horror of Gethsemane?

Murmurs of agreement with JOACHIM, *overcoming the other point of view.*

JOACHIM. Bishop Hosius tomorrow will not stand in battle-rank, eye to eye with his brother-in-Christ. Bishop Hosius did not stand against that onslaught in the northern plain. They put a hammer into my hand and I struck down that great warhorse and the man on top of it fell – his closed helmet rolled open: oh God I knew his face – I had broken bread with him at Christ's love-feast not two years since!

Several VOICES: '*Brother against brother – I say we will not do it!*'

4TH SOLDIER (*bursting in, very upset*). God of Grace, you're talking mutiny! Such talk among the regiments twenty years ago brought upon us the persecutions – I don't forget the enormity of Herculius, how he walked down the parade with the Chief Provost-Marshal and all his bloody crushers, smelling out the soldiers of Christ and hurling 'em into the garrison bath-furnace! I don't forget those days.

This produces silence.

JOACHIM (*adamant*). Because thou art lukewarm and neither cold nor hot, I will spew thee out of my mouth. If it is death, then we shall die. Christ will deliver.

General VOICES: '*Christ will deliver . . .!*' *One by one the voices pick up the slogan, until they are all shouting it.*

Scene Sixteen

Exterior: The cries of 'Christ will deliver' are heard continuously but now from afar off.

OFFICER (*urgent and annoyed*). Centurion – you're the guard-commander? – what in Hades is all that row about in the transport-lines?

CENTURION. It's the Christian rank and file, sir, praying themselves up into one of their frenzies. Best not to interfere.

OFFICER. Thank you, Centurion: carry on . . .

Scene Seventeen

Exterior: Back at the Christian meeting. The cries of 'Christ will deliver' begin to fade away as JOACHIM shouts above them repeatedly:

JOACHIM (*in an exalted crescendo*). The Cross of Light, the Cross of Light, the Cross of Light . . .!

VOICES. Quiet, quiet – he will prophesy – Joachim will prophesy – he is about to give utterance with tongues – quiet – (*Etc.*)

Silence falls again.

JOACHIM (*dropping his voice dramatically*). I see it: in the height of the heavens – oh Lord Jesus, answer thy servant – *answer* –!

As he speaks, he seems to be moving amongst the crowd, who respond to him with awestruck murmurs. His voice once again rises to a high pitch. When he finishes, 'amen' is taken up by everyone.

VOICES. Amen, amen, give answer, oh Lord, give answer to thy servant – !

All the VOICES suddenly shut off as though at a signal.

JOACHIM (*flat-voiced, quiet, in the sudden silence*). That's it then. That's it. Finished. He spoke. And I heard him. We know what we've to do. He showed to me the Cross of Light. Our Cross. I heard him say so. He said, wear it. In the forefront of the battle every Christian shall wear his Cross. Brethren, go back to your units, this very night: every man to paint his helmet, paint his shield, with the Cross of Light. And tomorrow morning, when they blow their trumpets, just you let them know you won't be there. Hallelujah.

The 'hallelujah' is spoken softly and with finality. It is repeated in the same tone by others, as the meeting disperses.

Scene Eighteen

KYBELE (*as narrator*).

> All night in the Constantine camp, murmur and stir:
> Last messages whispered, here and there, him and her –

Interior: a tent. Cries of sentries in the distance outside: 'post number one, present and correct and all's well:' and so on.
    SEMIRAMIS *and* JOACHIM *whispering, behind and between the next words of the narrator:*

SEMIRAMIS. Oh my brother, my spouse, my beloved is mine and I am his –

JOACHIM. My love, my dove, my undefiled – hallelujah, thou art mine –

KYBELE (*as narrator*).

> Joachim, first-rank pikeman, prophet of God,
> Loves and is loved by Semiramis:
> A term-bonded soldier and a slave of high price
> Both well aware it is not possible to wed.

SEMIRAMIS.

> We uncover nonetheless our nakedness together, we shed
> What might well be our last tears upon the ground
> Last hope for the day that the whole of our life
> Might at last be our own . . .

JOACHIM. And yet, after the night-time the sunrise: and oh! After *this* sunrise the world of flesh is riven in sunder!

SEMIRAMIS (*misunderstanding his passion*). Oh no, not tonight, we must not think of the battle tonight –

JOACHIM. Semiramis, not the battle, but what is to happen before it – epiphany in the eye of the Lord! Do you know what is the name of this place?

SEMIRAMIS. I heard them call it the Red Rocks.

JOACHIM. Red they may well prove: but that's not how their name shall stand. Oh, it has been written, John the Divine in the Isle called Patmos wrote it: Armageddon, there's the name! We challenge in the name of Christ both of these rival emperors: one great battle and then never again no more – oh thou that hast ravished my heart with one chain of thy neck, let me tell you of all that has been determined –

Fade out his voice under KYBELE*:*

KYBELE (*as narrator*). And he tells her; embraces her; she goes to the tent of the Empress.

Scene Nineteen

Interior: another tent. Some time later. Camp noises continue intermittently as before and fade out.

FAUSTA (*in a state, hitting* SEMIRAMIS). You left me alone, girl, where were you, I *needed* you –! Oh Semiramis – he has sent for me. (*in panic.*) He hasn't spoken to me since the march began, he has lived with his war-horse, his officers, the gamester's fury of his war – and now it has destroyed him, he has an ague-fever, he sits there soaking himself incessantly in hot water: Semiramis, I think he knows that my brother will win the battle, so why has he sent for *me* –?

SEMIRAMIS (*calm, reassuring*). Maxentius may not win, madam, he may not even fight. Christ is the one who will win.

FAUSTA. Constantine does not know Christ – unless Christ and the Unconquered Sun are the same thing, and they're not – are they? He is in pain from head to foot, and how do I know what to do to relieve him –?

SEMIRAMIS (*treating her as a little child*). Oh my lady, don't distress, sit on my lap, my lady child, when you go to him, take this oil, it's very special oil, you tell him that, and you rub it in, you rub it *here*, and you rub it *there* – and you tell him –

FAUSTA. I *have* seen him naked, once: but it frightened me, and I could not touch him – Semiramis, does he mean to make me a woman, upon the night before his death?

SEMIRAMIS (*still soothing her fear*). You tell him this is magic oil, it is designed to let him *sleep*: so he goes to the battle a new man, and there he will see how Christ is going to win! – tell him so, my Rose of Sharon, and then tell him this, which is a very great magic indeed –

> The Cross of Light against the sky
> Shall burn his head and dazzle out his eye
> Let him but follow where it shall travel,
> And there is an end to all his peril . . .

She has recited the verses carefully, slowly, improvising them on the spur of the moment.

FAUSTA. What does it mean?

SEMIRAMIS. Magic.

FAUSTA. From that woman to whom I gave the jewels?

Pause.

SEMIRAMIS. Go now to him.

Scene Twenty

Interior: Constantine's tent. Splashing of bath-water. Outside the camp noises intermittently continue.

KYBELE (*as narrator*).

> Terrible and bare and towering in the clouds of steam,
> There he is, quite alone, confronting the end of his life –

CONSTANTINE (*Crying out in a horror*).

> All my power has been one hopeless dream . . .!

Sound of FAUSTA *entering the tent.*

CONSTANTINE (*with hopeless contempt*).

> Who is that? Is that you?
> Child, I have sent for you: what can you do:
> *I* was only a boy when they sent for *me* and they said.
> 'Your mother from now on is as though she were dead.'
> My father's cold new wife had been delivered him by command
> From the house of Herculius, and in her parchment hand
> She fetched him the crown of Empire and he put it upon his head.
> And then, when he died, and I sprawled in his empty throne –
> God, but the grip of this cramp, every muscle and joint,
> Hot water, pour it quickly, girl, ha, I think I shall faint –

She pours water over him and he roars.

CONSTANTINE (*returning to his theme*).

> I was a young lion on a riverbank among bushes of green and gold,
> I was shouting aloud for joy, I had a wife of my own,
> I had Crispus, my son – and they were mine,
> And I loved them: until suddenly, contemptuous, cold,
> Herculius came: and he said,
> 'Look here, boy, your wife is nothing: my daughter is what you need
> If you truly are of use to rule this Empire at my side'.
> So I sent her away: it was as though she had died:
> And I took from the hand of Herculius – you.
Old snarling wolf-hound with the poison in his bite: is his little bitch-puppy any better, what do you say?

FAUSTA (*very self-contained, not to be intimidated*). Lord, let me rub your back with this bottle of magic oil . . . so.

She rubs him throughout the next speeches: he grunts now and then, as he begins to feel easier.

FAUSTA (*to herself*). He is huge and wet and hard and his skin is like coarse red leather, dark streaks of wet hair all over it, in unimaginable places; I am held captive in the cave of the Cyclops; but as long as I can soothe him he will not eat me – no –

CONSTANTINE. I asked you, what do you say?

FAUSTA (*speaking clearly and precisely*). When my father wanted to kill you, and he called on me to help: he said I was either his or yours, and I knew I was yours – I had to be, because I hated him, it was my secret, he could not guess. Neither could you: when I told you about the plot you didn't believe me, and then I proved it: and Herculius instead of Constantine went down. Not just your puppy – your watchdog.

CONSTANTINE (*as though he is regarding her carefully*). You have grown up since those days. How far have you grown? I scarcely see you from one month to the next, every month a different Fausta. This time tomorrow, a *quite* different Fausta. If I am dead, and if your revengeful brother should decide *not* to kill you for your betrayal of Herculius, you will be once more an Herculian, and they will use you as they will . . . Fausta: my little son, Crispus: he lives alone, as we all live alone, you have never seen him. I have given the secret order as soon as I am put to death, he too . . . what about *you*? You are either mine, or your brother's: you are bound to die for one of us. Which?

FAUSTA (*her voice trembling, but she controls it*). If you climb out of the bath, and lie on the camp-bed – let me rub you all over, not just your back . . . so.

He climbs out of the bath and gets on to the bed. She starts again to massage him.

FAUSTA. So: does the oil have virtue?

CONSTANTINE (*as though surprised to find it so*). Yes, it does . . . I think it does . . . I asked you a question: which? (*to himself:*) Her fingers against my limbs are trembling and I am trembling to feel them there, she could blind me in an instant with the pin of her brooch: more dangerous to me than either her father or brother, and I allow her, and she does not do it . . . doesn't she realise, in my despair, I have *given* her this chance?

FAUSTA (*matter-of-fact, as she rubs*). Your life was my gift when I saved you from Herculius, your life is my gift tonight, and tomorrow – Maxentius will not win.

CONSTANTINE (*scorning this optimism*). Every day since the north of Italy I have looked up to heaven in vain for my portent from the Unconquered Sun –

FAUSTA (*as a purely reasonable proposition*). Not in heaven. Here. A naked man beneath my hands and he has taken no harm: why shouldn't *that* be your portent? The Unconquered Sun is a great God, the God of the Christians is greater than he is, and the Mother of Christ is the Mother of the Living and the greatest of all: she was your own mother, sent away; the mother of Crispus, sent away; and you have searched for her ever since, all your life, in your imperial crown. Lie still, lie still, you helpless naked fellow. I will tell you how and when you will understand the gift of life –

> The Cross of Light against the sky
> Shall burn his head and dazzle out his eye.
> Let him but follow where it shall travel,
> And there is an end to all his peril . . .

CONSTANTINE (*Groaning*). No, no, no.

He shakes off, as it were, his superstitious acceptance of her spell-binding, and scrambles to his feet.

CONSTANTINE (*angrily contemptuous again*). No, this is nonsense, the most unscrupulous mountebank witchcraft! How much does your brother Maxentius pay you to arouse my blood and then extinguish it? By God, it is morning already –

Despite a small protesting cry from FAUSTA, *he plunges out of the tent.*

KYBELE (*as narrator*).

> And with that, out he goes, hardly a garment on his dripping skin:
> Maxentius must fight before Constantine can win:
> And before Maxentius fights, surely Helios the Unconquered Sun,
> If only for a moment, will condescend to shine –?

Scene Twenty-One

Exterior: after a passage of time. A field in the early morning outside the camp. Footsteps in the long grass, a jingle of armour.

CONSTANTINE (*furiously frustrated*). Dark, why is it so damn dark, so late into the morning –?

GENERAL. Troops very slow to respond to their orders, Emperor, they are nervous, they do not know what we are doing.

CONSTANTINE. Nothing but cloud, mist, fog . . . Yet, even so, even so, if Maxentius does march, we must be ready to meet him . . .! General-muster, prepare to advance – at least that looks like *something* – in the meantime, where's my uniform!

The cry 'General-muster! Prepare to advance!' has been picked up by other voices further away: and now bugles blow and drums start beating in the distance, with a general cacophany of orders.

GENERAL (*to himself, very sour*). He is mustering them for nothing. To hold them to arms miles outside the city, all day, and by the evening, tails turned, back to camp, nothing achieved . . . mutiny . . .

Scene Twenty-Two

Interior: a tent. The cacophony of orders continues, now loud and at hand.

PURVEYOR (*coming in and shaking someone in bed*). Bishop, are you in your tent? Oh God, you're not asleep –!

HOSIUS (*sitting up in his bed*). No no – who is that? Purveyor? What's the matter?

PURVEYOR. Urgent! A conspiracy: the Christian rank and file – they have in mind to refuse duty –!

HOSIUS (*fully awake and alarmed*). What! But it's too soon, we don't know yet what Maxentius will do – In the name of heaven, put a stop to it, Colonel –! This could finish our religion for ever: (*To himself:*) Lord Christ, fulfil thy purpose: in thy sight, O God, we are but worms . . .

Scene Twenty-Three

Exterior: troops clattering irregularly onto parade, a good deal of recalcitrant exclamation and protest.

GENERAL (*to himself, savagely*). *Götterdämmerung Feuer-und-Drecklichkeit, um Wotans Willen, was ist hier –?* Never in all my Roman lifetime have I seen such a muster as this, great gaps in every rank like broken teeth in a drunkard's mouth – (*He shouts in helpless anger:*) You, officers, what's going on, what's happening in your bloody cohorts – pull those men together –!

KYBELE (*as narrator*). Why, they slouched on parade like the animals into Deucalion's Ark, half of them missing, half of them half-dressed – and then out of nowhere –

A sharp repeated clear call of a bugle, quite different from the other ones that have been heard already.

KYBELE. – a sudden, new bugle, where was it from? Who had blown it? And at once, into every company, every cohort, all together –

The sound of running feet in a mass.

KYBELE. – maybe a third of his entire army, all of them running together, completing all of a sudden the gaps in the formations: and every man of these men, on his shield, on his helmet –

GENERAL (*to himself, horrified*). A white cross, bright new whitewash, why have they painted every man a white cross on helmet and shield . . .?

KYBELE (*as narrator*). And at that very moment, through the cloud, through the mist, the huge red brilliant sun –

CONSTANTINE (*as though seeing a vision*). General, it is a Cross of Light, look –! From one end of the army to the other the Unconquered Sun streams onto it and throws it back into my eyeballs –

GENERAL. It can only mean one thing: they have declared themselves for what they are: they are not going to fight for *you*.

JOACHIM (*some distance away: in a clear precise voice*). Christ will deliver.

'Christ will deliver' is picked up by those near him: and then is repeated all along the ranks.

GENERAL (*quietly to* CONSTANTINE). You see? Emperor, there are very few of these white crosses among the cavalry – we could turn the cavalry onto them, we could cut them down in scores –

CONSTANTINE (*with great intensity, to the General*). My eyes have been dazzled, my head begins to burn, the Cross of Light is to be followed, not cut down: oh, here *is* the portent!

He raises his voice to the group of staff-officers who are near him; and whose muttering voices and jingling armour we can hear as they gather round for his orders.

CONSTANTINE. Imperial decision: staff-conference orders, now! Dismiss the parade for one quarter of an hour: unit commanders draw buckets of whitewash from stores – *if* there's any left – and all ranks, *all* of them, whatever gods they worship, will adorn their equipment in the manner that you see. Yes: and we'll have it painted on my command-banner as well. If any of the regular religions complain, tell 'em it's the sign of the Unconquered Sun – Phoebus Apollo, Lord Mithras, Helios, tell 'em anything you like – but get it done!

The scout's pony galloping towards him.

SCOUT (*highly excited*). Sir – sir – General – Emperor – sir –! He's marching out of Rome, Emperor, two columns, horse and foot, across the bridges –

CONSTANTINE (*with passionate finality, among the* OFFICERS' *cries of excitement*). The Lord Jesus Christ, whoever, wherever he may be, has delivered him into my hands.

Bustle and shouting now as the OFFICERS *dismiss the parade and give out the new orders.*

GENERAL (*incorrigible*). It still does not mean that these Christians will obey you.

CONSTANTINE (*abruptly: he knows now exactly what to do*). Go find me that creeping Spaniard, the Christ-Bishop, Hosius – where is he?

Fade.

Scene Twenty-Four

Exterior: the same after a lapse of time.

HOSIUS. Emperor, I had absolutely no knowledge that all this was going to happen –

CONSTANTINE (*hard and abrupt*). Neither had I, Bishop. Neither had anyone: it was very cleverly done. How many Christians in Maxentius' army?

HOSIUS. A great many, certainly, I couldn't say exactly, but –

CONSTANTINE. But enough to destroy him, if they refuse battle at the sight of their own Cross? Bishop, that Cross is now *my* Cross and it means exactly what it says: Jesus Christ is my friend, and *he* gives the orders. Imperial decision: what are you waiting for? Run!

HOSIUS (*heroically persistent*). If Jesus is to be your friend, he requires more than the mere statement, he requires his official church to be officially recognised – an Imperial decree, complete toleration for the leaders of the Christian faith.

CONSTANTINE (*not without humour*). Ah, it began with magic, it ends with politics . . . I grant you everything you ask for, we'll look into it in detail after the battle. All that concerns me now is that Maxentius must go down!

Scene Twenty-Five

KYBELE (*as narrator*).

> Oh and he did go down.
> They beat him and they broke him
> And they threw him off his bridge.
> In the waters of the River Tiber –

CONSTANTINE (*exultant*).

> – I watched Maxentius drown,
> I watched his army run,
> I made his army mine:
> The Unconquered Sun is mine
> The Cross of Light is mine –!

KYBELE (*as narrator*).

> – said Constantine.
> And Constantine, with his wife upon his arm,
> Aloft in his golden chariot
> Through the trumpeting streets of Rome –

The harsh sounds and music of the battle are merging here with the more formal music and the cheers of the Roman triumph.

Through the rest of the sequence, in and between the speeches, the orchestrated shouts of CONSTANTINE'*s guard and its well-drilled* CHEERLEADERS.)

Shouts of the triumph

> All Hail Constantine Augustus!
> Hosanna: Hallelujah!
> Hail to the Lord Christ!
> Hail to the Lord Helios!
> Hail to the One True God!

The rumble and clatter of chariot wheels continuous throughout.
The following speeches are stylised, in time with the beat of the procession.

CONSTANTINE (*to himself*). I have it. Half the world. Who gave it me? I know his Cross: not his face. His power: not his history. Find out.

HOSIUS (*to himself*). The People of Christ are the people of a book. A God-dictated book. Read it to the Emperor. Teach him to read it. Teach him to teach it. Rule him that he may rule.

JOACHIM (*to himself*). New Heaven, new earth. New Rome, its name Jerusalem. New Jerusalem, its name is Rome. Now: is the Kingdom of God!

FAUSTA (*to herself*). I am alive. I gave him life. The new life of that girl-child in midst of the snowstorm brings life into *my* body. This very day my monthly blood, for the first time, begins to flow, washes out the blood of death: I am a woman.

CONSTANTINE (*to himself*). Find out his power and use it. Make war in the name of Christ: Maximin Daza must go down. My life is his death: it was given me by this Christ. I alone received the vision of the Cross.

KYBELE (*as narrator*). Which was thereupon proclaimed as the truth of Christ for all time.

CONSTANTINE (*to himself*). Christ, the Unconquered Sun, his truth includes all truth.

The music and slogans continue: and fade out.

Closing music.

2

CHRIST IS RISEN: CONSTANTINE

Scene One

KYBELE (*as narrator*). Constantine had defeated his Co-Emperor Maxentius and was ruler of all the west. Against him there had been three co-emperors, now there were only two. It was the year 313 AD. I was living in Naples. You in Hibernia have put me on trial to prove or disprove the genuineness of my philosophical calling; as I understand it, this means my constancy towards the obligations of that calling. Let you know, in Naples this did not seem a question. We accepted the cross of Christ upon our new ruler's battle-flag: he was tolerant, we were tolerant: and anyway was not the Cross also the symbol of Lord Helios the Unconquered Sun? A poetic concurrence, to enrich our spiritual life. Not so, in the eastern Empire, where Christians were in great numbers, and one of the two co-emperors, Maximin Daza of Egypt and Asia, was not at all tolerant.

The centre of his rule was Palestine: out of Palestine once came a strange disruptive god who said 'No other gods but me'. He used to be called Jehovah, now he was Christ, and Maximin Daza wanted him dead, he wanted all his intolerant followers dead.

Exterior: the song of the CHAIN-GANG, *working in a quarry: they chant a long drawn-out dirge to the beat of their hammers.*

KYBELE. He could not kill them all: so he enslaved them into his quarries and mines.

CHAIN-GANG (*chant*). Christ will deliver
        The promise has been given
        Christ will deliver
        The promise has been given
        Christ will deliver
        The promise has been given
        Glory will come
        Glory will come . . .

This continues through the narration.

KYBELE (*as narrator*). I was told that when the news of Constantine's victory came to the labour camps, the prisoners rioted for joy.

The chant suddenly dies away: there is a moment's silence as the hammers also stop. And then, first one voice, then another, and then one after another, MEN, WOMEN, *and* CHILDREN. *As it were all along the line, crying out the new phrase.*

CHAIN-GANG (*chant*). Christ is risen: Constantine!

KYBELE (*as narrator*). One after another they stood erect in their fetters and shouted out their triumph.

1ST GUARD (*furiously, as the new chant continues*). There he is, that one, at the end of the line –!

2ND GUARD. Another – over there! Shut his mouth for him – sharp –!

Running feet of the GUARDS, *blows, cries of pain: but still the chant is taken up.*

KYBELE (*as narrator*). And how had the word been brought there? Women, of course, inconspicuous, anonymous: imagine two women, I have told you about them before – upon Constantine's march from Gaul. A young dark-skinned mother, her child upon her back –

Rioting in background.

MELANTHO. I am Melantho.

MARY. My name is Mary the Companion.

KYBELE (*as narrator*). An impoverished nondescript pair, and somehow they had worked their way across half the world through every obstacle of bureaucracy and the secret police to bring this comfort to the camps of death in the forgotten corners of the desert. Where will they go next?

Scene Two

Interior: in a hut near the quarry, the riot heard faintly in the distance. Now and then, MELANTHO's BABY *gives a small cry and she hushes it anxiously.*

JOHN (*speaking in an urgent whisper: a strong middle-aged voice*). One more camp you ought to visit. The bitumen workings. Southern shore of the Dead Sea. Two hundred of our people there. The bedouin know the road. Put yourselves in their hands: it's a risk, but we have to trust them. And after that?

MARY. Antioch.

JOHN. Dangerous. Hardly any of us stick our head above ground in Antioch. I can give you a name, of a man keeps a safe-house, just inside the west gate. At least, he used to – I don't know now –

MARY. We have a name.

MELANTHO. My mother. Have you heard of her? I haven't seen her since I was a child. We are told she is in Antioch, a place called the House of the Women, her name is Oenothea.

JOHN (*his voice suddenly becoming hostile and wary*). Oenothea? The great Jezebel, high priestess of the abhorrent Babylonian Goddess . . .? Your mother?

MELANTHO (*simply*). If I went to her, she would help me.

JOHN. Oh yes, she might help *you*. You are a woman, she would think no doubt she could pervert you. Let me tell you the help she has given to the rest of us. Every man, woman, child, in this colony of death is here because of her. Every left leg has been lamed, every right eye has been put out, even mine, and I was a man blind from birth. Maximin Daza feels himself more intimate, more secure, with your mother than with any single heathen: she is his own personal sorcerer, she cured him of sexual impotence. When you see her, tell her this: Blind John of Antioch, five years upon the stone-gang, is now known among his comrades as John the Reader, because I have by heart and can repeat every word of Holy Scripture; in this place without books, I am the Book of God for all of them. Oh never can they murder the Word –

The sounds of conflict have died down. As he speaks, JOHN *has opened the door of the hut: voices of the* GUARDS *in the distance – 'over that way' – 'take a look at the huts'.*

JOHN (*hurriedly*). Ssh – I hear the guards: away from here, both of you. Blessing of Christ upon you – go.

Scene Three

KYBELE (*as narrator*). Antioch. It is said that in this city the Christians first found the name for their new cult: and that the man who brought it there – Saul of Tarsus –changed his own name on the way. He was out to change everything. And no better place than Antioch to begin.

Behind her narration build up a confused crowd-noise mingled with music – clashings of cymbals, woodwind, and snatches of exotic chants, as though a number of religious processions had got mixed up together in the street. Out of this turbulence, the VOICES *in the scene arise, isolated: this is not a naturalistic sequence.*

KYBELE. Every shape and size of god came ululating into Antioch: a city that compelled the most rational philosopher to be a mountebank magician, competing for an audience.

OENOTHEA (*late thirties: an eastern voice of intense authority*). My goddess, the fruitful Anna, mother of all living things, brought kings of Babylon to her golden bed in ancient days before the flood.

KYBELE (*as narrator*). The Priestess Oenothea had arrived in Antioch three years earlier, barefoot, from god knows where – she carried in her shawl a crude bejewelled image of a small white-toothed terrible woman, who, she said, brought life back to the dead, being indeed the very life of the heaven and the earth and the black waters under the earth. The Emperor became afraid of her: and the distinguished Theotecnus, High Priest of Olympian Zeus and Lord Mayor of Antioch, was infuriated by her rivalry.

THEOTECNUS (*elderly, self-important and crafty*). Olympian Zeus is the King of the Gods: this inconsiderable goddess is a scrub-woman in his kitchen. Maximin Daza should have more sense.

OENOTHEA (*fiercely*). Oh he grovelled, Maximin Daza, when I made it known to him how his huge masculine gods, the warriors' gods, the fathers' gods, had supplanted the ancient Mother and turned her into no more than a dutiful daughter, a servile bride, a rapacious horse-leech of a whore.

THEOTECNUS. Such a goddess as Anna of Babylon will respect no political reality, Babylon itself lies beyond the hostile frontier of the Great King of Persia: this is a cult that can only subvert the strength and good order of Empire.

OENOTHEA. I saw this proud Emperor stark naked and trembling, all his strength and good order dissolved when the trance came upon him: and I laughed at him, he heard my goddess laugh at him, till he covered his loins for very shame.

THEOTECNUS. How did she do it? – she built no temples of marble and porphyry and cedar-wood –

OENOTHEA. Humble and meek, I paid out coin in desultory handfuls from an old leather bag –

THEOTECNUS. And she bought for her ridiculous fetish a small house here, a disused shopfront there, a derelict shrine at some crossroad in the slums –

OENOTHEA. – I walked about the city: I talked to the women. Till today there is scarcely a woman's bedroom in Antioch that does not contain its veiled icon of my goddess –

THEOTECNUS. Always close beside the bed –

OENOTHEA. – where the white body of each trusting female is continually desecrated.

THEOTECNUS. – where every woman learns how to carve out her disgusting mastery from the deluded flesh of her rightful husband –

KYBELE (*as narrator*). In one respect only are Oenothea and Theotecnus in any sort of agreement –

The music and crowd-noises have now faded out almost completely.

THEOTECNUS. Maxentius has been destroyed in Italy by an alien creed –

OENOTHEA. The banner of a hanged man, an empty tale, an empty tomb, the empty hope of a eunuch carpenter who told his mother to get lost because the Son of Man alone – he said – is the one who will prevail against the abominable Woman of Babylon –

THEOTECNUS. Jesus alleged-Christ, a convicted criminal terrorist: that is to say supposing such a person ever existed. Maximin Daza must make war against Constantine – true religion against the false – if the Empire is to be saved.

OENOTHEA. Neither the Roman Empire nor its rival the Persian Empire is worth one drop of human blood. But among the people of these cruel dominions, ground-down, desperate, starving, the love of the goddess gives hope to the love of humanity. Let Maximin Daza open his heart to that love, or we will all of us wither to death under the dry dry whirlwind of the dogmas of Christ like a thornbush in the desert.

Scene Four

Exterior: outside a temple. CROWD *murmurings.*

KYBELE (*as narrator*). Theotecnus, in front of his temple, has endowed an ivory statue: eyeballs of precious stones: lips, teeth and tongue all wrought out of the purest gold: now and then the statue speaks –

HYMN.   Lord Zeus Omnipotent
               Olympian Omnipotent
               Lord Zeus Olympian
               Greatest and Best –

PRIEST (*smooth clerical voice*). Right Reverend, the oracular mouth is about to give utterance.

A new sound gradually makes itself heard, a kind of high-pitched buzz like bagpipes being got ready to play.

PRIEST (*to the people: who respond with excitement*). Hearken, o men of Antioch – now it begins to sing!

THEOTECNUS (*privately to* PRIEST). Make sure the transcript is accurate. Where is the shorthand-writer?

PRIEST (*also privately*). He is here, with his tablets. Choirmaster, silence.

The hymn breaks off at once.

PRIEST (*speaks again to the people*). Silence for the miraculous words!

The CROWD *falls silent. The buzz resolves itself into something like human diction.*

STATUE (*a deep buzzing boom*). Alent lontamine bor . . . alent Leftium bor bor bor.

The CROWD *gasps in wonder.*

THEOTECNUS (*interpreting to the* CROWD, *slowly, precisely*). Against Constantine, war: against Christians, war, war, war –

The statue begins to buzz again: and the PRIEST *again calls for silence.*

STATUE. Mithiniul sky lend . . . weather . . . bor.

THEOTECNUS (*again interpreting*). Licinius, my friend, together, war – write it down. Licinius, legitimate co-Emperor in Greece and Illyria, is the natural ally of our Emperor against Constantine: the statue confirms it! The Lord Zeus has commanded!

CROWD (*the beginnings of a political demonstration*). War against Constantine, war against Christians, Licinius is our friend – (*Etc.*)

THEOTECNUS (*privately to* PRIEST). The Emperor will read the transcript: and his policy will be *our* policy . . .

Peak slogans. Fade.

Scene Five

Interior: in the sewers. dripping water, echoing vaults, footsteps splashing through liquid and sludge.

HYMN (WOMEN's *voices*).
> *An*na great *la*dy of *Ba*bylon, *god*dess of *life* and of *death*
> *Life* and of *death* and of *Ba*bylon *god*dess, o *An*na ho *ho*
> *An*na of *Ba*bylon, *Ba*bylon *An*na, o *ho*-ho, ho-*ho* . . .:

Repeated as often as necessary, particularly the 'ho-ho' bits.

KYBELE (*as narrator*). Oenothea, having no temple, transports the image of the goddess to wherever it is expedient for the goddess to be. Beneath the streets of Antioch, a vast labyrinth of sewers, brought together in the middle in a wide subterranean vault, where Oenothea and her acolytes have assembled in secret to determine a new ritual.

OENOTHEA (*serious and intent*). Today this Roman Emperor, at last he has sworn it to me, he will *do it*! – he comes barefoot among slime and refuse, here in the thick clogged anus of Antioch: to make the whole world clean and new – as it were, in the twinkling of an eye.

The hymn comes to an end.

OENOTHEA. Nothing must be left to chance. The whole status of our goddess depends upon this ritual. Is the image properly dressed at the corner of the outfall-sump? With all the candles, as I said – and the collection-bowl?

1ST ACOLYTE (*the* ACOLYTES *are young women*). Holy Mother, it is.

OENOTHEA. And the images of the lesser gods, I said one against every archway where the drains run into the vault, you've left room for the pilgrims to walk round them?

2ND ACOLYTE. We have, Holy Mother.

OENOTHEA. The complete network of the sewerage channels has to be traversed by all the pilgrims, nine times, for each repetition of the liturgy. Absolutely crucial none of you lose count – do you all have your prayer-beads? – show me show me –

Murmurs from ACOLYTES *and clatter of beads.*

OENOTHEA. Good. And most important of all, none of the pilgrims must get lost – particularly the older ones – not even Theotecnus.

2ND ACOLYTE (*amid subdued giggles*). *If* he comes –

OENOTHEA (*grimly*). Oh he will come.

Fade.

Scene Six

Interior: a buzz of conversation round a dinner table as though something very disconcerting has just been propounded.

MAXIMIN DAZA (*aged 29: an excitable, irascible, arbitrary dangerous man, with a coarse barking voice still redolent of his earlier years as an NCO on the parade-ground. The nature of the voice suggests a big body and physical strength. His religious reflections are both ignorant and deeply sincere, and his self-contradictions are perfectly unselfconscious. He is now vehemently enlarging on the announcement which has just disconcerted the company*). Yes – in the sewers! After dinner you'll all come with your Emperor, *all* of you – ministers of state, staff officers, eunuchs of the palace, my wife and her women, priests of the recognised temples – *all*!

Three days and three nights, no food, no sleep, no drink, no shape or form of sexual indulgence, nothing but prayer, till the voice of the Goddess, the eternal infallible voice, conturb our hearts like an oracle: and then we shall know what to do! What's happened to the music?

Music is heard but very much in the background.

THEOTECNUS (*nervously unsure of all the implications*). Unutterable Refulgent Majesty – it is your wish we all enter into a vow?

MAXIMIN DAZA. Have you all got something to drink? The food will be served directly. Theotecnus, the vow is made, I made it, me, Maximin Daza, on behalf of my entire government.

Because you my government sit and look at me, whinge at me, bleat at me – 'what is to be done?' The corn crop in Egypt has failed, people in thousands are dying of hunger, Constantine has denied the gods, the great King of Persia is once again threatening our borders, utter bloody corruption in every department of state, and Licinius along the Danube in terror of Gothic barbarians – he demands I should send him soldiers, *how* can I send him soldiers –?

THEOTECNUS (*irritably pressing a perennial point*). Majesty, as I told you, the miraculous oracular mouth of Lord Zeus has already pronounced on these matters, he has made it quite clear that an alliance with Licinius exerted against Constantine will –

MAXIMIN DAZA. If *that* is an oracle, then I am a whirling dervish. Your miraculous mouth does not appear to have read a single foreign-policy report for the last fortnight.

What he now says is new to the company: and they respond to it with gasps and cries of alarm.

MAXIMIN DAZA (*very bitterly*). Licinius, my esteemed Co-Emperor, the ruler of my Dalmatian homeland, has thought fit to put out the word that he, an acknowledged Augustus, is prepared to make terms with Constantine! So even if I send him the troops that he asks for, how are we to know he won't use them against us?

General murmur.

1ST COURTIER (*a brisk military voice*). Majesty, it is all a question how many Emperors there are to be in this Empire. Constantine thinks there should be no one but him –

2ND COURTIER (*a sleek toady*). We think there should be no one but *you* –

There is some well-trained applause for this sentiment: and a little chorus of 'Maximin Daza, sole emperor: Hail!'

3RD COURTIER (*a dry cynical administrator*). Licinius will assist – in order to betray – whichever seems the most likely to prevail.

A murmur of agreement.

MAXIMIN DAZA (*bursting out passionately and rather pathetically*). Don't you see, don't you see, you damn fools, we are already most dreadfully betrayed! I cannot beat Constantine if Licinius is with him: but if Licinius is with *me*, all my effort is diverted into *his* bloody stupid war against the Goths! Don't you see human counsel is worth nothing in this emergency – religion – religion alone –!

Cross-fade.

Scene Seven

Interior: in the sewerage.

OENOTHEA. – religion will accomplish nothing, without practicality. Chariclea –

1ST ACOLYTE. Holy Mother?

OENOTHEA. – famine relief. While we wait for the Emperor, you and Vashti go back to the House of the Women. Be ready to take delivery of fifteen wagons of grain: from beyond the Persian border, therefore it's illegal; be careful – Theotecnus would do anything to discredit us. *His* relief operation has been a complete fiasco.

2ND ACOLYTE. Even some of the Christians are coming to *us*, they can get nothing to eat from their own people –

OENOTHEA (*as a matter of practical fact*). If they eat the food of the goddess, they will no longer be Christians.

Cross-fade.

Scene Eight

Interior. The EMPEROR'*s banquet again: music continues, as before: and* MAXIMIN DAZA *is holding forth.*

MAXIMIN DAZA. Christianity is not the problem, however much Constantine may think he'll encourage it, I have *dealt* with Christianity, in Antioch now it is a minority cult, we have arrested all the ringleaders — high time we had dinner, we must feed ourselves up in preparation for the ritual, bring in the dinner!

SERVANTS *are heard ordering other* SERVANTS: '*Bring in the dinner*' *etc., and there is a bustle.*

Positive affirmation, that's what this Empire needs: one god, female *and* male, inclusive of all divinity: and if, by the strength of her ritual, Oenothea can prove to me that her goddess alone exudes that all-embracing power, then I, as a religious man, am prepared to accept it, and you will accept it, and Zeus will accept it. Anna of Babylon will reign supreme.

THEOTECNUS (*highly alarmed by the* EMPEROR'*s resolute manner*). Refulgent Majesty, I adjure you, in the Name of Zeus Omnipotent, not to put your trust in this woman Oenothea! I am already uncovering evidence that her own secret doctrines are directly connected with –

MAXIMIN DAZA (*quiet and dreadful*). If you dare to finish that sentence, I will burn you alive.

A general gasp: they know he means what he says.

THEOTECNUS (*terrified*). Oh Majesty, I did not mean – I – Majesty – forgive me – I –

MAXIMIN DAZA (*ferociously forgiving*). The dinner is on the table, you are my guest, so think yourself lucky.

There is a clatter as dishes are laid, dish-covers removed, etc. The music and dancing has ceased upon his call for dinner.

Because of the famine, we do not eat with greed: porridge is all we eat, serve it out.

Ladling out of porridge. Some sotto voce groans and grumbles.

Theotecnus, I'll not have you abuse our liberalism in regard to religious doctrine. We don't even punish Christians unless they are proven criminals, in our labour camps there is not one single prisoner-of-conscience. What's happened to the music? Where are the dancing women?

He claps his hands.

Because of our sacred vow, they will not dance lasciviously, I have told them to keep their clothes on. Oh, we are well aware how great an effort of endurance – what else did Diocletian the great Augustus have in mind when he divided the Empire, gave command of each quarter of it to one of his own? Dalmatian frontier clansmen, peasants and cowherds, all of us, from the one hard northern corner, well capable of all endurance in the face of disorder, chaos. Yes, even Constantine, who now repudiates the honour of his ancestors. But Diocletian retired from office, great man though he was, founder of my fortunes, inspirer of my life. If the daft old devil had done what I'm doing, he'd still be on his throne. *He* abandoned his problems, *we* intend to solve them. Positive affirmation.

We are to take them to the heart of the goddess, and she will provide an answer. God knows, we've to get one from somewhere . . . Eat your porridge, gobble it up. Our Priestess of Mysteries will not be kept waiting!

Cross-fade: as they all begin to eat porridge in silence.

Scene Nine

Interior: the sewers. The HYMN:

> Anna great *la*dy of *Ba*bylon, *god*dess of *life* and of *death*
> *Life* and of *death* and of *Ba*bylon *god*dess, o *An*na ho *ho*
> *An*na of *Ba*bylon, *Ba*bylon *An*na, o *ho*-ho, ho-*ho* . . .!

Echoing murmur of a large congregation in the vault. At the last ho-ho . . .

OENOTHEA (*magisterially*). Lord Emperor, and all of you! Repeat the invocation: 'All gods become one god, female and male'.

ALL. All gods become one god, female and male.

1st ACOLYTE. Repetition nine-times-nine. At the end of nine-times-nine, stand upright, arms outstretched, repeat the affirmation: –

OENOTHEA. Power of the Mother, Power of the Spouse, Power of the Widow: Three in One and One in Three.

As they all begin to repeat this affirmation: cross-fade to suggest passage of time.

Scene Ten

Interior: the sewers. The CONGREGATION *is now moving off: the hymn is played on instruments, without singing. Their feet splash uncertainly in the channels, and there are groans and exclamations.*

OENOTHEA. Take it slowly, follow the acolytes, keep it moving, one step at a time –

ACOLYTES (*smoothly and efficiently stewarding the process*). A ledge under the water here, mind where you put your feet – follow the line of the torches, please – turn left at the next bend, please are there any more officers of the Antioch City Council, where's the Town Clerk? – keep your eye on the line of the torches, please.

The footfalls fade away, as does the music.

Scene Eleven

KYBELE (*as narrator*). Intimidated, amazed, the great men, the great ladies, burdened with their robes of office, stumble forth into the murk of the sewers. After a short while, the Priestess in secret leads the Emperor aside to a small foul brick-lined alcove where, dripping with filth, they press their ears against the floor: an acoustic abnormality, every echo of every word, muttered or spoken throughout the labyrinth.

Interior: the secret alcove in the sewers. The voices of the COURTIERS *processing through the tunnels come faintly but very clearly to this echo-chamber, against an incessant background of the invocation, endlessly repeated; and now and then – the affirmation.*

2ND COURTIER (*from the tunnel*). Steady, man, in the Name of Cerberus, you'll have us both bloody drowned!

A lot of confused splashing.

1ST COURTIER (*from the tunnel*). Why else d'you think he's brought us here?

MAXIMIN DAZA (*in a furious whisper*). I know *that* voice: my own personal military staff! Mark him down for a short interview with the Chief of Security!

2ND COURTIER (*from the tunnel*). I'm never going to last out three days of all this –

1ST COURTIER (*from the tunnel*). He's got a sentry at every manhole-grating.

1ST ACOLYTE (*from the tunnel*). Keep moving, gentlemen, please, don't interrupt the sequence.

1ST COURTIER (*from the tunnel*). Blood of Hercules, there's a rat!

2ND COURTIER (*from the tunnel, gloomily*). Scores of 'em, hundreds –

1ST COURTIER (*from the tunnel*). Look here – d'you suppose this is a new sort of government purge?

MAXIMIN DAZA (*gleefully*). Of course it is, of course it is, the *goddess* does the purging, I am but her instrument.

1ST COURTIER (*from the tunnel*). He's out of his mind.

MAXIMIN DAZA. So I am: so will we all be when we've all been down here three days.

OENOTHEA. Mere existence, that is all, swim like fishes in the waters of the womb of the Great Mother.

Fade out.

Scene Twelve

Exterior: a quiet street; occasional footfalls and carts in the distance: birdsong. Behind narration, chair-bearers bring and set down the sedan chair. Wicket gate opens, and footsteps of old lady.

KYBELE (*as narrator*). In a well-to-do quarter of Antioch, behind peeling whitewashed walls, an old house, once splendid, now neglected and dilapidated, the inhabitants never observed – although neighbours will tell you they think there are two of them: ladies, of great station and mysterious history. Only their servant, an old hobbling crone, occasionally emerges from the wicket-gate. Sometimes a sedan-chair stops outside the house, and a sealed letter is handed to her.

Crossfade to interior. Voices of PRISCA *and* VALERIA *muttering indecipherable prayers which stop as* OLD WOMAN'*s footsteps approach.*

KYBELE (*as narrator*). Indoors, two women kneel on the untended dishevelled floor. Hands clasped in prayer, ears pricked for the footsteps of the old servant. They are well-dressed, and of proud deportment, but look closely, their garments are threadbare, their faces lined with anxiety and suffering.

The last wrapping comes off a scroll.

PRISCA (*a firm stoical voice: she is in her sixties*). Read what he says to you.

VALERIA (*aged between thirty and forty: attempting to be as stoical as her mother, but unable to suppress her distraught emotions*). 'From Gaius Maximin Daza, Lord of Egypt, Syria and Asia, greeting: to his Most Noble and Beloved Relatives, to the Lady Prisca, Refulgent Spouse of Diocletian the great Augustus and to her daughter Valeria, Widow of our deceased uncle, the Divine Emperor Galerius. Most beautiful Valeria, you are the dearest of all the suppliant-pensioners who presently enjoy our compassionate protection. At ease upon my couch I recollect in such great detail each particular carnal vibration as you bowed yourself in grief beside me at the funeral of Galerius –'

PRISCA. We will hear no more of that. Detestable pornography. To keep us starving in utter poverty until you yield to his filthy desires –

VALERIA (*a sudden cry, as it were forced out against her will*). Is there no one on this earth to help us?

LUCUSTA (*from the far end of the room: aged about seventy, a voice full of slum-cunning*). Milady –?

PRISCA (*startled*). Lucusta? What is it, woman?

LUCUSTA (*approaching*). I'll tell you who will help you. Oenothea the priestess at the House of the Women will help you. There's no food distributed anywhere else: they've even closed the market . . .

VALERIA (*in some horror*). The Priestess! – but, mother, we cannot –

PRISCA (*cutting her short*). Thank you, Lucusta, you may leave us.

LUCUSTA (*curtsying herself out*). Most Refulgent, Most Noble . . .

VALERIA (*once LUCUSTA has quite gone out*). Oenothea is a heathen, any food she dispenses will have been offered to an idol, we have already denied Our Lord for the safety of our mortal flesh – not any more!

They fall to their knees and recommence their prayers.

PRISCA. Holy Mary, Mother of God, in thy infinite mercy, grant us a sign –! Grant us a sign, grant us a sign –!

A sudden flutter of bird's wings.

VALERIA (*in excitement*). Mother – look at the roof! at the hole in the broken roof! That bird was trapped in the house just as we are – and yet –

The wings' flutter stops and the bird sings.

– she pauses in her agony, and she sings!

The wings beat again: and disappear.

And now she flies out!

PRISCA. You are right, it is a sign. We will go to this heathen woman.

Scene Thirteen

Interior: the sewers, as from the secret echo-chamber, after a considerable passage of time. The ritual continues, with evidence of physical distress in its by-now broken rhythms.

OENOTHEA (*herself exhausted*). All sense of time lost, yet time is still with us. Two days, more or less. Further and further down into the depths of purgation. Emperor, have you trudged, have you prayed, have you prostrated yourself in the mire? Why do you return now to your priestess before she is ready for you?

MAXIMIN DAZA (*his voice cracking with thirst*). Oenothea, you have not told me, when the oracle is given, how shall we know it is given?

OENOTHEA. Because the words of it will be mingled with the mouthings of all the pilgrims, with your own mouthings, you will not be able to mistake it.

MAXIMIN DAZA. What are they mouthing now?

OENOTHEA. Nothing to the purpose, only their own weaknesses. Listen.

4TH COURTIER (*a woman, in the tunnel, approaching hysteria*). O Mother of the gods, I denounced my innocent neighbours as atheist Christians –

1ST COURTIER (*likewise*). O Mother of the gods, my embezzlements of the corn-subsidies have helped bring about this famine –

GENERAL VOICES (*in tunnel*). O Mother of the gods, have mercy, let our sins not be found out – (*Etc.*)

OENOTHEA. Go again, Emperor, bring forth the vomit of your *own* fear – go –!

A pause as he goes.

OENOTHEA (*calling quietly*). Chariclea, has he gone?

1ST ACOLYTE (*approaching*). He is back among the slime, Holy Mother.

OENOTHEA. Tell your sisters to begin the words – go.

KYBELE (*as narrator*). Oenothea's acolytes, amid the invocations and affirmations, now began to insert the message of her intended oracle.

Scene Fourteen

Interior: the sewers, moaning and splashing, and the ACOLYTES' *words re-echoing insistently along the tunnels.*

ACOLYTES (*one after another – distorted sound effects here*). All gods become one god, female and male, all empires become one empire, Roman and Persian . . . Power of the Mother, Power of the Orient, Power of Persia, Three in One and One in Three . . . Persia . . . Persia . . . Persia . . .

OENOTHEA (*to herself*). Let him hear enough of this, he will turn his policy eastward, make a treaty with Persia, and my goddess in her shrine at Babylon will control both the Empires: faced with which –

KYBELE (*as narrator*). Faced with which, Constantine, and Licinius, must needs submit without resistance: Maximin Daza will be a new Alexander the Great! But Oenothea had left the revelation too late. A confidential messenger, suddenly down in the sewers, upon his knees before the staggering exhausted Emperor –

Scene Fifteen

Interior: the sewers, a passage where MAXIMIN DAZA *is suddenly brought to a halt as the agent splashes down in front of him.*

AGENT. Lord Emperor!

MAXIMIN DAZA (*frightened*). What? Who are you? Are you a demon out of Acheron, throwing your torchlight into my face –?

AGENT (*flatly*). No, Lord, North-west Germany. The confederation of hostile tribes has accepted your privy subsidy, they can swarm into Gaul, take Constantine in the rear any time that Your Majesty chooses: and moreover they will need to. For Constantine has confirmed his alliance with Licinius against you, beyond hope of reversal. Licinius is to marry the sister of Constantine, and a Christian Bishop is invited to the ceremony and Diocletian the retired Emperor is invited to the ceremony and –

OENOTHEA (*furiously approaching*). No, Emperor, no, do not listen to this man – he is sent here indeed by demons to confound all the work of the goddess –

MAXIMIN DAZA (*shrewdly weighing it up*). Diocletian, shamed by a Christ-Bishop? Constantine, diverted by Germans and thereby Licinius laid wide-open to my attack? While the work of the Goddess urges me to turn my back on them and extend myself eastward? No, this is no demon but the strongest oracle I ever heard . . . I am guided by the Immortals, nobody else: I'm not going to argue: I return to the main vault, I shall make my imperial decision – now – back to the vault –!

General cries: 'Back to the vault!'

Fade out.

Scene Sixteen

The same, in another tunnel.

KYBELE (*as narrator*). Theotecnus, astray in the tunnels, has his own confidential visitor, old Lucusta from the house of Diocletian's wife and daughter.

THEOTECNUS (*surprised*). Who in Hades are you?

LUCUSTA. Oh you know me, I'd never have known *you* with all the muck smeared all over you: will you listen now, Oenothea is getting everyone along to that house of hers, I recommended no less than forty to go to her in the last few days – even ladies of very great place; purple, I say no more. Yet she refuses point-blank that Priestess job I'd hope she'd give me. What will *you* give, if I let you in to some certain definite fact that'd close down her operation for ever?

THEOTECNUS. Rubbish, you don't know anything.

LUCUSTA. Don't I? What will you give me? Chief Sacramental Widow in the annual Espousal Ceremony of the Lord Zeus, how about that?

THEOTECNUS. Only if the information is worth it.

LUCUSTA. Oh it's worth it, fair enough. Oenothea has a long-lost daughter, she is a Christian, she has just come to Antioch with a most notorious female Christian: and as soon as the ritual's over they will both be at the House of the Women. How about that?

Cries: 'Back to the vault' – 'Back to the vault'

KYBELE (*as narrator*). But the ritual has found its own termination. Overhead in the streets and markets, the multitude of Antioch, unable any longer to endure their famished existence, are breaking open the warehouses where the hoarded grain accumulates.

Scene Seventeen

Interior, the sewers, in the main vault. The sounds of rioting have begun to seep into the underground tunnels, and now rise in a fierce crescendo. The noise of the ritual breaks off amid cries of consternation.

KYBELE (*as narrator*). Down through all the sewer-gratings the clamour of the riot assails the Emperor's ear –

MAXIMIN DAZA (*in a panic*). Is everyone together, where is my bodyguard?

1st COURTIER (*his military duties reasserting themselves*). First company at the head of the shaft, second company down here – Lord Emperor, your security-personnel deployed and ready –!

Splashing footsteps and voices all converge.

MAXIMIN DAZA (*taking command of himself*). Imperial decision: one, we declare war upon the renegade Licinius, and, when he has gone down, upon Constantine, renegade and traitor!

OENOTHEA (*hard cold and precise, as the* EMPEROR *pauses to take breath*). May the Mother of All Living spit blood upon your genitals, Emperor, may you perish like a worm under a stone.

There is a dead moment of silence. MAXIMIN DAZA *stammers in superstitious terror: and then explodes with rage.*

MAXIMIN DAZA. Ah – ah – arrest that woman, hold her there, catch her you damnfool, don't let her get away –!

Splashing and scuffling, as OENOTHEA *makes her escape down the tunnel, with one or two following after her.*

VOICES. Hold her, catch her, after her, quick –!

MAXIMIN DAZA (*as the noise dies away*). Imperial decision: two. This terrorist attempt to destabilise our authority is inspired by the alien ideology of the renegade Constantine. We therefore reactivate the utmost rigour of every law directed against minority cults. The Imperial Guard will put everyone to the sword whom they find at large upon the street. In the meantime, look for a manhole leading up into a *quiet* street through which we can all be extricated. Go!

Orders given, general shouting, riot noise increases: the sound of the GUARD *trampling along the street: fighting and screams – fade down to serve as background for next speech.*

Scene Eighteen

KYBELE (*as narrator*). Maximin Daza moved his army, at great speed, out of Asia, across the Bosporus, and took Byzantium. No less speedily, law-and-order under Zeus was restored in Antioch, the police of Theotecnus having swooped upon the House of the Women and arrested all whom they found.

Riot is background to the following sequence of internal narrative monologues.

PRISCA. I am the wife of an Emperor: I walked on foot that day like a beggar-woman through the slums of the town. Every street was full of riot.

VALERIA. I am the widow of an Emperor: with my mother in the terrible street I walked on foot past the synagogue.
    The Jews inside were chanting: it was the Day of Atonement. They had a notice on the door: 'Food Distribution for the Children of the Circumcised Temporarily Suspended'. I saw the soldiers go in upon them: and kill them all.

A brief noise of violence and screaming: fade it out.

PRISCA (*she and* VALERIA *hurrying from the violence*). Beyond the next corner, the House of the Women. In a great crowd outside the gateway, hundreds of starving emaciated women –

A murmur of a crowd of hungry WOMEN.

PRISCA. – and then, before we could reach them –

VALERIA. How many months since it happened . . .?

MARY. How many months since our journey began? I, Mary had brought with me Melantho, the daughter of Oenothea, the young mother to the house of her mother, we could not get to the house –

Crowd noises build up.

MELANTHO. Every time the door was opened to let any of the women out, the ones in the street surged up against it to get in, I did not understand, I was frightened –

OENOTHEA. I had made my escape, I had fortified my house, armed all my eunuchs, put them on guard –

MELANTHO. My mother all of a sudden appeared in the doorway: my heart gave a leap, I knew she would surely help us, the child in my arms seemed to know that we were safe, she was no longer crying from hunger –

MARY. I was praying all the time to the Blessed Virgin: and when the crowd of women fell to their knees crying out 'Holy Mother!' –

Crowd cry out as described.,

MARY. – I thought there had been a miracle, I did not see Oenothea for the moment –

VALERIA. As they shouted 'Holy Mother!' – that was the moment the soldiers with Theotecnus at their head came down upon this house as well –

Sudden onrush of booted feet, screams etc.

VALERIA. Swords, spears, clubs, armed men out of every entry –

Confusion and violence.

PRISCA. Fighting with the eunuchs, slicing through the crowd with their weapons –

VALERIA. Lengths of rope flung round our necks, pulling us, dragging us –

MELANTHO. All together – all at once – mother, I must get to you –

MARY. I tried to call out – a man's hand in my hair, tearing it out of my head –

MELANTHO. The child out of my arms, in the fierce grab of a man's hand – Holy Jesus – what could I do – ?

The sounds of violence stop all at once: and there is silence.

Scene Nineteen

Interior: a prison. Iron door is slammed shut somewhere down a corridor, and a GAOLER'*s footsteps echo and fade away.* MELANTHO'*s* CHILD *cries.*

PRISCA. Ssh – ssh – we are all safe, and the child is safe: in the state-prison of Maximin Daza.

VALERIA. Safe enough, and peaceful enough, now the mother of Melantho has decided to go to sleep. May we settle to our devotions, or would the turbulent spirit of that goddess of hers wake her up to contend with us again?

MELANTHO. She did not know she had a Christian daughter: more of a shock to her than the Emperor's malice.

MARY. If we are constant and quiet, she may be prepared to trust us. Shall we sing about the Christ-child, how he was saved from the cruelty of soldiers?

She begins to sing, in a quiet crooning lullaby manner:

> Oh Egypt's road is long and hard
> And Egypt's land so far,
> Sleep sleep upon your mother's breast
> As she rides beneath the star . . .

Cross-fade to suggest passage of time.

Scene Twenty

Interior. The prison, the entrance lobby. Dragging of chained feet as PRISONERS *are brought in. Iron doors are opened and shut.*

GUARD. All right, Christians, move it, keep in line, down the stairs – turnkey receive admissions, five lengths of chain, fifteen live bodies to a chain; better count 'em all present and correct before you sign 'em in.

CHRISTIANS (*shouting dispersedly*). Glory to Christ in martyrdom, glory to Christ –!

GAOLER (*counting*). One two three four five, one two three four five – hey-up this one's dead, in'he? – I'm not taking *him* – one two three four five – (*Etc.*)

Scene Twenty-One

Interior: the prison: a cell into which the new arrivals are being brought. The cell-door is flung open and they shuffle in, the GAOLER *ordering – 'in you go, follow it through, in you go' etc. the 'glory to Christ' ejaculations continue.*

BISHOP (*already in the cell: an aged, infirm, but rigorous, voice*). New arrivals, Eumolpus?

EUMOLPUS (*already in the cell: young and self-conceited*). Yes, Bishop, scores of them, and some of them very strange company.

A group of WOMEN *singing with exuberance*:

SINGING WOMEN.   O the Blood the red red Blood
> O the red red Blood of heaven
> Pour it out and let it flow
> Now we know we have been chosen
> O the Blood the red red Blood
> Blood of joy and not of woe –

EUMOLPUS (*with disgust*). The Montanist sectarians. Throwing themselves upon martyrdom like courtesans into an orgy.

Overlapping with the WOMEN's *song, another one, sung by a few* MEN.

SINGING MEN.   The Holy Ghost is not God
> Jesus Christ is not God
> God the Father is not God
> But together let them be
> Three in One and One in Three
> God is all together: and so are we!

BISHOP (*with scorn*). Alas alas, the Sabellian sectarians too? Are we to have these monstrous tendencies day and night at each other's throats in this very small cell?

MYSTICAL FANATIC (*his voice rising up ecstatically out of the hubbub*). I have been in every heaven and in every heaven I took on a new shape appropriate to the ineffable flesh of the harlot of the great knowledge –

EUMOLPUS. That one is not even the shadow of a Christian: the false cult of Simon the Magician who would destroy the authority of Paul himself.

BISHOP (*hopefully*). Remember what Paul wrote: 'the authority of the Lord: if a man does not recognise this, he himself should not be recognised'. So that's what we do with them: they are in error, we do not know them.

Cross-fade to suggest passage of time.

Scene Twenty-Two

Interior: the prison. The cell where OENOTHEA *and the others from her house are confined. The* BABY *is crying.*

OENOTHEA (*shrieking and rattling the bars*). Oh wherever she is, she will not let them rest, do you hear me, do you hear me out there – Anna of Babylon will never let you rest in peace –!

MELANTHO (*very angry*). Mother, will you stop that – you're keeping us all awake and the gaolers take no notice – all night the baby's been crying and as soon as she drops off you start her up again –!

OENOTHEA (*uncontrollable*). They took away the goddess, they snatched her from my arms, may the man who has taken her burn inwardly from his bowels to his heart to his head till his whole body becomes –

MELANTHO. Mother, because of you they've stopped bringing us proper food for the baby. She's going to die, mother, die, your own granddaughter and you will have killed her! Of course, to you she's only a Christian and you hate her and you hate me and you want her to be dead!

OENOTHEA (*to the others*). Do you see how she treats me? My own daughter, she treats her mother the way all Christians treat everybody –!

PRISCA (*very much the* EMPEROR's *wife*). We *must* endure this prison without abusing one another like this. Where is our dignity?

VALERIA. Years ago, mother, you and I renounced Christ because of our dignity. Do you not think we are well paid?

Cross-fade to suggest passage of time.

Scene Twenty-Three

Interior: the prison. The main cell again. MELANTHO's *baby can be heard in the distance, crying.*

1ST PROLETARIAN PRISONER (*a sour young man*). That bloody child's still hollering down the passage.

2ND PROLETARIAN PRISONER (*cynical middle-aged woman*). They got women-of-the-purple in there, ha'n't they? Cause no end of disruption wherever they bloody are.

1ST PROLETARIAN PRISONER. That pair'll be out of here in no time, anyway: You heard bloody Daza's back in Syria after his victory over Licinius, he's not going to leave his auntie in a dungeon. The more so as she sprinkled the old incense once, din't she?

2ND PROLETARIAN PRISONER (*bitterly*). Right, and we don't none of us need to forget that!

Footsteps down the passage, and a cell door is unlocked.

GAOLER (*down the passage*). Christian detainees one-three-five and one-three-six, Prisca and Valeria, Refulgent and Distinguished, come on, ladies, let's be having you!

2ND PROLETARIAN PRISONER. See what I mean? They're bringing 'em out already.

Footsteps as PRISCA *and* VALERIA *come out of their cell: the door is shut, and they are heard walking off with the* GAOLER *down the passage.*

BISHOP. Exactly the kind of divisive social comment that called the holocaust down upon us in the first place. We'll have no more of it in this cell, if you please.

Scene Twenty-four

Interior: fade up into middle of conversation.

MAXIMIN DAZA (*as urbane as he can be*). – dear ladies, nobody told me; of course, the war, the civil emergency but no excuses, I am Emperor, I take the blame. Apart from all that, though: you are in health? The conditions in the prison were not too – ah –?

PRISCA (*frigid*). We were not put to the torture.

MAXIMIN DAZA. Dear Valeria, they didn't put *you* to the torture? I could not bear to think of your beautiful body under the hands of –

VALERIA (*wearily*). If this is why you've let us out, nephew, would you please send us back inside? I have no interest in hearing any more of your –

MAXIMIN DAZA (*bluffly*). Valeria, I'm a rude soldier, when I propose marriage, I must do it –

PRISCA
VALERIA ⎭ (*gasp of horrified amazement*). Marriage –!

MAXIMIN DAZA (*ignoring the interruption*). – must do it my own way. A few compliments first, and then down to the practical reasons. Now, to begin, if you –

PRISCA (*her mind boggling*). You cannot *marry* my daughter, you have a wife and family already.

MAXIMIN DAZA (*a sort of gallant apology, followed by what he conceives a thoroughly common-sense statement*). Madam, I'm proposing to Valeria, not to you. If you were of breeding age, certainly you. But there will have to be children, of the divine seed of Diocletian, and that is essential. You're his wife, his one flesh: you're his daughter, flesh of his flesh: and who am I? I am *him*.

PRISCA. You are – *what*?

MAXIMIN DAZA. The oracular statue of Zeus has informed me that when I have won my war – and it's very nearly won – the entire greatness of Diocletian will be transferred, by spiritual force, into the blood and bones you see before you. So, the sperm from my flesh, once I penetrate Valeria, will have gone back into *his* flesh, right? – the identity will be doubled, and our son will be – why, at the very least a demi-god. It's a reasonable proposition.

VALERIA (*hardly able to speak*). It – it – I thought it was just lechery – but this – this is *insane*.

MAXIMIN DAZA (*getting annoyed*). Your own – renounced – Jesus was surely just such a demi-god from between the legs of a mortal woman? If I'm mad, what are *you*, to believe so tall a story . . .?

VALERIA (*intensely*). Whether we believe, or we don't believe, has nothing to do with it. We must proclaim Christ: because – yes – we did renounce him!

PRISCA. It's no good telling him that, child, he will not understand it. To restore the integrity of our conscience, how would he know what that –

MAXIMIN DAZA (*trying his best to make accommodation with them*). Why wouldn't I know? When my uncle Galerius made me an officer and said that before long he might make me an Emperor, he sent me out of the regiment to a school – with philosophers and all sorts. I am educated, you know that. Diocletian persuaded you to give up your Jesus for the security of the Empire, and you did. I've far too much respect for the pair of you to believe that it was only because you were afraid of being burnt – I've seen the most miserable women, of the very lowest classes, burnt, crucified, chewed up by lions, singing out the name of Jesus at the tops of their voices. Hercules-god, but you're better than them. The integrity of your conscience told you to submit, because the integrity of your conscience knew that Empire came above all: and so it still does. Which is why you will marry me – security of Empire, security of dynasty, Diocletian's . . . (*With a sudden change of tone:*) No: I've got it wrong! Look at your faces: Hercules-god, you'd rather die.

VALERIA. Ten years ago we did not dare die: yet what have we gained from it?

MAXIMIN DAZA (*exploding into his crudest viciousness*). She says no, so I'll take the old one. Not to bed, no no no, far too raddled a bag for that: but the wife of Diocletian's got a hand, she's got a tongue, onto your knees, bag, let's have your services –

PRISCA (*overriding his fury*). Diocletian the great Augustus once said to Galerius that you, Maximin Daza, were not fit to take command of a latrine-fatigue in a transit-camp.

MAXIMIN DAZA (*bellowing*). Imperial decision: where's my staff, come in here, be ready to write it down –

Flurry and fuss as COURTIERS *come in.*

COURTIERS (*deferential and nervous*). Most Unutterable Refulgent Majesty – (*Etc.*)

MAXIMIN DAZA (*rhetorically positive*). We make no more martyrs. They'd rather die, so they won't die. Once they're dead, they gang together, all come back in thunderstorms to stale on my doorstep and the janitors don't even know they're there! No: you don't die. You are *banished*, the most remote internal exile for these two malevolent women, to a north-east frontier fortress where no one in the whole world except the barbarian border-guard will ever see them or hear them again – take 'em away!

Scene Twenty-Five

Exterior: an ARMY *upon the march.*

KYBELE (*as narrator*). He returns to his army, and, as he goes, he swears a great oath.

MAXIMIN DAZA (*crying aloud from his horse as he rides with the troops*). I pledge my word to Olympian Zeus, that if he grant me final victory, the perversions of Jesus Christ shall be exterminated throughout my realms! Once and for all!

Scene Twenty-Six

Exterior: another ARMY *upon the march.*

KYBELE (*as narrator*). Co-Emperor Licinius, at the head of *his* army, remembered how Constantine had designated the divinity who gave him the conquest of Rome.

LICINIUS (*on his horse riding with his troops – to himself: he is an elderly man, crafty and coarse*). If that young man is to be my brother-in-law, he must not be the only one in the family to get his visions from the new god. In *my* dreams, I beheld an angel who dictated to me the words of a prayer. (*He shouts aloud.*) Imperial decision!

His call is taken up by a succession of OFFICERS.

OFFICERS (*down the column*). Imperial decision, halt banners for the imperial decision! (*Etc.*)

The MARCH *halts.*

LICINIUS (*calling to the troops*). Every front-line regiment will chant the following verses before action commences –

> Highest God and One True God alone
> Our victory shall make thy glory known.
> Jesus Christ Unconquered Sun
> Hear our prayer, thy will be done.
> Amen.

Fade out as the ARMY *repeats 'Amen'.*

Scene Twenty-Seven

Interior: the prison. Night. Quiet murmurs, disturbed dreams, GUARDS' *pacing footsteps and voices down corridors,etc.*

KYBELE (*as narrator*). Bit by bit the tidings of Maximin Daza's decisive war drift in to the state prison at Antioch.

MARY (*slowly, meditatively*). They are saying there has been another great battle in Thrace, and nobody knows how it ended . . .

MELANTHO. This might very well be the last night we spend here together.

Scene Twenty-Eight

Exterior: Drumbeat. A battlefield. Distant shouts and gallopings. Heavy breathing and the clank of armour as a MAN *pulls himself, wounded, up a hill.*

MAXIMIN DAZA (*exhausted and despairing*). Sound it again, man, sound it again, blow the recall till your eyes fall out!

A faltering trumpet call, dying away – the TRUMPETER *too is exhausted. The battle noises diminish into wind on the hill.*

MAXIMIN DAZA. Is there not one squadron left to rally to my banner – even my guards have deserted me? Left me alone on this bloodstained hilltop, with only my purple robe to show the world I am their emperor. (*With sudden agonised decision.*) Very well, so pull it off – pull it off –

His armour jangles as someone helps him off with his regalia.

MAXIMIN DAZA. You: give me *yours* – name of the gods, and *let me go* –!

Scene Twenty-Nine

Interior: another cell.

DION (*a middle-aged intellectual*). My dear Eumolpus, even if this is the last night we spend here alive, I insist upon refuting your insupportably absurd contention that 'the first day of creation was intelligible light', a premise, esteemed colleague, you ascribe to Theophilus of Antioch, but which is, I submit, no more than an adaptation of Philo of Alexandria who maintains –

EUMOLPUS (*a young man, equally passionate in his long-running argument*). Most excellent Dion, before you can refute it you must first clarify your own definition of 'intelligible light': do you contend it means the 'Divine Word' or do you take it to imply the all-inconclusive concept of 'Pre-existent Wisdom', because according to (*With rising inflection*:) Cleanthes of Assos, Chrysippus, *and* Panaetius –

A protesting noise from the BISHOP.

DION. Ssh, you have awoken the old Bishop –

BISHOP. If the victory in Thrace has gone to Zeus and not to Christ, all of us, philosophers and otherwise, will have all our definitions only too thoroughly clarified: think of that, my children, and pray.

Cross-fade to another part of the prison.

OENOTHEA. Whether Zeus wins or Christ wins, my Goddess must inhabit the waste places of the earth: she will live among the puff adders and she will sting, oh how she will sting . . .!

Scene Thirty

Exterior: drumbeat. A waste place: wind.

MAXIMIN DAZA (*addressing a small group, who murmur a sympathetic response*). I, Maximin Daza, fugitive, in the ragged cape of a common soldier, a slave who stayed to die when his emperor ran away, I am recalled by the voice of my ancestors to my duty: a cup of poison among my friends. Before I drink it, my last orders: swear by Zeus to carry them out!

A low muttering as they swear.

MAXIMIN DAZA (*viciously*). First: Theotecnus and every other priest and soothsayer who urged me to this disastrous war shall immediately follow me, companions for my journey, my safe-conduct through the miasmas of the River Styx. Second: as I drink –

Sound of pouring out and drinking.

(*His voice now benevolent*) – in two minutes, I am a god, with a new wide understanding of the errors of humanity: therefore all prisoners from minority cults to be at once released, including the cult of Christ. For it is possible the Galilean is himself an Immortal: he may wish to thank me when he meets me . . .

His last few words are failing as the poison grips him.

Scene Thirty-One

Interior: the prison. Running feet along the passages, cell doors flung open, a crescendo of shouting and excited movement.

KYBELE (*as narrator*). And his orders were obeyed. As they swarmed out of the prison, the captives stared bewildered at the bright blue Syrian sky –

CRIES. Freedom, freedom, we are free, Lord Jesus has made us free–!

Scene Thirty-Two

Exterior: the street outside the prison. General noise of PRISONERS *saying goodbyes to each other, and dispersing.*

MARY. Whatever the future holds, we can say with certainty, that we know who we are: we made the choice.

OENOTHEA. My goddess leads me back to where she belongs: the ruins of Babylon within the frontiers of Persia.

MELANTHO. Mary and I to the west: the land of the wife of Constantine. I shall preach in Christ my gratitude to her for the life of my child.

A group of determined REVOLUTIONIST-CHRISTIANS *have formed up together and are shouting slogans preparatory to parading through the town.*

REVOLUTIONISTS. The meek shall inherit the earth! Ours is the Kingdom! Neither Constantine nor Rome shall rule! No Rome, Christ alone!

EUMOLPUS. And what about you, friend Dion, I cannot persuade you to come with me to Rome? The theological reputation of Bishop Hosius is already –

DION (*excitedly*). No no, Alexandria! And not to waste my time there with political bishops. Dr Arius of the Christian College is a very humble class of priest: but his profound dialectic can only be ignored at peril of abandonment of intellectual consistency. Alexandria for the great debate!

EUMOLPUS (*with a slight laugh*). My dear friend, you'll never learn. Hosius has the ear of government: order – control – power.

REVOLUTIONISTS (*shouting*). 'No Rome, Christ alone!' (*They repeat their slogan over and over as they set off on their march.*)

Closing music.

3

BURDENS OF EMPIRE

Scene One

Opening Music.

KYBELE (*as narrator*). [Here in Hibernia, to talk of the Roman Empire is difficult, because we have no maps. But consider, all this side of the Empire, from Italy westwards, was ruled by Constantine: from Greece to the east, as far as Persia, by his Co-Emperor Licinius. This was the settlement of] 313 AD. Constantine was young, his Co-Emperor Licinius old: they would not agree for long. On matters of religion they did agree: Jesus Christ was allowed full place among all the other gods.
    On family matters they agreed. Constantine would marry his sister to Licinius. Both Co-Emperors knew one or other must go down, to leave one man alone at the head of united Empire.
    Disunity had created two capital cities: [no longer Rome, but] Nicomedia in the east, Milan in the west. While Helen the mother of Constantine lived in no city but on her estate in northern Gaul: she was not invited to the wedding of Constantine's sister.

Exterior: a bright morning in a country garden. Various appropriate sound effects: a peacock screams, a PEASANT WOMAN *is singing a folksong in the distance, someone else is calling out, an ox-cart lumbers down the lane, cows, sheep, chickens, etc. close up, we hear the feet of a large* WOMAN *among brambles, heavy breathing, snipping of stalks, tearing out roots, the raking of garden rubbish (not all at once: there is only the one gardener involved)*

HELEN (*aged in her seventies, strong testy voice betraying peasant origins, but with the authority of an upper-class lady. Her accent could have a slight tinge of Welsh*). That's you, you little bugger, out you come, off – nasty horrid briar, strangling all about you, oh I'll nip you off, root you out, so I will.

She uses the spade for a minute, panting with the effort.

HELEN. You've caught my clothes? Tear them then, I'm stronger than any of you. What's a tear – I was born naked, I don't mind being naked once again. Wife of an Emperor, mother of an Emperor, I am Helen – and you don't like it! I am Helen, I am on my knees, I am getting at your roots: and you know that you are *nothing* . . . (*Calling out to someone.*) Sextus! Over here!

SEXTUS (*an old servant: approaching at a hobbling run*). Your ladyship –?

HELEN. You can sweep all these brambles, on the bonfire immediately.

SEXTUS. Y'r la'ship.

HELEN. The whole estate's in rack and ruin: no wonder you're all such a pack of rotten rascals, if you do nothing you get nothing, there's nothing to get. Did you send out the wagon to fetch that Carrara marble from the abandoned house across the valley? If we don't put our hands on it, those damned German squatters will. And when you bring it, stack it in the yard, I want a day-and-night watch over it till I find where to use it. Talking of Germans, has Wolfgang been to see you about his lease of the upper vineyard?

SEXTUS. Not yet, y'r la'sh –

HELEN (*not letting him finish*). Don't you deal with him, send him to me. Off with you, about it, whoosh!

HELEN *returns to her briar-trimming.* SEXTUS *is working at a little distance.*

HELEN (*addressing the briars again*). Oh, you are nothing: and you think *I'm* nothing: but that's where you are *wrong!* Helen's eyes, Helen's ears, are wide wide open to all of it. Such a wise and determined Emperor, son of Helen, lord of Rome, lord of half the world, look at him! My Constantine the conqueror, my Constantine the peace-maker, my Constantine just like his dad, always too slow,

always too careful, always in the wrong place at the wrong time! And don't tell me I
don't know it! Don't you tell me I can't see the bad blood creeping back. The
children of Herculius, brambles, brambles, around his limbs; strangling him dead
before he even begins to stretch himself. Herculian wife: Herculian half-sister, and
yet he still believes he is ruling his own empire! Gods . . .! Don't you tell me, you
nasty thorn bush, that my son killed Herculius. He has left all that matters of him
alive. Half-sister sent off to marry Co-Emperor Licinius: Constantine will use her,
she will use Licinius, my Constantine will use Licinius. But her grandfather was
Herculius: and Herculius used everybody! Him, and Diocletian . . . And what about
my Constantius? Assistant-Emperor to Herculius, faugh! Would he complain . . .?
Not he. 'It's not the title that counts' he always said, 'but geography of the office',
the administrative calibre of the man that fills the office . . . Herculius told him that
his office would do better without his wife, without Helen, and would he
complain . . .? The geography demanded that the new wife for my Constantius was
the daughter of Herculius, the new mother for my little boy . . . Constantine . . .
my baby.

She sits heavily down and rustles something in a basket.

(*addressing her 'doll'*). Baba knows everything, [don't you . . .? Baba has seen it all,
haven't you, Baba? Baba says nothing, do you, Baba?] You have never opened
your mouth, so no one banished *you* – you have never been whipped – you just stay
with me. 'Take the good-luck doll with you,' said old Olwen in Colchester – 'Baba
has seen all and said nothing: she's the one to bring you luck,' she said. So I took
you down from behind the bar and carried you off in my basket, to marry my
Constantius. Remember Baba . . . when the young bruisers of the Dalmatian
Regiment came in for their drinks and women . . . that bad blood Herculius he
never said a word, sat on a stool with his head in his hands, the girls swung
themselves past him and laughed, I gave a laugh too – I don't know why. Olwen
was mad as a rat, she laid the full of her whip into all of us – 'You never never
never laugh at a customer – even though he's only a sick-drunk Dalmatian that can't
hardly speak Latin – more to the purpose *because* he's a Dalmatian, oh they use
everyone and they never forget. Bad blood,' she said, 'Bad blood.' But my
Constantius was a Dalmatian and like a fool I allowed him to bring me out of
Britain in the baggage of the regiment and like a fool I thought I was his wife.
(*Suddenly jumping up in alarm.*) Sextus, the cats –! They're all among the bushes –
they'll be after the peacocks – Sextus!

What are they doing . . .? They've all turned upon the ginger tom! Ah! I see it
now: they're freezing him out. (*She calls out softly to the cat.*) Stay put, you bugger!
Don't let them upset you, stay there, stare 'em out, they'll give up –! Oh, but he's
leaving, he's banished, they're all getting up now – . . . off to the wedding: [all of 'em
off to the wedding, all of 'em off to Milan,] the great wedding in Milan . . . mark
my words, Licinius after this wedding is going to rule over the whole world. He'll
take hold of every title, geography of all the offices – but administrative calibre,
integrity of purpose, trust? My Constantius had trust. 'Diocletian alone of all of us,'
he said, 'brings back *respect* into this Empire: Herculius', he said, 'is nothing:
Diocletian has the brains, and the courage, and the strength . . .'

Scene Two

*Exterior: a quiet day with the muted sound of the sea not far away and some gulls now
and then crying.*

KYBELE (*as narrator*). Ancient remnants, retired, forgotten, digging the garden on a
government pension in shabby clothes in far-off places – [Helen, in Gaul, who never
had power:] Diocletian, in his fortress palace in Dalmatia, still alive, and very
frightened, as he stoops among his cabbages.

DIOCLETIAN (*in his seventies: an embittered old man, too long alone, suspicious and nervous, but still acutely intelligent. His voice is that of a man long accustomed to instant obedience: not cultured, but not by any means ignorant*). Black spots, mildew, an orange tinge upon the green leaves! Oh yes, there is no doubt of it, it is happening yet again. (*He calls out abruptly.*) Hello there – call the Captain, call the Captain of my Guard, damn you! – where is he – Infortunatus –!

Someone afar off – an old man's voice – takes up the cry 'Infortunatus!'

KYBELE [(*as narrator*). Diocletian, son of a slave, in twenty years of ruthless bureaucratic rule, himself and his three chosen colleagues, had restored the Roman Empire. He bore a very heavy burden on behalf of all humankind, any wonder he was glad to abdicate?]

DIOCLETIAN (*angrily shouting*). Infortunatus!

KYBELE [(*as narrator*). From the vegetable patch he can see nothing except high stone walls on every side, unless he were to climb to the top of the battlements. But he never goes up to look, because out there would be the Empire, and the Empire is no longer his.]

DIOCLETIAN. Where *is* the bloody man – never here when I want him – In-fort-u –!

Before he has finished his call, INFORTUNATUS *replies from just beside him.*

INFORTUNATUS (*an old soldier, nearly as old as* DIOCLETIAN: *with a long-standing intimacy towards him*). 'Course I'm here, I'm always here, I'm the only one that is . . . You've got beetles in them cabbages. I told you, you want to piss on 'em, one at a time, saturate each leaf, you see, that'll soon –

DIOCLETIAN (*angry and positive*). By god this is not beetles. These plants have been poisoned. A man's hand in this garden, who was he, how did he get here? One of your squad must have been suborned.

INFORTUNATUS (*gently ironic*). Oh dear, oh dear, oh dear, after all of these years, can't we do any better than that? You still believe that one among your own could be in someone else's pay? Whose pay? Constantine? Licinius? What the devil use'd that be to any one of *us*?

INFORTUNATUS' *plodding footsteps, withdrawing.*

DIOCLETIAN (*calling after him*). So how did my cabbages get their death? (*To himself:*) How did my *wife* get her death, will you tell me that? And my daughter?

He begins to walk.

KYBELE (*as narrator*). He picks up his trowel and basket, walks toward the palace entry.

DIOCLETIAN (*to himself*). Because you don't need to answer. Licinius killed them. And if them, why not me . . .?

Scene Three

Interior: action continuous. The footfalls – he is wearing boots with grit and soil on them – change as he passes onto a marble floor, and re-echo from the ceiling of the palace.

KYBELE [(*as narrator*). – walks through the foyer to the stair-hall, up the great stair, into the long gallery.]

DIOCLETIAN (*panting a little as he climbs: to himself*). They asked but the one thing: my protection. As though they thought I could protect *myself*.

KYBELE (*as narrator*). It is now growing dark. [All alone on shuffling feet he walks up and down, up and down.] Dumps his basket on the pedestal of a statue: the goddess Roma. [He looks up at her.]

PRISCA *laughs. It seems to be coming from a long way off, as it were inside his head.*

KYBELE (*as narrator*). She laughs at him, marble teeth, marble lips. He hears the scornful laugh of Prisca, his wife.

PRISCA (*the voice of a ghost in his mind*). We were fugitives, we had loved you, we thought once you loved us. Or so we told ourselves when there was no one else to come to. We had to come through the lands of Licinius. We had declared ourselves Christian, it was proclaimed that *he* had, so why not?

DIOCLETIAN (*angry, trying to brush it all aside*). Let Christian protect Christian, is not that what it's all about? Is not that the very reason why I could not defeat them?

KYBELE (*as narrator*). [Snarling with anger, he turns his back: and there, across the hall, another statue, the goddess Pax. Marble lips, marble teeth.] He hears his daughter Valeria.

VALERIA (*another ghost-voice: not scornful, like* PRISCA's, *but with a certain affectionate irony*). Christianity you sought to defeat, or human intelligence, human affection, the flesh and blood of your own family? In Nicomedia you raged like a trodden scorpion at the great prayer-hall built for Christ: but nothing to the fury that contorted the glands of your neck when you walked into my mother's drawing-room and found philosophers, poets, and – yes – he was a Bishop, we were debating together, women and men as equals – you stamped so hard in your soldier's boot you nearly broke your right leg on the threshold.

DIOCLETIAN (*in great distress*). Flesh and blood, in my own house, I was betrayed, I am always betrayed. How can you say I did not love you! If I did not love you, how could I have been so angry? And Christian-loving Licinius hunted you down and caught you, oh my darlings, he cut off your heads . . . And now he and Constantine will do their best to murder *me*, because I am the last man alive of all the ancient world: and then they will murder each other, how can they not?

PETER (*a soft confidential-secretary kind of voice: but a ghost-voice like the other two*). If *they* can't help it, *you* couldn't help it.

DIOCLETIAN (*crying out*). Ah –?

KYBELE [(*as narrator*). His bent torso jerks in a sudden fit of terror. On the end wall of the gallery, lit blood-red through the western clerestory, a mosaic mural of the god Apollo, hard violet eyes in the great golden head . . .]

PETER (*compassionately*). Of course you could not help it, you made the rules and the rules were broken. And when you found out that I, Peter, your trusted Chamberlain, to whom you breathed your closest confidence –

DIOCLETIAN. I always knew you were a Christian: but I thought you were a loyal Christian, if you broke my rules you nevertheless loved me and would do nothing to hurt my government – but then –

PETER. You were told I was the man who set fire to your private apartments, and all but burnt you to death in your bed. Of course it wasn't true and you knew it wasn't true: but Christianity was against the rules, so all Christians were capable of anything. By the terms of Euclid, Q.E.D.: you burnt me to death.

DIOCLETIAN. There may have been injustice, there was certainly imprudent haste, I will admit that in the emergency –

PETER. You had no choice. You made a holocaust. If those who have come after you decide to destroy *you*, they too will have had no choice. That's what Empire is all about, it has nothing to do with Jupiter, nothing to do with Christ.

PRISCA. Or with love . . .

VALERIA. Or with hope.

DIOCLETIAN (*as who should say 'I am glad this point is raised'*). Ah, hope. They always asked me: 'in your new Empire', they kept on pleading, 'where have you left room for a little bit of hope?' This was nonsense, let me explain to you –

Fade down to suggest passage of time.

Scene Four

Interior: the same, a little later.

KYBELE (*as narrator*). Perhaps an hour, two hours, later, Infortunatus the Captain is sent for by a distressed servant – the ex-Emperor, it seems, will not go to bed, [he walks up and down the empty gallery, holding a single candlestick and haranguing the deep shadows as though his entire Senate had assembled there in the dark . . .]

DIOCLETIAN's footsteps, up and down. INFORTUNATUS' feet approach with a jingle of his armour.

DIOCLETIAN (*in the middle of his speech, pressing a point obsessively*). – it is emphatically necessary to explain again and again that nothing in all my policy has been proven incorrect . . . of course I underestimated the idiotic inability of individual co-emperors to rule in harmony with their opposite numbers – idiotic, individual – individual, idiotic – (*Etc.*)

The needle has, as it were, got stuck. INFORTUNATUS takes advantage of this to insert himself into the situation.

INFORTUNATUS (*as DIOCLETIAN continues to repeat himself*). Do you realise what the time is?

DIOCLETIAN (*takes no notice: but the needle comes unstuck*). I am asked about hope. In that regard I can do no better than refer you to the distinguished work of Porphyry the philosopher – oh yes, I don't discriminate against philosophers, I never did, only if they were meaningless mystics, in which case they were subversives, in which case –

He breaks off, sensing dangerous ground: and then starts again from his original point of departure.

Porphyry states, and I quote: 'The greatest fruit of piety is to worship god according to the tradition of one's fathers'. How is that not ground for hope? But Constantine and Licinius have refused to accept it: and therefore they unhinge all the rational social balance I so exhaustively restored – exhaustively – exhaustively – (*Etc.*).

The needle is stuck again, and again INFORTUNATUS intervenes.

INFORTUNATUS. Come along, old chap, old Emperor – it's long past dark. You come to your bed. (*To himself.*) I could have a try with his old name and his old rank, before he got hold of all his notions . . . (*Aloud, parade-ground voice:*) Regimental-Quartermaster Diocles, *to* your bivouac, dis-miss!

The result is not quite what he expects. DIOCLETIAN stops his 'exhaustively restored' at once – but –

DIOCLETIAN (*as though dealing with an idiot*). Oh dear oh dear oh dear, what the bloody hell are you talking about? Do you think I've gone soft in the head?

INFORTUNATUS. No, Emperor, I don't.

DIOCLETIAN (*with asperity*). You don't? That's not correct. For if I hadn't, why would I abdicate? My gall-bladder, chronic, oh yes. But no: the *real* reason! I constructed a system, constructed it for all of us: it was my job to save it: so therefore I must persecute. But persecution went against my considered prior conviction, so therefore it was *incorrect*. And nonetheless I found myself totally unable to see what else I could have done . . .! With the result that the Christians will take over my system, for their illogical god alone, and for every twist and turn of the imaginary secret soul that this god, according to Porphyry, so gruesomely devours – no, but not god, it's their own selves eating themselves . . . Bed, did you say, sleep? From before the beginning, we have slept. Then we wake for so small a short time: then we sleep until the end, until after the end, until after the end of the end. We don't twist, we don't turn, we don't eat, we don't drink: and from now on, *neither do I* . . . You are, Infortunatus, so much of an old loyal comrade, you will not attempt to dissuade me. Just one last bowl of wine, I'll pour it out for a pious libation . . .

Scene Five

KYBELE (*as narrator*). Diocletian went down, by self-starvation, 316 AD. I'd say his pangs were as nothing compared to the intellectual starvation he had imposed on all of us while he ruled. He banished my beloved teacher and kinsman Lactantius, professor of rhetoric at Nicomedia, and closed down his school, which is why I went to Naples. But the worst hurt of all for me was that Lactantius became a Christian, turning his back upon us all. We saw him exchanging the rational exploration of the reality of the world for a primitive and superstitious panacea of eschatological redemption. Of course, looking back, I should have felt happy that Lactantius had found happiness, for does not Epicurus say, 'our highest duty is to secure happiness in this world, for there is no other'? But where was *my* happiness to come from? [What philosophical school would employ me? I was tainted by Lactantius's Christianity. I became isolated. The economic rigidity of the Diocletian system meant that, without realising it,] I had become just one of a mass, alienated from the state, alienated from the state's gods, conscious only of never-ending taxation . . . In the year 324, Licinius went down, [after years of dispute, conspiracy, finally war, between himself and Constantine.] Not known whether he killed himself or was murdered. Constantine, now supreme, thinks his mother should come to court, to counter-balance the Herculians.

Exterior: coach-wheels bowling along a well-made road.

KYBELE. To sound her out, he sends Bishop Hosius of Cordova, his most trusted Christian adviser, a distinguished man of celibate life, [well-placed to give impartial judgement upon the demeanour of royal females.]

Scene Six

Interior: inside the coach.

HOSIUS. The difficulty is, my dear Eumolpus, whereas in North Africa the Donatists are more a nationalist schism than a heresy, the Sabellians in Alexandria are more a heresy than a schism –

EUMOLPUS. Which means they must each be handled in quite different ways. Surely if you explain to the Emperor –

KYBELE [(*as narrator*). His travelling companion, consultant, assistant: The Emperor Constantine has his conference-table, Eumolpus has his library, and Hosius moves in between.]

HOSIUS. As I said, the difficulty: His Majesty sees everything as a political or military problem, his well-intended solutions are dangerously pragmatic. I wish we could establish a more fundamental philosophical strategy.

EUMOLPUS. Dialectical consistency above all –

HOSIUS. Above all.

KYBELE (*as narrator*). Hosius is making himself, as it were, the intellectual father of the father of his Fatherland, leading the Emperor to splice together the Sermon on the Mount and the traditional corpus of Roman Law.

HOSIUS. I did suggest to His Majesty that the decisions of the Council of Elvira should be partially introduced among the provisions of his new Codex Civilis. Elvira made quite clear the distinct responsibilities of our Priesthood: at that time of course only in relation to the Christian laity. Now we have to relate them to the entire commonwealth, both Christian and heathen. [The moral foundations of Canon Law from within our own community to eventually replace the basely materialistic concepts that underlie all the old judicial assumptions –]

EUMOLPUS. Man as an ethical being, the inherent possibility of redemption as well as retribution, the differential definition of *sin* as opposed to *crime* –

HOSIUS. *Opposed* to? Not always clear . . . (*He is slipping into self-colloquy here.*) How to categorise the behaviour of those clergy who surrendered their sacred books to Diocletian's police . . . saying they did it to prevent bloodshed . . .? Was it a crime against church-property, or a sin against their own souls . . .? Or the legitimate craft of the serpent together with the gentleness of the dove?

EUMOLPUS (*fiercely*). Legitimate? It was never that! *Never –*!

HOSIUS (*anxious not to get involved in a distressing argument*). Ah: do you see over there?

EUMOLPUS. The building-site?

HOSIUS. The new cathedral of central Gaul, I organised the government grant – excellent progress! . . . One thing that particularly pleased me about Elvira: we determined once and for all a very strict regulation of marriage among the clergy. You have no idea how casual were our sexual conventions in Spain at that time.

EUMOLPUS. We must strengthen and discipline the priestly order.

HOSIUS. And totally detach it from the carnal world. Yes . . .

A pause. Hosius abruptly changes the subject, as though he is worried.

HOSIUS. . . . When we are with the Lady Helen, don't be too ready to offer your opinions. Police-agents . . .

EUMOLPUS (*startled*). You mean, *she* will be under surveillance?

HOSIUS (*drily*). Of course: she *is* 'family'.

Scene Seven

Exterior: a country-house courtyard. A babble of noise from a group of WOMEN *in a deputation. . . . A kind of broken Welsh accent, or Irish (they are Celts.)*

DEPUTATION (All overlapping their cries). Oh Lady Helen, you are greatest queen, you are greatest queen-mother, you are emperor's womb and breasts of his milk, save them save them, save them . . .

HELEN (*dominating the hubbub*). I damn well can't save anybody unless all of you stop talking at once! Your husbands and sons are guilty of terrorism, convicted by the District Court, condemned to be burnt at the stake, and oh my daughters I am not a court of appeal, so what in the name of the gods do you want me to do?

AN OLD WOMAN. In the name of God-Jesus, lady, not to burn, not to burn –

against religion, if they burn, for how shall burnt bodies rise again at the third day?

EUMOLPUS (*slightly aside from the main dialogue, to Hosius privately*). Bishop, d'you think these ragged petitioners can be Christians?

HOSIUS (*ditto*). Of a garbled and barbarous sort, perhaps yes . . .

HELEN (*to* HOSIUS). Hosius, d'you hear her? She calls on God-Jesus, you're his man, you'd better advise me. (*To the Deputation:*) My daughters, this nobleman is a very great Christ-Bishop, sent expressly to my estate, at my request, by the Emperor, to hear my people's grievances.

EUMOLPUS (*privately to* HOSIUS). That's not entirely true.

HOSIUS. But very diplomatic.

EUMOLPUS. Any chance, out of this, we can get her to accept Christ?

HOSIUS. Wait . . . wait . . .

OLD WOMAN. Lady Helen, let me tell you, my man was on this land here living before ever came that German man to try to put him out –!

WOLFGANG (*a serious middle-aged German*). Ladyship, please! I am Wolfgang son of Walther, very well-known as righteous man to the Emperor in this land. I have parchment from my father from Kaiser Constantius, ladyship, your own dead husband, to tell me I have right here to make my farm, me *und meine Leute*, my sword-fighters, *nicht wahr*? for the warfare we have made as soldiers of Rome in time past. But these others, who are *they*? When I found them I said to them, 'Go! Make your thorpe-place, your village, where you will, but not here!' But year after year they would not go, and in the end they take weapons, turn terrorist, give it out they will rob and kill to be able to hold my fields, ladyship, they are not land-born peoples, they have come without reason from all the world over.

HELEN. Is this true? You: where does your man come from?

OLD WOMAN. Why, he was soldier, wasn't he? In Britain, in the rebellion-days, didn't they help Lord Constantius, and then didn't he tell them: over the water, find land and work it, free men for ever in Gaul?

HELEN (*expansively, pleased by their trust in her husband*). Lord Constantius was never anything but true to his word . . . (*Aside, to herself: with some scorn, as Deputation applaud:*) If he knew what his word was. Did he give it to *both* of 'em? Oh he would. (*To the petitioners:*) If your men had been soldiers they must not become farmers unless they have papers of permit.

WOLFGANG. Ah ladyship, *I* have permit, see, here it is –

He flourishes his documentation.

OLD WOMAN. But lady, they were starving. They walk one hundred mile to see the Inspector-General for welfare-distribution, he say to us, 'No!' He say that we must –

HELEN. If he said so, it was the law. You must obey the law.

MARY (*coming up from the back of the hall*). Gracious lady, may I speak in Christ on behalf of these people?

HELEN (*sharply*). What have *you* got to do with them? You don't come from these parts: and certainly your companion does not – whose is that child? Ethiopia? The East?

EUMOLPUS (*privately to* HOSIUS). I have seen these two women before – now where on earth . . .

MARY. Gracious lady, you are quite right: from the East, yes. With permission, may I take the time to explain?

HELEN. Take time or waste time? What are your credentials?

EUMOLPUS (*privately to* HOSIUS: *this and* HOSIUS' *following speech spoken while* HELEN *is talking to* MARY). Antioch! In prison, the persecution, that's where they were! How *did* they get here?

MARY. I admit I have no paper of identity: after all the Christian soul is not made out of police-paper, my words are as true or as false as those of anyone else.

HOSIUS (*privately to* EUMOLPUS). The more we listen, the more we shall learn . . . [just what we came to find out – the legal confusion, the irregular creeds, unaffiliated hedge-preachers, female too . . .]

HELEN (*after thinking about it for a moment*). No, no, not good enough –

HOSIUS (*privately to* EUMOLPUS). Oh she mustn't dismiss her – (*He speaks aloud, now, to* Helen:) Refulgent Excellency, may I intervene? The young woman should be heard, fatiguing though it may be: this judgement is important, it will be taken note of by the Imperial Court. Your Ladyship's opinion will be of inestimable benefit to the Emperor, I know that.

MARY (*helped by this*). – yes, because the Emperor now rules within the embrace of Jesus Christ, and his judgement is as the judgement of God, when his mother shows mercy, it is the mercy of the Mother of God –

HELEN (*interested*). Ah?

MARY. – giving comfort to all those who cry out under the weight of their burdens.

HELEN (*gratified*). We will listen: continue.

MARY. I am Mary the Companion, I am from Spain and I travel the world: I minister to the People of Christ in the Name of her after whom I named. The woman with me is Melantho.

MELANTHO. Great lady, I accepted the True Way because a great Christian lady saved the lives of myself and my child. She gave me her jewels to provide warm clothing, food, shelter for us, at a time of such hardship and dread. Great lady, she was your daughter-in-law, Fausta the wife of Constantine: and I have called this girl Helen-Fausta in tribute to her goodness and to the goodness of the mother of her husband.

EUMOLPUS (*privately to* HOSIUS). I did not think Her Ladyship had ever met the Empress Fausta?

HOSIUS (*privately to* EUMOLPUS). No more she has: it is as though her face is frozen by a blast of winter. She wants urgently to put questions, she does not know *which* questions: ah, she smiles at the child, fondles her hair, she is thinking to herself very fast. So am I. I do believe I now know what all this is all about. When Constantine marched upon Rome, [I was with the army, I heard the story, there was indeed a woman gave birth in an unseasonable snowstorm as we crossed over the height of the Alps. It became one of those legends spread by the camp-followers:] (yes, they said the Empress had struggled through the snow to help her, had performed a kind of miracle: in some way there is confusion between the wife of Constantine and his mother – the wife being young and helpless, forsaken by her father; the mother alone and old, forsaken by her husband – you understand the sentiment of these quasi-cults among the soldiery?]

EUMOLPUS. Helen has heard the legend?

HOSIUS. It looks like it . . . Ssh –

HELEN (*feeling her way rather carefully*). You came down the mountains into – Liguria, is that not so? And you stayed there until – the child was weaned:

MELANTHO. Great lady, that is true.

HELEN. And no man hindered you: you found, as it were, all roads smooth and open before you?

MELANTHO. Until we had to travel again to the east, yes we did.

HELEN (*complacently and perfectly dishonestly*). Then the work was done well, and my servants are to be commended.

MELANTHO. Oh lady, it is true! You worked in secret for our safety and health.

EUMOLPUS (*privately to* HOSIUS). Oh crafty crafty Empress Dowager, she does not *claim* the credit, just allows it to *drift* towards her . . . Oh yes we must have her at court!

HELEN. We don't seek your gratitude, daughter, just your thanks to the Lord Jesus and to the Mother of Lord Jesus.

EUMOLPUS (*privately to* HOSIUS). She's not saying she is a *Christian*?

HOSIUS (*privately to* EUMOLPUS). Did the Emperor say he was a Christian when he put the Cross on his banner? She has declared in our presence the greatness of Christ: that's all that we need.

MARY (*excited by* HELEN's *remark*). Lady, if you are Christian, then regard these poor people with the pity and the hope of Christ. [Oppressed and confused with inordinate regulation, helpless, as has been said, from all the world over, soldiers, bond-servants, evicted share-croppers, who knows what? –] who knows indeed who *is* the rightful owner of all these fields after so many years of war and pestilence? Everywhere ruined houses, abandoned villages, broken stones. In your own courtyard, a great pile of broken stone: where did that come from?

HELEN (*highly displeased*). Are you trying to tell me that my Carrara marble has been fraudulently obtained?

HOSIUS (*anxious not to have* MARY *in trouble*). Refulgent Excellency, perhaps we are being a little too specific? I am sure she does not mean that your marble has anything to do with . . .

WOLFGANG (*angry*). Oh she is meaning! She is meaning to say that not one of these bad peoples in fact can be criminal! Because bad peoples are all poor peoples and for poor peoples we must weep? I am Wolfgang. I weep only for good order and law that is not kept by *all* the peoples. For what else do I live in this Empire but because of good order? For what else do I say to you Jesu-Christ is one great God? He did not kill, he did not rob, he did not tell his twelve good friends: 'Band together, take up weapons, pull me down from the tree of death! No: but they *were* poor: even so they kept in order, so do I. For if not, I must be punished. Ladyship, I demand of you, equal hand, these men are punished!

General wailing from the deputation.

HELEN. I'm not the judge: I do have influence, everyone has the right to ask me to use it, if there is ground for mitigation. I am not sure the judges *have* fully understood all these confused circumstances –

DEPUTATION. She will plead, she will ask mercy, great lady, we thank you, (*Etc.*)

HELEN. That'll do. I'll speak in private with the Emperor's advisers. In the meantime, food and drink for you all in the outer courtyard. Gentlemen . . .?

Scene Eight

KYBELE (*as narrator*). Despite her denial, Helen did make a judgement. A Christian judgement: strongly influenced by Bishop Hosius. It introduced the next world to heal the ills of this one: and helped reconcile the poor and meek to their continued oppression.

Interior: HELEN's *hall again.*

HELEN (*speaking with careful formality*). The men condemned by the district court must die: I cannot prevent it.

A great moan from the deputation. HELEN's *voice continues, over-riding it:* WOLFGANG *can also be heard ejaculating in satisfaction.*

But I can and will ensure that they are hanged rather than burnt so that their bodies remain complete for the final resurrection.

Some of the moans turn to sighs of relief and gratitude.

HELEN. Hanged by a rope, not crucified –

All the moans turn to sighs and ejaculations of relief and gratitude: and there is some clapping of hands. Christian terminology is new to her: she speaks words like 'Golgotha' with hesitation . . .

HELEN. – my son has abolished that punishment in deference to most holy Golgotha. At the same time, Wolfgang the plaintiff has agreed to accept Christ, and his own responsibility not only as a landlord but as a spiritual preceptor.

WOLFGANG *utters 'ja ja' in agreement.*

HELEN. He will build a church upon his land and Bishop Hosius will consecrate a priest to administer it . . .

Fade out.

Scene Nine

KYBELE (*as narrator*). A few days later, Helen, Hosius, and Eumolpus set out upon the Rhine in an Imperial state barge. Their eventual destination: Milan.

Exterior: on a large vessel rowing up the river. The OARSMEN's *song is heard in and out behind the narration, and behind the dialogue of the subsequent episodes. Lines 1 and 3 of each verse from the* SHANTYMAN: *2 and 4 from the* CHORUS. *Also a drum-tap, continuous, to keep time.*

OARSMEN (*sing*).

> We're rowing up river and why do we row?
> *Count your stroke and keep to the line:*
> The heart of Queen Helen is white as the snow
> *Out, and in, and all up the Rhine.*
> Queen Helen is dressed in the silver and gold
> *Count your stroke and keep to the line:*
> She's lived all these years yet she never grows old
> *Out, and in, and all up the Rhine.*
> Queen Helen is dressed in the silver and blue
> *Count your stroke and keep to the line:*
> Wherever she looks she sees all that you do
> *Out, and in, and all up the Rhine . . .*

KYBELE (*as narrator*). Messengers have been sent on ahead with the momentous news that Helen is now a Christian. Meanwhile, with horror, Eumolpus recollects that Melantho is the child of a notorious heathen priestess. Bishop Hosius is greatly disturbed, he needs to keep his eye upon such uncontrolled wandering women, he therefore persuades Helen that Mary, the Companion, Melantho, and the little Helen-Fausta, should be included on the journey as members of her household. At the head of the river they are to be received by the Empress Fausta and an assortment of Herculian relatives. Constantine will not be there: these days he finds it politic to keep a splendid distance. His representative will be Crispus, a distinguished young general, his son by his first marriage.

Scene Ten

Exterior: on board the Imperial barge. The OARSMEN's *song and the laughter of* HELEN-FAUSTA *and* HELEN *playing on the poop-deck.*

OARSMEN (*sing*).

> The heart of Queen Helen is lighted with joy
> *Count your stroke and keep to the line*:
> For Caesar Augustus her own darling boy
> *Out, and in, and all up the Rhine.*
>
> We bring her to meet him in Italy's plain
> *Count your stroke and keep to the line*:
> He never will leave her not ever again
> *Out, and in, and all up the Rhine.*

The song continues intermittently behind the dialogue.

HELEN. That's enough running about, child, let old Helen sit down, poof! I'm out of breath. Why don't you and your mother sing one of the songs of Jesus?

HELEN-FAUSTA (*an excited little girl, about 12*). Shall we sing about the water into wine?

HELEN. Water into wine sounds lovely. Was it Rhine water? Because Rhine wine is the best in the world.

MELANTHO. Galilee water, madam.

HELEN. Galilee, where is that? Never mind, you'll tell me all about it. Go on.

MELANTHO
HELEN-FAUSTA (*singing*).

> O the water in the jar
> Shall be wine, mother dear
> Pour it out into the cup
> Fresh and clear:
> Let 'em drink until they're tipsy
> At the wedding of the gipsy
> For the Coming of the Kingdom
> Is so near! O so near
> For the Coming of the Kingdom
> Is so near . . .!

Applause from the royal party, HELEN *laughing with pleasure.*

HELEN-FAUSTA. Now I can do riddles: shall I do riddles? I want to do the burning-riddle. I need the torch for the burning-riddle.

MELANTHO. Here you are, I've lit the torch. Quiet, everybody, please: do you all see the burning flame?

HELEN (*nervously*). Do be careful naked lights on board ship are –

HELEN-FAUSTA (*reciting with great seriousness*).

> Bright flame hot flame
> Waving and tall –
> I put in my hand –

Shocked gasps from the AUDIENCE.

HELEN-FAUSTA (*triumphant pay-off*). And it never hurts at all –!

HELEN (*amid exclamations of wonder*). Good heavens, you will injure her –!

HELEN-FAUSTA.   Gentle flame kind flame
                  Flame without danger

Tell me its name
As it lies in the manger?

HELEN (*indulgently, aware this is show-business, not sorcery*). The child is a magician!

HELEN-FAUSTA (*as no one gives her the answer*). The answer: is – the Love of Jesus!

Applause.

HELEN-FAUSTA. Look, I can do another one with water – will you get me the bucket of water –

We can hear HELEN-FAUSTA *beginning some trick with splashing water, and laughter at it.*

Scene Eleven

KYBELE (*as narrator*). In the cabin, as the voyage proceeds, Hosius attends to his current correspondence.

Fade up conversation. Interior: the OARSMEN*'s song drifts in to the cabin, intermittently behind the dialogue. So do* HELEN-FAUSTA*'s fun and games.*

OARSMEN (*sing*).

The river is long and the river is strong
Count your stroke and keep to the line:
There's many a rock where the boat can go wrong
Out, and in, and all up the Rhine.

If the boat it goes wrong and we're drowned in the tide
Count your stroke and keep to the line:
Not even an Empress can swim to the side
Out, and in, and all up the Rhine.

HOSIUS (*dictating a letter*). '– in conclusion, beloved colleagues in Christ, the two points that effectually sum up my foregoing discourse –' I'm not going too fast for you, Eumolpus? But we must draft these documents before we reach the landing-place –

EUMOLPUS. No, no, I am coping very adequately, 'Foregoing discourse' . . .?

HOSIUS. In conclusion two points. 'one: we must ensure that all Christian practice throughout the western provinces is thoroughly supervised by properly-consecrated Bishops. [I need not remind you that the Laying-on-of-Hands was instituted by Our Lord himself, and that the Apostolic Succession is therefore an historical absolute.] Two –' All this to be written in cypher – 'Two: His Imperial Majesty is *not* a baptised Christian. A total reversal of his attitude toward us is always a political possibility. Bear in mind the apostacy of renegade Licinius.' That's it: and a copy to every Bishop.

EUMOLPUS (*hushed voices in this part of the scene*). 'Total reversal'?

HOSIUS. We must allow for it: and attempt to forestall it: [thus.] Second letter: to the Emperor. 'Your Majesty will know [from the appended examples, the influence of Christian Law upon Civil Law is gravely impeded by disunity of Christian doctrine.] The highly important precedent of the Council of Elvira; [limited though its terms of reference were,] which leads me to suggest a General Council of the entire Christian Church, to be called together by Your Majesty, at such time as Your Majesty thinks would best serve . . .'

EUMOLPUS (*writing away: suddenly he breaks off*). It is the Herculians you fear most at the Imperial court? [But Fausta's cruel father has been dead for many years, all the rest of them are Christian.

HOSIUS (*significantly*). Purportedly. But nothing is permanent. Also,] an Emperor may change his wife. He cannot change his mother. Christian Helen is a rock of stone. Once we place *her* under the corner of the temple, she will be there for all time.

HELEN-FAUSTA*'s splashing and squealing suddenly gets much louder, there are running feet on the deck and gusts of general laughter,* HELEN*'s voice dominant.*

EUMOLPUS (*listens to the noise: and comments in disgust*). If all that up there is allowed to continue, your rock will be totally eroded.

HOSIUS (*worried*). Debased rural primitivism, pure superstition, we ought all to have outgrown it . . . [she has that fetish-doll of hers talk back to the child, you know.] And yet she gets the woman Mary to recite the true gospel to her –

EUMOLPUS. Can you separate Mary from the conjuring-woman?

HOSIUS. With diplomacy, perhaps. I'll go on deck and try something.

He leaves the cabin and mounts the companion ladder.

Scene Twelve

Exterior: on deck HELEN-FAUSTA *is laughing and playing with her* MOTHER *and* HELEN *further along the barge:* HOSIUS *in private conversation with* MARY. *The* OARSMEN*'s song has died away: but the drum-taps continue to mark the time for their strokes.*

HOSIUS. Such a beautiful dark child, she performs her innocent magic with such hope and joy, does she not? The old lady is enraptured.

HELEN (*from a little distance*). Why don't we let Baba splash the water as well?

MARY. Which is how we'd make contact with any others of the True Way, every town that we came to. And ones who did not know Christ, they'd see the magic tricks, they'd hear the Name of Jesus: all so warm and friendly that –

HOSIUS. That they'd have no fear of sorcery when they saw it was only a child. Our Lord himself loved children, I've no doubt he would have approved –

MARY (*suddenly very sharp*). The execution of those starving men in Gaul, would he have approved *that*?

HOSIUS (*taken aback: but ready in an instant*). Ah . . . Easy but foolish to pity those poor men. Daughter, we should envy them: [in their deaths they came closer to Jesus than you or I can ever hope for on this earth. Was the law that condemned them wrong? Yet they knew as they died that their Saviour was also the victim of an unjust law –] I spoke with them at the gallows' foot, they were exultant in their new faith. Oh but last night I could not help weeping for the slow slow progress that we make in this cruel world. When oh when will we be fit to receive the Bridegroom at his coming? Our lamps are not yet lit, our garlands not arrayed –

MARY. I have long since stopped weeping: but I pray to our Mother for strength –

HOSIUS. To our Mother –?

MARY. Oh yes, I found her before I found her Son.

HOSIUS. Ah . . . and Melantho? She too found the Mother first?

MARY. Yes. The Mother of Christ, she said, must be greater than any goddess: she saw her Son die on the Cross, and did she not then suffer as Melantho herself was suffering . . .?

HOSIUS. You are an excellent teacher: there is great work for you in Milan, we must not lose touch. After all, we are both Spaniards, kinfolk, you might say . . .

MARY (*to herself*). Oh he is gentle, he did weep for the cruelty of law, he understands that Christ and Caesar are as far apart as water and fire. I wonder how much will Caesar understand him? Perhaps in the halls of princes there is no way for the True Way but in the footsteps of such a man?

Cross-fade to suggest passage of time.

Scene Thirteen

Exterior: on the Imperial barge, once again beside HELEN *on the poop. The* OARSMEN *are singing again.* HOSIUS *is in conversation with* HELEN.

OARSMEN (*sing*).

> Queen Helen she wears her crown on her head
> *Count your stroke and keep to the line*:
> But we pull at her oars until we are dead
> *Out, and in, and all up the Rhine.*

HELEN. Hello there, bring a footstool for the Bishop, he will sit by me.

BARGE-CAPTAIN (*as he speaks, the stool is brought*). Ya'r la'sh'p.

HOSIUS. To have my unworthy comfort taken care of by the mother of the most powerful man in the world! Be assured his greatness of spirit is *your* spirit – history proves it, even profane history, the mother of the Gracchi, the mother of Achilles – and our most pertinent sacred chronicles, you will soon come to hear of the mother of Moses, of Samuel – you know already, do you not, of the agony and joy of Bethlehem and Golgotha. No Emperor has been blessed as Constantine is blessed, in you.

HELEN. Because I come from the people, the people know the likes of me will never be changed by power and glory.

OARSMEN (*sing*).

> The boat of Queen Helen is heavy as lead
> *Count your stroke and keep to the line*:
> And we pull at her oars even after we're dead
> *Out, and in, and all up the Rhine.*

HOSIUS (*after a short pause, during which we hear the words of the song*). There are those who will try to change you. Your son has occult enemies, as well as his open ones. Consider Licinius. He intrigued against Constantine's throne, sent subversives into the west to undermine the agreed settlement, renegued upon the oath he had taken before Christ, and then began to persecute.

HELEN (*crabbily*). He was married to an Herculian, what else would we expect? The old bugger was transparent, *I* foresaw his treachery, why did not Constantine? Of course, now that he's gone down, they're pleased to invite *me* to come into their palaces. Nobody else left for me to warn 'em against, that's what they think: Licinius was the last of the danger. My arse was he the last of it!

HOSIUS. Dear lady, before he died, he made sure that he was not. Do you know that Licinius notified the Great King of Persia that our Empire was ripe for oriental infiltration? The agents of Persia are everywhere, as silent as cats on the prowl . . .

HELEN (*with sharp distaste*). Cats?

HELEN-FAUSTA *and* MELANTHO *are sitting sleepily further down.*

HELEN-FAUSTA. Now can I sing the song of how Jesus caught the fishes?

MELANTHO (*sleepily*). Very well, my darling, sing the song –

HELEN-FAUSTA (*singing*).

> Fish little fish in the deep blue sea
> Will you never never swim to me?
> Fish little fish in the wave so cold
> I am swinging my net till the day grows old.

HOSIUS (*significantly, as the song proceeds*). Mother and daughter: the cat and the kitten. There is a grandmother as well. She was in gaol in Antioch: not for Christianity, but for over-competitive heathenism. And *her* vile goddess came from Babylon.,

HELEN (*taking this in carefully, and with mounting alarm*). Babylon is ruled by the Great King of Persia . . .? Why, Bishop, do you tell me that black bitch has attached herself to me in order to murder my son! The very next town we stop at, she and her brat go straight to execution! The miracle-child, oh yes: and bad-blood Fausta was there at her birth . . .

HOSIUS (*slightly deprecating her extremism*). I do think you should be rid of them . . . Execution . . .? Perhaps not prudent . . . But Mary the Companion, a truly holy woman, we need to keep *her*. In all matters, remember, I am your friend.

HELEN. And the trusted friend of my son, who needs every friend he can get.

HOSIUS *gives a sudden little sign*.

HELEN. What's the matter? Are you ill?

HOSIUS. The sunshine – too hot . . . When Herculius put me in prison –

HELEN (*sotto voce as he carries on talking*). The father of Fausta – bad blood, bad blood –

HOSIUS. – the resistance of my constitution to all extremes was destroyed – the continual torment, the water-torture, they forced urine and liquid filth into our throats by the gallon to persuade us to deny Christ. With your permission, I will go below . . .

She murmurs an indulgent 'of course, my dear friend . . .' He leaves the deck.

HELEN (*to her 'doll'*). Oh but Baba is my friend, my son's friend as well, he's all alone, Baba, with no one to watch over him: but we'll watch, we'll be vigilant, and not let those torturing Herculians anywhere near him!

Cross-fade to suggest passage of time.

Scene Fourteen

Exterior: on the Imperial barge, the poop-deck. HELEN *murmuring: 'Baba, my friend: good Baba, quiet Baba, Baba my friend': Etc.*

OARSMEN (*sing*).

> If we had a Queen as could walk on the water
> *Count your stroke and keep to the line:*
> We'd never need row this damn boat ever after
> *Out, and in, and all up the Rhine.*

HELEN-FAUSTA (*running up onto the poop*). Lady Helen, Lady Helen, do you want me to sing about beautiful Queen Esther and the cruel King of Persia –?

HELEN (*startled out of her musing*). What –? What! No! Go away from here. Off!

HELEN-FAUSTA (*horrified by the rebuff, bursts into tears*). No I won't go away, you're a nasty old woman, I'll put the evil eye on you, you don't believe I can? But I can I can I can –

HELEN (*in shock at this*). You said *what*?

BARGE-CAPTAIN (*coming over*). A bit of trouble, ma'am?

HELEN (*furiously*). What is this child doing on the poop? Where is her mother –? (*Calls out:*) You! – woman, you –!

MELANTHO (*running aft in alarm*). Oh lady, she did not mean it, she is only very young, she did not intend –

HELEN. Get out of my sight.

MARY (*also running aft to them*). Gracious lady, I beg you to pardon –

HELEN. You're the one that brought them here, I hold *you* to be responsible. Take them both below decks, this instant, do you hear me, and find them some work to do. Captain, you will take care of it.

BARGE-CAPTAIN. Cert'nly, y'r la'sh'p. Go on there, get for'ard, move!

The three of them are hustled forward.

HELEN (*in a high state of nerves, reciting a rapid charm to her 'doll', over and over*).

> Baba good, Baba kind, Baba always in my mind
> Take it off, take away: take away the evil day
> Baba good, Baba kind . . . (*Etc.*)

Scene Fifteen

Exterior: the wind in the trees and the sound of the running river. A crowd of people gathered on shore: A CHOIR is singing 'KYRIE ELEISON'. A good deal of bell-ringing etc., to present the idea of a highly elaborate ritual. At intervals, congregational responses.

FAUSTA (*to herself: she is now in her mid-twenties*). So they came up the river, between the steep of the pine-clad mountains: his mother, white and motionless in her towering golden barge. Upon the shore we all kneel, she sits, and they sing about God. Across the river, on the right bank, smudges of smoke: and I know what they are . . . I am Fausta, I was six years old when my father took me over there, he carried me out of the boat on his shoulder, he said: 'Now, child, we will meet the wild men who live like wolves in the unconquered German forest. You are not to be afraid, because I am Herculius Augustus, I walk into their woods to show them they must be afraid of *me* – and of you, you are Imperial.' Five of them, black-faced charcoal-burners, crouching round their smouldering fire. My father laughed, and they jabbered at him in a strange barking language. I could not believe in the tongues that had uttered it. I reached forward and opened the mouth of the youngest one – oh, his tongue was just like mine, pink and wet. So I put mine out to him: and our tongues touched. My father saw it: reversed his stick like a spear and lunged it out against the throat of the young man. He fell back with a dreadful gasp and lay croaking on the ground . . . From that day forward my father never spoke to me again: except to order me to kill my husband. I never looked him in the eye until the day he lay down dead.

When Helen stepped ashore, how could I have known she would bring with her – Mary! And Melantho – and the child . . .! I would have run forward to embrace them – but Melantho and her little girl were grabbed hold of by the chamberlains, all in a flurry they were gone: and the stiff embroidered ceremony continues, with prayers, and bells, and the bishop gives his blessing, and Crispus covered in jewels embraces Helen covered in jewels . . . and Mary looking as though she were dead. There is the banner with the huge face of Jesus Christ – Look at his eyes.

A great ringing of bells marks the embracement of HELEN *and* CRISPUS.

Last week, in Milan, my youngest son upon my lap, Constantine, Crispus, at table. Constantine watching me, wide-open eyes like the eyes of Christ. He told us that his sister's son, Licinianus, child of the renegade, child not ten years old, had that day been put to death. 'Rule of warfare', he said. 'We won the battle. If Licinius had won it, then Crispus would be dead.' Eyes of Christ, eyes of Constantine, eyes of Herculius when he tore the throat of the charcoal-burner. Two round eyes in the head of Herod and all the mothers of Bethlehem screamed.

There is a sudden rush of wind and rain.

FAUSTA. The wind blows, the rain comes down, the pavilion tears at its ropes. Cold cold cold on the edge of this Empire, and we must all cross the mountains to Milan . . .

Scene Sixteen

Interior: CONSTANTINE *in his study at dead of night, poring over documents. There are occasional muffled sounds in the corridors of the palace. His soliloquy is a series of broken thoughts, interspersed by passages of silence: all very quiet.*

KYBELE (*as narrator*). In Milan at dead of night, his round eyes wide and wakeful, Constantine watches the world . . .

CONSTANTINE. 'At such time as Your Majesty thinks would best serve' . . . Diplomatic Bishop Hosius. And ambitious Hosius. Which means, devious. I must be careful . . .

NIGHT-WATCHMAN. Fourth watch of the night and all's well: in the Name of the Most High God, protection to the Imperial Household.

CONSTANTINE. There is a direction, to which his deviousness will be pointing him. [Not *my* direction, though no doubt he would wish that I would think that it was] . . . He would like my Roman Empire to be overtaken and controlled by the Christian Priests, that much is clear. Christian discipline: [what *is* it?] Do this and do that . . . to what end . . .? Salvation of all men. Am I therefore to subordinate my sovereignty upon earth, now, to the rule of Christ, he who will be imposing himself over me once I am dead? 'Thine is the Kingdom' . . . that's his kingdom. [Well-ordered: and Hosius requires for it well-ordered people . . . So do I, for *my* kingdom . . .] but where will I be in his? Alongside fishermen, shepherds, the lowest ranks of the Revenue Service? if so, a poor reward for exhausting years of the Imperial burden . . . Is it conceivable my Imperial burden is morally insufficient? Already I am beginning to think like a Christian. How insidious this religion, it invades my most intimate sanctuary . . .

A group of CHRISTIAN PRIESTS *passes along the corridor, one of them muttering prayers and all of them giving the responses.*

PRIESTS.   Almighty God, in the watches of the night,
                          guard over this palace
                          (Lord God hear us)
                          Preserve the soul of thy servant Constantine
                          (Lord God hear us)
                          And all those of his household, inasmuch O
                          Lord as they are thy dutiful servants
                          (Lord God hear our prayer) . . . (*Etc.*)

CONSTANTINE. Half of my subjects do not accept Christ. I myself, initiate of Mithras, still eligible for eternity, a highly *select* eternity upon the terms of Lord Mithras . . . My officer-corps: Mithras-men: loyal: they still believe I am still the son of my father who was indisputably one of them. Through their loyalty I am at last the one and only Emperor: Maxentius went down, Maximin Daza went down, and now Licinius has gone down . . . I AM THAT I AM . . .

Cross-fade to suggest passage of time.

CONSTANTINE. [Undeniably, if the Christians are not in good discipline,] there will be challenge against me from more than the Mithras-men. 'I am the true Christian' . . . any one can say it, '*Mine* is the Kingdom', anyone at all . . . My own household . . . Fausta and Mary talk and walk; Helen walks and talks with Mary, who, they say, is a Christian holy-woman who walks where she will. Hosius walks and talks with Mary . . . Hosius never told me what Fausta told me – that it was Mary who interpreted an oracular text that somehow led forward to my vision of the cross . . . 'Disunity of doctrine', he constantly repeats and expects me to know, every time, all the time, which doctrine, where, who asserts what, how many disputes . . .? Oh yes: his 'general council' could be very instructive . . .

Interior: CONSTANTINE's *study, as before. The* PRIESTS *pass by again, muttering the same prayers and responses.*

CONSTANTINE. But where to hold it? [Rome will not do, not central . . . Byzantium? I have plans for Byzantium, not to pre-associate them with sectarian dialectic . . . Somewhere else . . .?] Nicaea?

CONSTANTINE. Nicaea . . .! Imperial Decision!

NIGHT-WATCHMAN (*afar off down the corridor*). First watch of the morning and all's well: in the Name of the Most High God, the Imperial Household has been protected this night!

Closing music.

4

LETTERS, DISCREET AND INDISCREET

Scene One

Opening music.

Exterior: CRISPUS *composing a letter. He is in his early twenties: serious, intelligent, fresh voiced. Sounds of evening on a river bank: the murmur of the water, the odd fish jumping, birdsong, a light breeze in foliage, etc. Also, from a distance,* TROOPS *drilling, and the occasional sound of a bugle.*

CRISPUS (*letter*). From Crispus, Caesar and General, son of Constantine Augustus, to the revered Lactantius, at his house in Naples: greeting. Dearly beloved tutor, father of wisdom – or do you suspect my sincerity when I address you as that? So many years since I sat at your feet and imbibed your acerbic wisdom, since you last had cause to correct my inattention – why should you suspect that your giddy and careless pupil has become at last not only commander of the frontier-army, but also a thinking being?

Scene Two

KYBELE (*as narrator*). When Crispus wrote his letter he did not know that Lactantius was dead. The year was 324 AD. Constantine had moved his court to Nicomedia, the eastern capital. Preparations were well advanced for the Christian Council at nearby Nicaea. For so many years, Constantine's policy of toleration for all beliefs ought to have lifted my spirits, restored my intellectual energy: but it soon had become clear that to the Christian belief alone, was benefit to accrue. I had sunk back into my depression, even worse when I heard that the Emperor's son Crispus had been given for a tutor Lactantius, my old professor; who was now reaping his reward for turning to Christ, and had achieved the highest place a philosopher should look for – fatherly mentor of a brilliant heir-apparent. I had gained nothing but gloom and self-pity, and was being kept alive by the state's welfare-rations, and was squatting in an old summer-house at the back of Lactantius' vacant villa a mile or two out of Naples just beside Virgil's tomb.

Fade in sound effects: the seaside, gulls etc.

KYBELE. Even though Lactantius had Christianised, he had not forbidden his old students this privilege: but I was the only one who stayed on there. I had no will to go elsewhere. One morning I was hurrying along to pick up my bread-dole, with my head bent down as usual: suddenly my arm was clutched –

Laughter: music of cymbals, rattles, tambourines etc.: not too loud, just enough to give an atmosphere.

– and a voice said – 'You're coming with us to pay your dues to Kybele!' – I was surrounded by a giggling crowd of market-women, running and shoving each other – one of them put a gaily-coloured rattle in my hand and a garland on my head – and at once I was part of their exuberant procession. Behind us the sea was sparkling and blue – I realised that summer had come: and off we went through the countryside to a primitive village shrine, where we ate and drank and laughed until we all lay down in a stupor. The men of the village came leaping down out of an olive grove: 'We pay honour to Kybele,' they cried, 'Do not reject us.' A shy young lad in soldier's uniform spoke to me: 'Help me, auntie, to fulfil my respects to the goddess,' he said: which I did. All my gloom had been lifted. From then on I called myself 'Kybele', after the goddess-mother of the earth. Hope came pouring into me: I would write at once to Lactantius and heal the breach between us. I hurried to his villa to enquire from the caretaker where he was. 'Haven't you heard?' he answered 'Lactantius died last night.'

I burst into tears. He sat me on a chair while he got me a drink of water. On the table there was an unopened letter, with the imperial seal, addressed to Lactantius. I still do not know by what power I was seized: but I did a most dangerous thing – I took the letter and left. When I got home, I opened it.

CRISPUS (*letter*). As you yourself used to put it, Lactantius: continuity of learning, enlightenment of civilisation, is as the soft summer rain, invisible, imperceptible – and yet the landscape comes to its inevitable flower, the leaves hang heavy on the tree – here I am beside the Danube, gentle rain, circling flies upon the surface of the water, the anglers rejoice, a volume of Tacitus lies open beside my elbow.

KYBELE (*as narrator*). Here was an omen! My change of name, my amorous tribute paid to the goddess had brought me good luck. And not only good luck, my faith was restored in my philosophy: 'Do nothing unless it brings happiness to oneself and to others.' I had had part of an ancient rural ritual, had ceremonially recognised the seasons of nature, had made a young soldier happy in his flesh, and now to another soldier I had the opportunity to give happiness of intellect. I suddenly remembered it was the birthday of Epicurus – we were supposed to have kept a perpetual candle alight as a sign that his teachings would never die – I had allowed mine to go out: but now I would light it and it never *would* die because now I was going to write a reply to Crispus! I would influence him, I would encourage him, I would lead him – oh so subtly – away from Lactantius's Christ and back again to the old old truths. And I would begin by signing my correspondence with my new name. Was this deceit? Subversion? Egotism? Or a genuine Assertion, of my right to my ideas under the emperor's pledge of toleration?

CRISPUS (*letter*). History speaks to the creator of history, I can save or ruin the Empire in one moment of quick decision, so should I not also call myself the creature of history? And where does that leave my father, in his palace at Nicomedia, dependent every day upon the competence of my soldiers . . .?

KYBELE (*as narrator*). Had I been more of a politician than a philosopher I would have realised that toleration was only possible because of the efficiency of the state police. Later I found out that Crispus's letter, before it reached Naples, had passed through the hands of Colonel Jaxartes, the newly appointed, thrusting Director of the Imperial Secret Service. He showed a copy of it to the Emperor.

Scene Three

Interior: a bath-house. Bare feet on marble floors and an echo for the voices of the MEN.

KYBELE (*as narrator*). No secret agent, even your own, can ever be trusted. The only place where Constantine would venture to meet *his* was in the bath-house, strictly private, attached to the Imperial apartments: complete nudity, no concealed weapons. [Assassination would have to be by bodily strength; Constantine could out-wrestle the meagre frame of Jaxartes in any environment. They stood together, upon the edge of the cold plunge.]

CONSTANTINE. He's a perfect right to read Tacitus if he wants. I *need* an intelligent General.

JAXARTES (*a keen young voice, with an eastern liquidity*). But if from his reading he goes on to draw conclusions –

CONSTANTINE. I put you in your job to clear out the dead remnants, all those leather-and-sweat soldiers and superannuated bureaucrats who didn't know a plot from a prayer-meeting. They all but allowed renegade Licinius to usurp the whole Empire. The entire security network was idle and corrupt, half of the present establishment used to work for Licinius. That's what you're supposed to be doing, check the loyalty of your own people: you are *not* to invent conspiracies just to make yourself important – Hercules-Helios, Crispus is my eldest son!

JAXARTES (*he has an almost impertinent familiarity with the* EMPEROR, *permitted as a sort of perquisite of his position*). So we intercept his letters, essential routine. Do you order me not to?

CONSTANTINE. Of course you intercept them, but you don't bother *me* with them. Not unless – (*He breaks off from a disturbing thought.*)

There is a great splash, closely followed by another: both followed by wallowing noises.

JAXARTES (*they are now both in the water*). It wasn't only the letter.

CONSTANTINE. Then what the devil else?

JAXARTES. As you said: prayer-meetings. Have you any idea how many discordant groups of Christians there are in your empire, all praying against each other, cursing each other, invoking their Christ in every possible shadow and shape?

CONSTANTINE. Do they invoke him against me?

JAXARTES. Not as far as I have yet discovered.

CONSTANTINE. Then it's none of your business. Bishop Hosius deals with that. Bishop Hosius is calling a council to deal with it thoroughly. What I want *you* to do is to take particular note of immediate priorities. First, my new city.

Flounderings as first one and then the other climb out of the pool.

CONSTANTINE. Warm-water room, follow me.

Scene Four

Exterior: as scene one.

CRISPUS (*letter*). Tacitus says: 'The concentration of power in the hands of an autocrat caused truth to suffer in more ways than one. Adulation bore the ugly taint of subservience, detraction and spite had a ready audience'. Am I not preparing myself to be an autocrat? I have to write all this down, now, to you; or the little biting insects that infest this great river will eat into my brain and grow there into Furies, consuming me, devouring my reason . . .

Scene Five

Interior: The bath-house. A different room. A soft lapping and paddling as the two MEN *lie in the warm bath.*

JAXARTES (*airily*). Your new capital in Byzantium will not be ready for use for five or six years. The surveyors are only just beginning to put pegs into the site. No problem whatever to reorganise our eastern network in that space of time.

CONSTANTINE. Oh but there is. In my opinion Antioch and most of Cappadocia have been infiltrated by the Persians.

JAXARTES. *I* told you that. I showed you the files . . . This protest in North Africa, against the bishops whom you have approved – it purports to be a hangover from the days of persecution, but –

CONSTANTINE (*ignoring the change of subject*). Let me make this quite clear. The city of the New Rome will have an equally new security service: and Cappadocia, Antioch, Egypt, anywhere else in the east, will be rearranged in accordance, *not* the other way round. So you can begin your advanced planning now, and submit your proposals one by one as they come up. (*His voice drops suddenly into a preoccupied murmur.*) What on earth did he mean – biting insects in his brain? D'you think he's got the swamp-fever? (*Business-like again.*) Now I want to discuss my jubilee.

JAXARTES. The twenty-year jubilee is more than a year ahead. Sir: I *must* talk about North Africa. We have had a schism in the Christian cult there since before the defeat of Maxentius. Two whole regiments of regular soldiers, totally tied up to preserve the peace among the 'children of peace', and they can't do it. Before long the schismatics will be proclaiming their *own* jubilee –

CONSTANTINE (*reverting to the main issue*). My jubilee will be in Rome. It has to be in Rome for very ancient historical reasons: and I must perform sacrifices, as Supreme Pontiff of the traditional gods. Two areas of potential trouble. One, from the Christians who will resent the traditional gods. Two, from the Romans generally who will resent the Byzantium project.

JAXARTES (*swiftly, anxious to get all this out of the way*). Security in Rome is no problem, long-established foolproof routines there –

CONSTANTINE. That's what they told Julius Caesar.

JAXARTES (*briskly acknowledging the Emperor's wit*). I take the point. I'll let you know my dispositions every stage of procedure. (*He changes his tone.*) Did you *read* the files we sent you about Christian dissidence?

CONSTANTINE (*heaving himself out of the water*). If they've allowed the steam-room furnace to burn down as low as this one, by Pluto I shall have to –

Scene Six

Exterior: As scene one.

CRISPUS (*letter*). Did not Socrates ask, how can the soul attain to truth, when the fallible body which must help it is so obviously led astray? How to tell the difference between the Ideal and the Concrete? Would you call the power of Empire Concrete?

Scene Seven

Interior: the bath-house: the hot water is bubbling and there is a hiss of steam.

KYBELE [(*as narrator*). The furnace under the steam-room is fully as hot as it should be. The Emperor extends himself and hopefully closes his eyes. Colonel Jaxartes has *his* eyes wide open, dark and glowing in his sharp swarthy face.]

JAXARTES (*reeling off his facts without mercy*). The Gnostics are almost everywhere; [in the most remote regions God alone knows what they believe.] The Donatists in North Africa are in my view more of a social-revolutionary nationalist group, but on the surface they object to clergy who evaded martyrdom in the old days. The Novationists are much the same, but have connections with the Montanists. The Encratites and the Apotactites seem concentrated in Phrygia, where the Montanists originally came from – I daresay there's a connection, though they all denounce each other. The Sabellians are intellectuals: they have a view about God the Father. Sub-divisions of all of these: I would calculate more than a hundred. Did you read my provisional analysis of Valentinus on church government? He stated in so many words that –

CONSTANTINE (*cutting him short*). My dear man, I did *not* read it. I gave it to Bishop Hosius. *He* is in charge of the Secretariat for Christian Affairs. The first thing you must learn is to delegate responsibility –

JAXARTES (*deceptive mildness*). It will all be sorted out at the council?

CONSTANTINE (*complacently*). At Nicaea, among all the bishops. In twelve months' time. I've even allowed them travelling expenses and a grant for their accompanying clergy.

JAXARTES (*not putting any significance in it*). You won't attend, yourself?

CONSTANTINE. I can't attend. I assumed that being Supreme Pontiff I would be expected by Jesus Christ to be his chief bishop as well, but it seems the great vision I had before my victory did not quite indicate that: the Holy Spirit has its own route whereby it is conferred. I didn't ask questions. The Ideal of Toleration means that some things have to be accepted, however odd they may appear. (*He changes the subject: a brooding note in his voice*.) Why was Socrates condemned, d'you remember?

JAXARTES (*lightly*). Corruption of youth, I believe . . .

CONSTANTINE (*still brooding*). And Tacitus was a republican . . . None the less, it is undeniable that my son has more than mastered the hostile German tribes . . . He does remember, he is not the only son I have got . . .?

Scene Eight

Exterior: as scene one.

CRISPUS (*letter*). Continual slaughter of Germans, I have believed this was success, their incursions would come to an end, their motives being sheer barbarian greed – if it was not worth their while, they would no longer risk themselves. But now I find it is not so: for they are *driven* against us, by the Huns, who themselves have been *driven*, by the Chinese. To save our frontier, dear Lactantius, we must first conquer *China* . . .?

Scene Nine

Interior: the bath-house, the hot water still bubbles and the steam hisses.

CONSTANTINE (*a note of disquiet and annoyance*). Are you trying to tell me the bishops cannot be trusted?

JAXARTES. They seem, according to my informants, to be putting together a most cogent political structure . . . Now, you brought in regulations to inhibit their accrual of personal wealth. Did it occur to you, first, that the regulations would be widely evaded; second, that the personal wealth could quite legally be converted into corporate wealth to build up factional power?

CONSTANTINE (*worried*). Factional? Against whom?

JAXARTES. That remains to be seen. I am proffering a suggestion. The bishops on the whole represent what one might call the Pauline tradition of Christ-worship. It is one among many traditions. We know very little about how they all came into being.

CONSTANTINE. Bishop Hosius says it is all in the books. The Gospels, the letters of Paul himself, the –

JAXARTES. The books that *he* gives you. Factional books. There are others. The Pauline bishops, I submit, constitute a certain tendency, which aims to establish an élite corps within the broad organisation – if indeed we can call international Christ-worship an organisation at all.

CONSTANTINE. You said, an élite corps.

JAXARTES. Ssh, here comes the eunuch with fresh towels . . .

CONSTANTINE. He's more than a eunuch, he's a deaf-mute: we can talk.

Soft footfalls of the bath-attendant.

JAXARTES. I said an élite corps, intended to operate outside the normal relationships of cult-members with one another and with God, and largely unaccountable to the individual congregations. Also, these bishops have been deliberating in secret.

CONSTANTINE (*alarmed*). Have they? How do you know?

JAXARTES (*cooling it*). Perhaps too strong a term . . . Shall we say, 'without publicity'? Of course, they don't keep secrets from your Secretariat of Christian Affairs.

CONSTANTINE (*after a troubled pause*). Hosius?

JAXARTES. I don't know. He could be implicated.

CONSTANTINE (*now thoroughly startled*). Godsake, man, implicated in what?'

JAXARTES (*level voice*). In whatever is going on. I don't *know* what it is. Not yet. Which is why –

CONSTANTINE (*rushing to the worst possible conclusion*). Do you mean to tell me Hosius and the bishops are attempting to take control of the empire? A *coup*?!

JAXARTES (*soothing, but still seriously concerned*). Why, surely that's most improbable? No, no, but they could take over the whole of the Christ-cult.

CONSTANTINE (*relieved, but not satisfied*). Isn't that what they're supposed to do?

JAXARTES (*laying it on the line*). Sir: you are the Emperor, you make your own political judgements. My job: to provide you with enough information so that whatever you say will be well said, for the common good of all the citizens.

Scene Ten

Exterior: as scene one.

CRISPUS (*letter*). Now that my father has declared the first day of the week a public holy day [– day of the Sun God, or the Sabbath of Christ, according to inclination –] our German auxiliaries, a very thorough set of Christians, assert the Sabbath; and make use of it for the communal debate of military duty in the light of scripture. I found one of their texts – took it away and hid it – think of Tacitus again, the sufferings of truth – for it said: 'Any candidate for baptism who wants to become a soldier shall be rejected, for he has despised God'. How could I let men under discipline discuss the implications of *that*? And then again, they understand that other Germans, the hostile tribes, are themselves becoming Christian, converted by their own captives. Which does not stop them being hostile, and just as barbarous as ever.

Scene Eleven

Exterior: a courtyard, with a paved floor. Echoes of handball being played by two men with bare feet.

CONSTANTINE (*as the ball bangs against the walls*). So what is it you want me to do?

The game stops.

JAXARTES (*enthusiastic*). Fault! My point, sir.

CONSTANTINE. It was in!

JAXARTES. No sir, out: I was nearer the ball than you were, my eyes don't deceive me.

KYBELE (*as narrator*). They have moved into the gymnasium-yard, they are playing a game of handball.

CONSTANTINE. All right, I'll grant it you. I'm out of breath. Talk.

JAXARTES. I don't know, you don't know, just how much of all this is a present and urgent danger. But my department can find out for you, if you will approve the allocation.

CONSTANTINE (*disturbed, his mind moving turbulently*). I see. I see. Yes. I had a great vision, the sunrise of my day of victory. You can't question visions. But by God you can question the men into whose hands they deliver you! Do you know what I was going to do? Actually going to allow them to baptise me, before even the council had met. Oh yes, of course, you *must* have your allocation. What do they all believe, why do they all believe it, what does it mean for the concrete world – *my* kingdom, not *his*? High-priority investigation, keep it under cover, don't confine it to the empire – Persia, extremely significant – Germany, too – oh yes, Germany . . . God, but it's going to cost thousands. And already the advanced estimates for the construction of the New Rome –

JAXARTES (*very excited*). Sir, I can do it! Since I took over I have been careful to recruit an altogether new type of operative, men and women who understand all these new things in our ancient world, they will *know* what they are looking for! And I myself, with your permission, will go out into the field on this – chiefly the east – I'm very well experienced in the east –

Scene Twelve

Exterior: as scene one.

CRISPUS (*letter*). I was interrogating a young German, I threatened him with the torture, do you know what he said? 'Why do you call me an alien?' he said. 'Has it not been written, every foreign country is the Christians' homeland and every homeland is our country. We are all one people together, bound in the Holy Spirit, and with no property. Neither military booty nor secret information. All I have is yours, General,' he said, 'you don't need to torture me for it. But then all you have is mine. My tribe needs ten wagon loads of the most up-to-date Roman weapons. When can you send them?' I killed him then, without torture: and tried to forget what he said.

Scene Thirteen

Interior: sounds of accoutrements being put on: belts, jewels, etc.

KYBELE (*as narrator*). In the dressing-room. Half-a-dozen valets on hand for the Emperor. They adorn him in full regalia [for the morning's formal work. Jaxartes must wait, naked, until the room is empty: his master is still taking no chances.]

JAXARTES. About the letter from the Danube. What do you want me to do?

CONSTANTINE. Nothing. Send it on to where it was addressed.

JAXARTES. I did. There was a reply to it. From a woman. She signs herself with the name of 'Kybele'. She calls herself a philosopher: but I think she is a prostitute. Her imagery is very lewd. She is not Christian.

CONSTANTINE. Oh don't waste my time with his erotic diversions.

JAXARTES. You did take note of his post-script?

Scene Fourteen

Exterior: as scene one.

CRISPUS (*letter*). You see, the nature of the debate is changed, as between Christians north of the river and those to the south. Words like *property*, *duty*, do not have the same meaning. Change your place, you change your truth. How is it, beloved teacher, you never told me this would happen? When the heathen emperors died, and the Christian Emperor came, did you not notice it then? Because, at that time, it seems, surely all of you crossed the river . . .?

Scene Fifteen

Interior: as scene thirteen; the dressing-room.

CONSTANTINE. Let me read, from now on, *all* of his letters. And those from the woman – but only if politically relevant.

JAXARTES (*lowering his voice when he says 'bishops'*). Which reminds me: I do have one other paper to show you. It's a report about – some of your Pauline bishops.

Paper rustled etc.

KYBELE (*as narrator: sound effects appropriate to what she says*). When Constantine reads it: his face fills up with blood. Without his robe, without his diadem, his sceptre grasped in his hand like a cudgel, he flings himself out of the bath-house, down the corridor, through the curtains –

Scene Sixteen

Interior: a hall. The murmur of MEN *assembling: then* CONSTANTINE's *furious footsteps into their midst.*

KYBELE (*as narrator*). – and appears, an avenging angel, amongst the members of his privy cabinet just as they are coming together in the foyer.

CONSTANTINE. Where is *Hosius*!!

KYBELE (*as narrator – with appropriate sound effects*). They fall prostrate, they are thunderstruck, never such departure from protocol –

CONSTANTINE. On your feet –!

They rise to their feet.

CONSTANTINE. I want that bishop – there! Now, sir, what is the meaning of *this*!

Crackle of document flourished.

CONSTANTINE. Did I not tell you that this ridiculous argument between the Patriarch of Alexandria and his disobedient clergyman was to be settled without delay? Did I not tell you I was all ready to embark for my pilgrimage to the Holy Land, the Waters of Jordan? And who was to baptise me?

HOSIUS (*terrified, but facing it out*). Refulgent Majesty, the revered Eusebius, Bishop of Caesarea –

CONSTANTINE. Then why has he been condemned for taking part against the Patriarch? Is this what you call reconciliation, is it, is it? – *well*? – And moreover, we were *not informed* . . .!!

HOSIUS. I am well aware, Majesty, Bishop Eusebius is your close friend, your official biographer: but his provisional condemnation is only until the whole matter is cleared up at the council –

CONSTANTINE. Who says there's going to be a council? Who even says there's going to be Christianity any more in this Empire? Do you think I cannot see why Diocletian and Herculius were so determined to root you out?

There is a sensation among the assembled dignitaries at these appalling questions.

– You go at once to the east – now – Imperial post – and get this most monstrous condemnation reversed!

HOSIUS (*going down to the floor*). I prostrate myself dutifully upon my dismissal –

CONSTANTINE (*ignoring him*). The rest of you – inside the cabinet-room!

Scene Seventeen

KYBELE (*as narrator*). About this time, in Nicomedia, appeared Ate the goddess of strife, in the unexpected shape of a small fat man, a master-baker from southern Italy, his name was Physcon, he was an ex-slave, and, when a slave, he had been married to another slave, Semiramis of Palmyra. Now he was mayor of his Calabrian township, priest of Jupiter, tax-collector. Alas, he was liable for all default in revenue, and alas there were grave arrears, for the town was not prosperous. He sat in his bakehouse and brooded: by what divine injustice was he so cruelly harassed, when he had worked so hard for his freedom, his independent business; and by what bribed advocate to fortune had his sometime wife so unworthily improved *herself* . . .? For rumour had come to his shop –

Scene Eighteen

Exterior: street noises, wagons, footfalls, dog barking, conversations etc., as heard from an open-fronted shop.

RUMOUR 1 (*a pseudo-genteel commercial-traveller sort of voice*). She's living in Nicomedia.

PHYSCON (*crafty fat middle-aged voice*). Semiramis!

RUMOUR 1. Royal hairdresser no less: [her coiffures among the ladies of the court are making her more famous than Constantine himself.

PHYSCON. She's still a slave?

RUMOUR 1. . . . but she's allowed an unlimited clientele, as they call it, and half of her profits are her own.] Of course she'd never have got it if she hadn't turned Christian. [I suppose it's the same woman . . .?

PHYSCON (*gloomily*). She *was* milady's hairdresser, yes, in the old days, at the house of Cornelius Dolabella in Rome. I never heard who they sold her to. Nicomedia . . . Nicomedia . . .]

KYBELE (*as narrator*). And then, one day, another rumour, of a far more hopeful kind . . .

RUMOUR 2 (*a cocky know-all*). Oh there's nothing in Milan now, nothing at all, they've cleared the lot out, [government, war department, everything, even the eunuchs and the ladies and the ladies' maids, and next they'll be doing the same with Nicomedia:] anything that's worth anything's shifting, straight to Byzantium, the New Rome, except o'course the church, all that lot's for Nicaea; [at least till the council's done with – all the west's left abandoned for these Germans to bloody take hold of.] Mind you, the New Rome'll be a *Christian* New Rome, oh they'll take care o'*that* at Nicaea, be sure o' that – – –

PHYSCON (*to himself*). If all this good luck is going with this new god, maybe my bad luck belongs to the old ones, damn stupid not to ha' seen it before. Don't these Christ-people keep saying that wise men will follow a star? Was it *from* the east, or *to* the east . . .?

Scene Nineteen

Exterior: street noises as before, but we are now in the street itself.

KYBELE (*as narrator*). A week or two later, he was seen, and he was *heard*, for the first time in his term of office, walking and talking arm-in-arm with the local bishop.

The feet of the two MEN *heard above the background noises. There are some voices, also, in the background, registering reactions to* PHYSCON's *words.*

PHYSCON (*deliberately and loudly*). You will not take offence, bishop, if I go to Nicomedia to receive *Holy Baptism* there? Such an open demonstration, *at* the seat of government, will give much-needed publicity to this *town we are all so proud of*, to the *investment* opportunities we make available to the most *forward-looking* magnates . . .

Fade out effects.

KYBELE (*as narrator*). Thereafter half-a-dozen applications for Christian instruction from solid members of the municipal council, and all of them joined Physcon on his journey to Nicomedia.

Scene Twenty

Interior: a church full of worshippers; many feet moving about, murmuring prayers, people holding conversations, a choir singing some way off and occasional phrases from the baptism service: 'I baptise thee in the name of the Father, the Son, and the Holy Ghost'. Etc. (These latter, more than once, there are a succession of baptisms going on), all echoing in the big building's spaces. A gradual build-up of these effects as the NARRATOR *speaks.*

KYBELE (*as narrator*). – where they first enquired about building-plots in Greater Byzantium: and then they presented themselves for mass-baptism in the new basilica. Innumerable priests waist-deep in holy water at every crowded corner of the huge baptismal pool.

They are now in the baptistery: the baptisms are immersions, and there is a good deal of splashing as well as ritual intonings: and some informal laughing and joking as well.

BAPTIST (*abruptly – breaking off from an 'I baptise thee' routine*). Can't attend to you till this afternoon, don't you see how many people –?

PHYSCON. If you'll just be so good as to open this letter, from the bishop of –

Crackle of letter being opened. PHYSCON's *friends prompt him in a whisper: he recollects his manners and introduces them.*

PHYSCON. – ah – these gentlemen, my fellow-councillors.

BAPTIST (*obviously impressed by the letter*). Your bishop says you have pledged you and your colleagues henceforth to devote ten per cent of your business-profits to the endowment of a church in your home town . . . Indeed, extremely liberal.

FRIEND OF PHYSCON (*Rumour 2*). That was before –

PHYSCON (*officiously*). Ssh-sh, let me tell it. That was before we made up our minds to move ourselves and businesses to the New Rome, where ten per cent will *not be chicken-feed*: and another ten per cent to the basilica *here*.

BAPTIST (*more impressed than ever*). My dear sir, praise be to God, this is liberality one-thousandfold –

General buzz among the CROWD *who have heard all this.*

BAPTIST (*now very jolly with them*). Now the question of sponsors: we must certainly find some notable sponsors for *you* . . .

The previous sound-effects have faded out, to indicate a lapse of time. Now a CHOIR, *close-up, is singing.*

KYBELE (*as narrator*). But Physcon has a sudden scruple. The ceremony cannot go on.

The singing breaks off, raggedly.

PHYSCON. Wasn't about to mention it until afterwards, but then I saw as it were an angel, forbidding me to enter the water.

Ooohs and aahs from the BYSTANDERS.

PHYSCON. Here, d'you see, I wrote it all out – if you'd care to look over this statement.

Crackle of another document.

KYBELE (*as narrator*).

> The baptist takes one short glance,
> Observes legal complication
> Without end, far beyond
> His subordinate jurisdiction –
> Here is a matter
> For the bishop to pronounce.
> The bishop is not pleased:
> So many problems all at once . . .

Scene Twenty-One

Interior: a small office. Sounds of rustling papers as the BISHOP *clears his desk for the document.*

BISHOP OF NICOMEDIA (*crossly: he is a very business-like prelate, nothing at all churchy about his voice: he is also a contrast to the smooth* HOSIUS, *being sharp and tetchy*). Oh no, not another. He holds government office? He must perform heathen ceremonies? You surely know the rulings –

BAPTIST. He is moving to the New Rome, he will resign his government office –

BISHOP OF NICOMEDIA (*as he takes in the document, and realises that his first impression was incorrect*). Oh yes, ye-es . . . oh-oh, so what's this . . .? 'My scruple is about slavery'. He is not one of these zealots claiming Christ demands all slaves to be incontinently set free? 'Holy Paul' he says, 'writes to Philemon that the Christian slave of a Christian is a dear brother but he must not run away: in my case, a sister, or, as you will see, wife. I Physcon was born in slavery, in the same household as an infant female slave, of Palmyran origin. We grew up in carnal intercourse to such an extent that she and I made an uninstructed written contract of what we thought – though illegally – was marriage. I kept a copy of this, as appended as per margin.'

Rustle as he detaches the appended paper.

BISHOP OF NICOMEDIA. Even as a heathen he had some moral sense. 'We were separated by the exigencies of slavery. I have since found she is still alive, still a slave, but now a Christian.' Ah –! '– and belonging to a family of devout Christians.

My second wife has contumaciously refused to convert.' So he feels his first marriage is the only valid one . . . *I* see. Quotes Holy Paul again: 'The head of the woman is the man.' *He* needs to be *her* head, otherwise, as he says, he's living in concubinage and she in temptation. But of course he cannot marry her unless she is sold to him . . .

The BISHOP*'s comments here are a summary of what he is reading and we can hear him turning the pages as he goes on.*

BISHOP OF NICOMEDIA. 'Would Holy Church therefore authorise to her proprietors the purchase, as conducive to good morals and theology? Until we can both be brought thus into a state of grace – I do feel –'

BAPTIST. They *all* feel they cannot go through with the baptism.

BISHOP OF NICOMEDIA (*considering the implications, calculating*). If we fail him on this issue – you did say Guild of Bakers, you did say an Alderman, you did say, ten per cent . . .? – if we fail such a man, we fail an entire class; the very heartbeat of the lifeblood of the church. I am sure, without prejudice to any secular legal ramifications, we can annotate his document as Episcopally Seen and Approved.

KYBELE (*as narrator*).

> Seen and Approved:
> And Physcon's proud immersion
> At once can take place
> Before the whole congregation.

A burst of 'Gloria in excelsis' from the CHOIR.

Scene Twenty-Two

Interior: the bustle of the church porch.

KYBELE (*as narrator*).

> Afterwards he proposes
> To his friends a discreet diversion –

PHYSCON. The hostelry they call 'The Salutation of the Virgin', a very low class of place until the people became Christian – now they have this African woman, she does magic in the name of Jesus, and she demonstrates a flying child – they say it could well be a genuine seraphim: at all events, a marvel, why don't we go and see . . .?

Snatch of MELANTHO*'s cabaret-music.*

Scene Twenty-Three

KYBELE (*as narrator*). [So they went and they saw, it being already too late to present themselves at the palace. But,] the next morning, all in a body, they handed in the baker's letter, addressed to Semiramis: and departed once again for Southern Italy, to settle their affairs.

Scene Twenty-Four

Interior: the palace. During the first verse-speech of KYBELE, *sound effects appropriate to what she describes: and then the quiet of the* EMPRESS*'s private boudoir.*

KYBELE (*as narrator*).

> Semiramis in the midst of her busy assistants,
> Hard at work in her opulent saloon,
> Takes one look at the portentous letter,
> Catches her breath and begins to run –
> Till at last she is alone with the Empress –
> Spirits of heaven, what *is* she to do –?

FAUSTA. Don't do anything, this letter is meaningless.

SEMIRAMIS (*she is frightened and outraged*). He means *nothing* to me now, I will *die* if I have to leave here, oh madam, I cannot *do* it, I will *kill* myself, I cannot *do* it –!

FAUSTA (*sharp but compassionate*). Semiramis, where is your dignity? And where indeed is your good sense, rending your blouse, tearing your hair? This man is rich and rising, he loves you: if he and I agree to liberate you, you'll be the wife of a noteworthy citizen: and what is to stop you continuing to work for me? I could put it in the contract. Your business will expand even faster than his.

SEMIRAMIS (*realising Fausta has forgotten the crucial element*). But what about Joachim? He and I are one – without him I am lost, I am lost – are men and women to copulate like goats and rabbits? I found a marriage-bed, I will not change it for a brothel –!

FAUSTA (*understanding: she speaks with a certain envy*). Ah, Joachim . . . I had forgotten. Your fervent ferocious soldier, when we marched with the army from Gaul, front-rank javelin-man, catechist, prophet of God, who transported you, body and soul, with love; and then went away, discharged from his regiment, and who knows where he is now?

SEMIRAMIS (*growing into an ecstasy*). But *I* know, he writes to me, from the far regions where he gives witness for Christ. (*Incantatory:*) Oh my brother my spouse, my beloved is mine and I am his, and no one else shall lay a hand on me, no one else defile me, the virginity of the great spirit that has bonded our flesh together, oh rhua rhua rhua –

The 'rhua rhua' is a proper incantation, not simply emotional noises.

KYBELE (*as narrator*).

> She lifts up her voice in the ancient oriental keen
> Whereby the ecstatic women call on the divine being,
> To descend on them in mystery like a great white female
>   bird –
> She pulls open her breast, with red finger-nails ravaging
> Her quivering skin, the cry of her stretched throat swells
> Through all of Fausta's apartment, and beyond the closed
>   door
> End to end of the female quarters, till every woman in the
>   palace has heard
> The insistent ululation –
> The Empress takes action,
> Calls for help that can contain
> Such unlooked-for passion and pain –

Scene Twenty-Five

Interior: the general space of the palace corridors; the sounds of WOMEN *hurrying together.* FAUSTA *opens the door.*

FAUSTA (*loudly, above the growing tumult*). I want Mary the Companion – we need the Spirit to guide us – find her – bring her –!

Sound effects appropriate to the NARRATOR's *next description.*

KYBELE (*as narrator*).

> Bare feet upon marble floor
> Scurry here, scurry there,
> Voices calling, 'Mary, Mary,
> O Mary why do you tarry?'
> Contagion of energy, tumult and haste,
> To bring forth Mary the woman of Christ –

Scene Twenty-Six

Interior: a small room, outside which the gathering hubbub in the corridors becomes gradually heard, particularly voices calling MARY's *name.*

KYBELE (*as narrator*).

> Who repeats the Gospel in her private cell
> To Helen, mother of the lord of all,
> Helen for whom great Constantine is still
> Her little son, a wayward child
> Misusing and abusing his governance of the world –

MARY (*fade up: she is in the middle of telling the story*). '– the family of Jesus were told that he was out of his mind. His mother and brothers sent in a message to ask him to come out to them. He replied, 'Who is my mother?' ' – oh, lady, they are calling for me – d'you hear them, I must go –

HELEN (*bitterly, to herself, as Mary moves to the door*). 'Who is my mother . . .?' Whoever she is, she is born to be discarded . . . Wait, child, I will come too –

Scene Twenty-Seven

Interior: the corridors, and then in FAUSTA's *room, with the door left open.* HELEN *and* MARY *hurry towards the hubbub's centre: 'rhua rhua' is now become general with 'otototoi' as a counterpoint to it.*

KYBELE (*as narrator*).

> And so they go, they go great speed together
> Where all the women of the household gather
> Outside the door of Fausta, every one
> Infected by the cries they hear within –
> Naked flesh and torn-out hair,
> Orgiastic joy or black despair,
> Old Helen must be part of it and she
> Begins as well to rip her raiment and let flee
> Her own harsh croaking –

'Otototoi' now from HELEN, *close-up: the sounds of the* WOMEN *in the corridor are somewhat left behind, although* SEMIRAMIS's *'rhua rhua's' are being given full nearby vent. Cross-fade, to suggest a few moments' passage of time.*

> Fausta tells Mary what has been said,
> Mary grips hold of Semiramis' rigid head –

MARY. Put faith, put faith, put faith in Christ and his great Lady, you will *not* be sold to the baker!

FAUSTA. Will you not go to Bishop Hosius, get *him* to explain to her – name of heaven, where *is* he –? He *is* back from Caesarea –?

HELEN (*coming over the top of Fausta*). *I* will go to Hosius, Hosius knows, Hosius knows, otototoi – (*Etc.*)

MARY (*as excited as the rest of them*). Hosius knows, Hosius knows, we must all put faith in God, in the man of God, Hosius –

FAUSTA (*infected too*). Otototoi, rhua rhua, if he knows if he knows if he knows, why isn't he here –? She will *not* be sold to the baker! Rhua rhua rhua –!

KYBELE (*as narrator*).

> And now the clothes of Fausta are shredded on the floor –
> The hands of Fausta now pull her own jewels from her own
>   hair:
> Dowager Helen sees it. Sharp reversal: Helen cannot bear
> Her son's wife should thus display herself in parallel with her.

HELEN (*cutting it all short*). Debasing hysteria, get yourself together, girl, think of your husband, think of your children –

FAUSTA *and* MARY *fall silent.* SEMIRAMIS' *cries have scaled down more towards the dimension of moans.*

HELEN. Mary and I will sort it out, only one man to prevent her being sold to the baker and that's Hosius. I'll find him! Out of my way, sluts and strumpets – move –!

She walks away: the door shuts, the crying of SEMIRAMIS *is thus silenced.* HELEN *passes through the incantatory crowd of* WOMEN, *(who are now chorusing: 'She will not be sold!'), and their noise breaks off as she does so: we hear her 'shooing' them, and their hasty footsteps, running away.*

KYBELE (*as narrator*). The disordered palace resumes good order and the women return to their work. But a voice has been heard, a female voice has been shared: the voice of an old, free, world; long buried, yet, just now, if only for a moment, brought out alive and as loud as ever into the full glare of the trans-Propontic noon . . .

Scene Twenty-Eight

Interior: a small study. A rustle of paper as CONSTANTINE *reads carefully through a document.*

CONSTANTINE (*reading: his voice slowly taking in the words: and then speeding up at intervals on the less important phrases*). 'Directorate of Imperial Secret Service, for hand of Emperor only. Investigation into varieties of Christ-worship. Agent's Report: code-number Alpha-secundus.'

KYBELE [(*as narrator*). A conscientious scholar, well known to Colonel Jaxartes, employed in the Ptolemaic Library at Alexandria – his assertions may be trusted, by the Emperor, as he studies them, so long as they remain academic . . .]

CONSTANTINE. 'Subject of report: the woman-Christ of Samaria. Historical findings. This Christ was proclaimed by Samaritan philosopher, Simon the Magician. Fifteenth year, approximate, of Emperor Tiberius. She was Helena, alias Selene, alias Mary Magdalene. Word *Christ* being merely a title, "the One who is Anointed", to wit: as transcendent saviour, as rescuer from imperial rule. Political context: imminence of Great Judaean Rebellion causing multiplicity of Christ-claimants throughout the province. Comparative archival reference, the histories of Josephus.' Multiplicity . . .? '– the devotees of the woman-Christ were known as Christian' . . .?

KYBELE (*as narrator*). As soon as he reads that, Constantine sends for Bishop Hosius – who finds himself confronted with an unspoken charge of concealment of evidence. He stands his ground.

HOSIUS (*very firm*). *Christians* did not call them Christian.

KYBELE [(*as narrator*). Has he not been asked to arbitrate, by Helen and Fausta, in the very core of the household, upon a matter affecting both body and soul of one of Christ's people. He knows that the Emperor's women know that Holy Church is more than an errand boy.]

HOSIUS (*suddenly and portentously*). Emperor: who gave you life?

CONSTANTINE (*taken unawares by Hosius' confidence*). Who gave me –? Why, Fausta did –

KYBELE (*as narrator*). The name is scarce out of his mouth before Constantine knows it should not have been said. [Unsolicited recollection of pillow-talk twelve years ago: how in the name of Helios did it jump between his teeth just now?]

CONSTANTINE (*hasting to correct himself*). No: I'm talking nonsense. It's just that the Empress saved my life, as you know, when her father would have had her murder me . . . Of course my life was given me by *my* father, who else?

HOSIUS (*with a strong precision*). `Exactly so. And he had told you you were needed, to save the Empire, which is why your wife's father had to die instead of you. And your father became an Emperor because Diocletian had needed *him*. Always the authority passed on from man to man. Emperor: this document, whatever it is you are reading – it describes those who maintain that the supreme male authority – I mean God – is out to destroy the world! And that is why we say that they are *not* Christian. They do not recognise God, they do not recognise the Emperor, they do not recognise the authority of bishops, priests, deacons, or even municipal councillors. All structures of authority are anathema to them. They say that anyone anywhere can get up upon hind legs and prophesy that *you* are the devil! And such prophecy, they say, is divine.

CONSTANTINE (*very interested*). So they do still exist? They still follow this – this woman – this –

HOSIUS. Oh yes, we have been cursed with them from the very beginning. Our Lord Jesus, the true Christ, who appeared to you himself in his miracle vision, was speaking of these when he said 'wolves in sheep's clothing'. The holiest and most profound of our Christian thinkers have refuted them time and again – Paul, Clement of Rome, Irenaeus, Tertullian in his early days. And all they have done is to turn around and laugh and say to their dupes: this is just the devil talking!

CONSTANTINE (*rustling, as he leafs through, the report*). I think they've done more than turn around and laugh. I have a list here of their own philosophers. 'Marcion of Pontus, who hoped to bring the two traditions into harmony so he revered Paul and denounced Jehovah . . . Valentinus of Egypt, an initiate of occult Christian mysteries, initiated his own pupils, allowed hierarchical officials, including women, to be chosen by lot, i.e. the divine spirit. There is a text attributed to him: "God says he is a jealous God, there is no other God beside him. But by announcing this he shows the angels that another God must exist: for if not, of whom was he jealous?" '

HOSIUS. That text was not from Valentinus but Marcus – if you want, I can find you the reference –

He begins to shuffle through his books.

CONSTANTINE. While you're finding it I'll carry on with the next one, Montanus of Phrygia –

HOSIUS (*pausing in his book-rummaging*). Montanus was a libidinous madman!

CONSTANTINE. Perhaps: but he 'gave honour to women as inspired prophets and hierarchical leaders', it names two of them, Maximilla and Prisca; Prisca, it says, 'claimed a personal visitation from Christ iin female form'.

HOSIUS (*grimly*). She claimed a great deal worse than that. She made out that Lord Jesus in his lifetime, actually met the woman-Christ of Samaria, at the well –

CONSTANTINE. I remember that story, he asked her for a drink of water?

HOSIUS. And he offered her the water of life: she was in fact only a poor peasant woman. But according to the Montanists, *she* gave *him* the water of life, that is to say, initiation into her obscene cult: and he and she thereupon consummated what they call a sacred marriage.

CONSTANTINE (*brooding, as* HOSIUS *searches the books again*). She said – she gave him life. . .?

HOSIUS (*finding a useful reference at last*). Ah, I have found Valentinus: here is what he *did* say. 'There is only one rule: which is that there are no rules at all' . . . I think you should understand, Emperor, all this derives from ancient irrelevant quarrels between two sets of Jews. The Samaritans were not recognised as regular Jews, and so, in revenge, they suddenly produced their own pseudo-Christ to spite the Jewish disciples of the authentic Messiah, Jesus. Everything *he* said, *she* said the complete opposite.

CONSTANTINE. And occult initiation? The Great Knowledge she is alleged to have passed on?

HOSIUS. They used it to justify their part in the Rebellion against Rome. The Great Knowledge, in brief, is political support for the serpent that taught Eve to eat the forbidden fruit. Their entire doctrine is thus founded upon rebellious conspiracy, which they see as a virtuous act. Why, it was these so-called Christians, obeying no rules, not even in private morals, who provoked the persecutions. And of course, because they had no rules, they had no duty either to submit their own bodies to martyrdom. While men like me – under Herculius I was kept in the vilest dungeons, tortured, half-poisoned, while these rebels, these heretics, walked up and down the streets of Cordova, swopping jokes with the police; and furnishing them with *names*! (*He breaks off in confusion, aware he has got carried away*). Your Majesty, forgive me, I was –

CONSTANTINE (*graciously*). You were carried away by remembrance of your suffering: we know about it and we honour you for it.

HOSIUS (*catching advantage from the moment*). In our suffering we were guided by the truth of the Holy Spirit and the authority of the church, as ordained by the Holy Spirit. Just so, when you were wandering, as Paul of Tarsus was once wandering, lost and alone at the head of your soldiers, the Holy Spirit guided *you*. Mithras had failed you; the oracles of Mars had failed you: but the vision came, the miracle, and you destroyed the foul persecutor and all his heathen hordes!

CONSTANTINE. Did I? (*to himself, very troubled:*)

> They say, they say, the vision in the sky,
> Day in, day out, they say it and so do I.
> Do they not know it is a dreadful thought,
> That dream I had, that miracle – it was not sought,
> It flew on me from nowhere out of the rising sun,
> And now amongst its clutching tongues of fire I'm caught,
> Trapped, held and tripped every way I seek to run –

(*With a reversal to his previous sardonic manner: to* HOSIUS:) Heathen hordes? Those heathen hordes are today my tax-paying citizens. The Holy Spirit that guided me to a decision whereby you, the Christian Church, are relieved from paying the state any taxes at all.

HOSIUS. And do we not show our gratitude? Emperor, we believe in toleration. We also believe in obedience.

CONSTANTINE. There is a tension between the two.

HOSIUS. Why else do we have the council? So that we, the bishops of Christ, may tolerantly examine all the tensions, amongst ourselves.

CONSTANTINE (*very formal*). We shall await with the utmost interest your final report from the council.

KYBELE [(*as narrator*). There is such a distance in the Emperor's voice that Hosius concludes the interview is at an end. But he will not leave without giving Constantine one last proposition to think about.]

HOSIUS (*turning pages*). The book of Samuel, first volume. King Saul had a sort of vision, he was numbered among the prophets, he made promises to God: and he defaulted. And what did God say to him through the mouth of Holy Samuel? He said, 'Rebellion is as the sin of witchcraft: because thou hast rejected the word of the Lord, he hath also rejected thee from being king' . . . (*he reads the quote in a deathly voice*).

KYBELE (*as narrator – after a pause*). And when Constantine heard that, instead of executing Hosius for offering threats against the throne, he gave him an agreeable light lunch on the terrace of his garden, and let him go with many compliments. It was as well that he did so, because Hosius already had set up a text for himself, in case he were to be arrested – it would wreak a moral havoc, he believed, in the court-room at his trial.

Scene Twenty-Nine

Interior: the palace corridors: HOSIUS' *feet, walking.*

HOSIUS (*to himself, as he goes: with stout self-congratulation*). 'Behold a great priest, who in his days pleased God and was found just: and in the time of wrath he was made a reconciliation . . .'
· (*But with a change of tone, he is in fact very worried:*) Where has this Emperor obtained all his reports? For what is he searching, and now much else has he found? He reads of a woman-Christ . . . the Emperor's mind dwells upon Fausta . . . Who can tell what goes on, behind all these doors and curtains, when I and my fellow-clergy are peacefully at our prayers . . .?

HOSIUS' *footfalls die away.*

Scene Thirty

Interior: the small study.

KYBELE (*as narrator*). Meanwhile Constantine still studies, with quivering hand, his agent's report.

CONSTANTINE. So he comes to his political conclusions. 'This heterodox tradition, he says, presents no danger to the state. Its exuberance has declined, as an improved class of person is now joining the Christian cult, educated men of administrative experience, well able to induct the masses into harmonious behaviour, under a wise and tolerant Emperor, while they await the divine harmony to be looked for at the Second Coming.' Do they not tell me, Christ is not now expected back until his word has been preached to all nations under heaven? But perhaps nowadays, with all these experienced administrators taking part in the good work . . . Could it be possible that – *I* – am – the Second Coming . . .? I *did* have my vision, I am at least the Second Paul . . . If Christ has been called Helena, and Christ has been called Jesus, why should he not – then – *Constantine* . . .? Ah . . .? Can a police-report contain a divine revelation . . .?

Pause.

CONSTANTINE (*with a rustle of paper*). 'Local observations from security-surveillance, Nicomedia. The hairdresser Semiramis, intimately employed by the Empress Fausta, is known to attend a conventicle – the House of the True Way – where there is hidden talk of a female saviour'.

CONSTANTINE *mutters to himself, his voice rising as he continues, he is all confused and upset.*

CONSTANTINE.   My life would be her gift, she said,
[The knowledge of the Cross of light
Whereby from that day forth I have been led . . .

And] Semiramis so many years ago lived in the tent of Fausta, and Fausta was only a child. What sort of path was this to lead me into the midst of a miracle . . .? No, we won't think of it.

KYBELE (*as narrator*). But he thinks of it all day.

Scene Thirty-One

Interior: a chapel. A CHOIR *sings the Magnificat.*

KYBELE (*as narrator*). In the evening, in the Empress's chapel, Bishop Hosius sits and listens to the song of the Blessed Virgin, [she first made it on the day she saluted the Blessed Elisabeth.] An agèd deacon, [verger of the chapel, a cripple with one blind eye ever since the persecution, is hobbling about in the choir. He] stumbles past Hosius, who reaches out to prevent him falling –

Scuffling sound, briefly, amid the music.

KYBELE. When he has gone past, there is a paper in Hosius' hand. The bishop looks at it, furtively.

Sound of small paper being unfolded.

KYBELE. He reads of [a Christian picture of the Salutation – the signboard of] a dirty wine-house in the slums of the town. [Not so long since, it replaced another picture, two bold girls, stark naked, Helen of Troy saluting Aphrodite. What he reads there makes him wonder, how far has the house changed its nature with its name? What he reads there . . .]

There is a different music now, swelling up over the choir: an oriental dance-music.

[A dark bar-room, a dancing woman, black-skinned, between the torches, the thudding of drums, the screech of an Arabian flute . . .]

The music fades away again, and the CHOIR *anthem continues from behind it.*

HOSIUS (*to himself: his worst fears confirmed*). Melantho . . .! He found out the name! The child with her – magic power – flying, it says; the name of Christ, it says; [uncanny tricks with a huge pair of jewels – real emeralds, and the people of the house boasting they were a gift from the Empress Fausta . . .] Of *course* it's the same Melantho. Mary the Companion knew her. Does she know she's in Nicomedia? Why hasn't she told me? Does Fausta know?

KYBELE (*as narrator*). He steals a glance at Fausta, upright in her gallery, painted like an icon, jewels and cloth-of-gold.

HOSIUS (*to himself*). How much of all this can I use, *should* I use, to safeguard the truth of Christ . . .? (*With a sudden surge of panic, aloud:*) Oh merciful God, bring about this most crucial council, quickly quickly quickly, before it is all too late . . .!

KYBELE (*as narrator – as we hear it happen*). He bursts from his seat, falls prostrate on the floor of the chapel, a sudden most terrible agony, astonishing the congregation who believe he must be a very great saint, in furious search for the spirit of God.

Scene Thirty-Three

Interior: palace corridors. HELEN's *soft footfalls padding about.*

KYBELE (*as narrator*). That night, in the women's quarters, Helen is in search. Unable to sleep, her strange little doll Baba clutched to her bosom, the Dowager Lady pads up and down along the corridors, listening at doors, looking for someone to talk to, someone to assuage her irremediable sense of loss. [The armed eunuchs of the night-watch are used to her ramblings and take no notice.] She comes to Fausta's door, pauses outside –

Sound effects as appropriate to the narration.

KYBELE. – she wonders if her son is there. Inside the room, Fausta is lying alone in her big bed, thinking of the son of Helen, and asking herself how did Semiramis find the way to such magnificent self-abandonment, such love? All *she* can remember is the exquisite joy she felt as a child-bride, when Constantine would come to her by night, smile, and gather her up tightly in his arms as though she were a precious doll. Helen passes on. She goes to the door of Semiramis: and enters. The two women fall into one another's arms. Helen now knows what she has been looking for: to comfort and be comforted. Semiramis for the loss of Joachim; Helen for her husband Constantius, dragged from her bed years and years ago by political expedience. Mary in her cell can hear the two women weeping. She utters continuous prayer:

MARY (*a fervent whisper*). The spirit of the Lord has sent me to bring the good news to the poor, to proclaim liberty to captives and to the blind sight, to set the downtrodden free . . . The spirit of the Lord has shown me this day that the downtrodden are to be found as much among palaces as hovels. [Did not Jesus himself eat with the Emperor's tax-collector? Oh thank you, sweet mother-of-god for confirming me on my path . . .]

Fade out.

Scene Thirty-Four

Interior: FAUSTA's *bedroom. A door softly opens and shuts. Feet on the floorboards.*

CONSTANTINE (*as narrator*). Two hours after midnight, I the Roman Emperor visited my wife, like Jupiter out of a golden cloud full of lust for a supine nymph: except that Fausta did not wake up. I held a lamp near her sleeping face. I thought of a sudden question. (*Aloud: sharply.*) Fausta!

FAUSTA *gives a sleepy murmur, rolling over in the bed.*

CONSTANTINE (*with intensity*). Who gave you life? (*As narrator:*) She turned, she replied, one word, without waking.

FAUSTA. Eve.

CONSTANTINE (*as narrator*). I said no more. I got into bed. I slept.

Scene Thirty-Five

Interior: FAUSTA's *bedroom.*

CONSTANTINE (*as narrator*). An hour or so afterwards, I had a dream, a dream of panic, I held in my arms a twining twisting serpent. She was my wife – she cried out –

FAUSTA *gives a strangled terrified yell.*

CONSTANTINE. I awoke: my hands were tight around her throat; at once I left her bed. As soon as it was morning, I called for my secretary.

Scene Thirty-Six

Interior: CONSTANTINE's *study. The Emperor's hand-bell is ringing violently. Running feet already coming towards the room, successive doors open and shut as the hurrying* SECRETARY *bursts through them. Final opening and shutting of the study door:* CONSTANTINE *is already speaking.*

CONSTANTINE (*with great urgency*). Draft a letter to Bishop Hosius: 'We, Emperor Augustus, in our capacity as Supreme Pontiff, are happy to announce that when the Council of Bishops convenes, we ourself will take the chair. All these matters must be settled under our own eye and ear. Otherwise, chaos and anarchy!' Underline the last three words.

Closing music.

5

FOWLERS' NETS

Scene One

Opening music.

KYBELE (*as narrator*). 324 AD. When the Emperor Constantine decided personally to take the chair at the forthcoming Council of Nicaea, the Bishops did not know whether to be appalled or delighted. [Was Caesar usurping the prerogatives of God? Or had God at last captured the power of Caesar for his own purposes?] Already one sign which way the wind was blowing: Christian people were consulting the authority of bishops in affairs hitherto legal and secular. Even non-Christians would be affected by the decisions. To the private quarters of Hosius, Bishop of Cordova, in the palace at Nicomedia, just such a delegation.

Exterior: a paved courtyard with an echo. Sounds of birdsong: the soft footfalls of a SERVANT *dispensing refreshments.*

The Empress Fausta; the slave Semiramis, her hairdresser; the holy-woman, Mary the Companion: and Helen, the mother of Constantine. Hosius has been asked to rescue Semiramis: Physcon the baker is claiming her as his wife – she recognises only her marriage to the soldier Joachim. An easy matter for Hosius? But weeks have elapsed, they have heard no word from him, and this morning he sends apologies, he is bound to keep them waiting. In the meantime, his solicitous servants at the elbow of the Empress –

SERVANT. The Bishop has requested –

His voice dies away to a murmur as FAUSTA*'s thoughts take up the matter.*

FAUSTA (*to herself*).

          – has requested fine wine in fine crystal glasses
          To be served to the fine ladies, wine from Cordova the
             bishop's birthplace,
          As sipped there of an afternoon by the mother, the sisters, the
             aunts
          Of the apologetic and courteous bishop, who –

SERVANT. Regrets his inexcusable delay –

FAUSTA (*to herself*).

          – but alas he has been intercepted by another arrival of
             visitors –
          Ex-prisoners of the persecution, ex-comrades of the bishop's
             own suffering,
          Unexpectedly from North Africa, where outrageously they are
             driven out
          From their Christian community by outrageous fellow-
             Christians.
          And they bring with them bones.

SERVANT. Venerable and venerated relics –

FAUSTA (*to herself*).

          [– all that is left on this earth of those who died at the hands
             of the heathen.
          Old bones to bring grace, endow churches, transfer sanctity.]
          Dowager Helen, dreamily waiting, eating a sweetmeat,
          Awakens and opens her eyes. Bones: she has heard, as though
             she heard
           Of Carrara marble, saved from an old house to dignify her
             latest edifice . . .
          Semiramis, made nervous by the courtesy of the absent
             bishop,
          Is drinking the wine too fast, speaks rapidly, weeping and
             laughing –

SEMIRAMIS (*confusedly*). He understands, of course he does, sweet Jesus, he will understand –

FAUSTA [(*to herself*).

> She tells herself, 'I am saved': but must wait till the bishop
> can say so –

SERVANT *offers the* LADIES *more sweets.*

> Old Helen has her eyes closed, rocks her chair back and forth
> in the sun,
> Her fingers never missing the dish. For Mary, bolt upright in
> *her* chair,
> No dish, no fine wine. Head on her thin neck darting
> Sharp like a bird at every smallest sound.
> And I am the Empress. How is this correct?
> That I should sit and wait. Were I Emperor would I sit and
> wait?
> Herculius my father,
> Would *he* sit and wait, my mother wait? But Helen does:
> She sits and waits and looks at me: also sideways
> Do I look at her; mouse at the cat or cat at the mouse, which?
> Should I stand on my dignity, go to the Emperor and say,
> 'Your wife was waiting: till the wine-tasting bone-smelling
> bishop
> Had time to inform her whose hands he would permit
> To dress the hair upon her head!' And suppose he said, 'yes,
> That is what bishops are for' – suppose he said –?
> Helen is watching:
> Sip wine, Empress Fausta, sip and grin like a cat.
> These are the men who have always been the men
> To convey and contrive and collude for the man
> Who will kill when he chooses. And he does choose.
> The men that he has killed: the women he has not yet killed.
> [Constantia, Emperor's sister, wife of a murdered Emperor.
> Eutropia, my mother, mother of a murdered Emperor, wife of
> a murdered Emperor.
> Helen, Emperor's mother, castaway wife of a dead Emperor.
> Fausta, murdered Emperor's daughter, murdered Emperor's
> sister, Emperor's wife.
> Child of Constantia killed, child of Eutropia killed, child of
> Helen rules: and kills.
> Children of Fausta have *not* died, they just wait:
> And she waits: here is a courtyard of a palace where I
> command;
> And I am commanded, to wait.]

A sudden bustle of feet as HOSIUS *makes his hurried entry.*

HOSIUS (*effusive*). Forgive me, dear ladies, thousandfold forgiveness, unforgiveable delay.

FAUSTA (*to herself, as* HOSIUS *murmurs greetings and apologies*).

> So at last he comes, Hosius, comes running, the distracted
> bishop
> Hands stretched, face puckered with dutiful anguish –
> [Both my hands taken into his, fine bones of his fingers,
> Warm and dry, like glass fragile:]
> His greeting to Helen –

HOSIUS. Most excellent mother of excellency – what honour –

FAUSTA (*to herself*).

> And to Mary: to Semiramis –

HOSIUS. Beloved sisters in Christ –

FAUSTA (*to herself*).

> And we wait. And he speaks. But speaks
> what? This is a cataract.

HOSIUS (*a cataract*). [From north Africa, from Carthage,] oh terrible most terrible, barefoot, humiliated, Christian men, my old comrades –

FAUSTA (*to herself: coming in over* HOSIUS' *cataract*). A floodtide, a cascade, proving to distressed women that the world has greater sorrows than we are able to suffer, and that he, the pastor of God, must take as much care of his wolf-lacerated sheep on the mountain as he does of his fretful she-goats, safe in their well-fenced garden. [On the other hand, he must also encourage us: we are women of the Emperor, and he always encourages the Emperor.]

HOSIUS [(*his cataract continuing*). – and how did they blame these good men? Why, the old old wicked libel that because they rejoiced in our Lord Emperor's glorious victory, they were therefore not sincere in their previous martyrdom – 'No Rome, Christ alone!' – the heretical cry, as always, of those who want nothing but disorder –]

HELEN (*consolingly*). But dear bishop, they did rescue the bones of their saints –

HOSIUS. Oh they did, they did, the sacred relics of the noble victims of cruel Herculius –

FAUSTA (*to herself*). He recounts yet again the cruelties of my family, [and I, the daughter of Herculius, sit pressing my long painted fingernails so hard into the palms of my hands, there is blood on the fringe of my sleeve.] It is not quite the bishop I am hating, but Helen. She is ready to betray Semiramis just as she betrayed Melantho.

> [So greedy she is for old bones, see how she wraps
> The old bone of her right arm right across the bishop's arm,
> Grips his hand in her hand –]

HELEN (*angrily*). No account must they get them back, *we* must look after them: build a church in my son's new city, make it truly a *Christian* New Rome, where, if they want their relics, they must crawl upon their knees to the shrine and cry to be forgiven!

FAUSTA (*to herself*). She gives money for churches the way I would give money for jewels. But Hosius knows better than to ask her direct.

HELEN. [Oh but, old friend, it must be done – you have told your need to ready ears and surely the Lord will provide –

FAUSTA (*to herself*). The cash-box is as good as open, Helen is on his side, now it is time for the real business.

HOSIUS. Ah, when suffering is shared, how quickly relief is afforded. For have we not all suffered – the slave, the free woman of God –

FAUSTA (*to herself*).

> He has told us of his bones and his Africans –
> Now he tells us of ourselves –?

HOSIUS. The mother whose son was torn from her –]

FAUSTA (*to herself*). *When* will he tell us what it is we want to know –?

HOSIUS. [The daughter who sits here, refulgent Empress of all our lives, when it might have been another in her place –

FAUSTA (*to herself*).

>So politely he insults me with the memory of *my* forced marriage,
>Of the expulsion of my husband's first wife . . .]
>Mary the Companion is red and white and shuddering with growing rage of inspiration
>Semiramis is looking at me, why can I not speak? I will speak!
>(*Aloud: and sharply*:). Bishop Hosius, your fellow-bishop, of Nicomedia, signed a letter, to allow an Italian baker to lay claim upon my slave –

HOSIUS (*adopting at once a clearly unhelpful judicial tone*). Ah . . . Ah, Majesty, your slave. It is a claim. Oh yes. Who has the documents to prove the original purchase? And to whom the jurisdiction? A question, do you see, of an intense archival search. Which city, and what date? You do understand, difficulties. You do understand, I have undertaken to look into it. But –

FAUSTA. But?

HOSIUS (*starting philosophically and working towards a personal attack*). But, madam, what *is* a slave? insofar as we are in Christ, we are assuredly free: insofar as we are of the world, then all of us are slaves. A small piece of paper, most difficult to be found, might bind or loose a body, it cannot liberate a Christian *soul*. And yet, with the church, as you have heard, in such torment, tearing itself to pieces, the ministers of Christ must prowl and prowl around for this one small moth-eaten fragment, who owns or does not own a beautiful lady who has already in the beauty of holiness given herself to God –?

MARY (*who has been making expostulatory noises for some time, now breaks out in an angry cry*). The spirit of the Lord –!

HOSIUS (*ignoring her*). Do I dare to rebuke? I do not rebuke, no, I am aware that to a woman's heart such worldly trivialities –

MARY. The spirit of the Lord –!

SEMIRAMIS. The spirit speaks in the mouth of Mary – oh be silent and hear it!

MARY. The spirit of the Lord has sent me to bring the good news to the poor, to proclaim liberty to captives and to the blind sight, to set the downtrodden free –

She repeats this again: singing.

HOSIUS (*in a sudden rage: not letting Mary finish*). Ignorant insulting women – 'I suffer not a woman to teach, nor to usurp authority: judge in yourselves, women, is it comely that a woman pray unto God uncovered, she dishonoureth her head,' – it is written, 'if she be not covered, let her also be shorn!' Oh vanity of vanities, saith the preacher, all this coil about a hairdresser: And you think fit to ask *me* to make busy my dedicate fingers in so worldly and discordant a purpose! Oh madam, madam –

FAUSTA [(*to herself, as he goes on*).

>Why, the tears are running down his old face like streams down a mountain,
>Am I to swim, am I to drown, how to struggle against such a deluge?]

HOSIUS. – madam, you are Empress, I speak to you what I must, take my head upon a serving-dish like the head of John Baptist, take my head, take my hands, take my heart – take all that is mine and devour it in your vainglory, but I shall not be silenced: my voice is the voice of Paul unto the madwomen of Corinth, my voice is the voice of Elijah unto the queen of iniquity –

FAUSTA (*to herself, above* HOSIUS' *reproachful torrent*).

> [Why should he be silenced?
> Let him roar in his elegant courtyard till his lungs break out
>   into blood,]
> I have one arm for my friend Mary, one arm for my friend
>   Semiramis,
> Three in one and one in three we turn our backs and walk.

As she rises, and MARY *and* SEMIRAMIS *rise with her,* HOSIUS *stops talking abruptly. We hear the clip-clop of the three women's feet going away.*

HELEN (*to herself*). So they walk, and leave him standing. But Helen stands with him. Bad blood of the murderer Herculius, [bad blood of.the murderer Herod, bad blood of Herodias.] Hair on her head like serpents, gorgon-head of her infected blood: [old Helen observes her proud backbone as she goes, old Hosius observes the agitation of her wicked hips –]

HELEN's *feet are heard walking, after the others.*

HELEN. [Yet I cannot stay with Hosius.] If Fausta is a gorgon, she is a gorgon in the bed of my son: she must be followed, she must be watched.

HOSIUS (*hurrying after* HELEN). Lady Helen – your excellency – wait – oh my goodness, this is terrible –

HELEN (*still walking: to herself*). Good old friend, but he must not keep me, who but I can bring all of this darkness to light?

Scene Two

KYBELE (*as narrator*). It will be remembered that the Emperor has let loose Colonel Jaxartes, Director of his Secret Service, upon the history of Christianity. Jaxartes is loyal neither to the new religion nor the old but only to his own caste, the subterranean servants of imperial power.

Scene Three
Exterior: the noises of a busy waterfront.

KYBELE (*as narrator*). He arrives in Alexandria. A city of Greeks and a city of Jews: the enlightenment of Greek philosophy had from here become absorbed into the Roman Empire: and had absorbed into itself the farouche enthusiasm of the Jews. Philo of Alexandria was a Jew with a Greek mind, and had philosophised his primitive faith. And when Mark the Evangelist brought Christ to the city both Greek and Jew had welcomed him with sophisticated receptivity. Jaxartes knows one thing about the present state of Alexandria.

JAXARTES (*to himself, as he walks through the port*). A Christian man called Arius, near seventy years old, of huge and cadaverous appearance, has mortally offended the Christian establishment by announcing that Jesus of Nazareth was not God.

KYBELE [(*as narrator*). Nonetheless, Arius, with his impeccable morals, his austere dress – he wears nothing but sackcloth – is the very print and picture of a gospel-impregnate saint. Here is indeed a strange reversal, has the whole city turned upside-down?] Jaxartes, the instinctive hound-dog, sniffs the air as he walks up from the port.

He is now away from the sounds of the dockside and in echoing narrow crowded streets.

JAXARTES (*to himself as he walks*). Far too many armed civilians . . . Church-porch militia, temple-gate militia, old gods against the new one, the new one against the old. Usual barricades between the ethnic ghettos: these days Jews and Greeks indistinguishable from each other but *we* don't live where *they* live, cross the boundary you get your throat slit. Fair enough, I'm an obvious stranger, they're not going to slit *my* throat. And yet, I don't know . . . I don't know . . . there *is* something . . . not *quite* usual . . .?

KYBELE (*as narrator*). At last he sees what it is. The lower orders: that is to say, neither Greek nor Jew but the ancient natives of the Nile, dark mud-coloured compost upon which civilisation grew, the subsoil, which hitherto he scarcely noticed. Today, however: he sees them everywhere. And they all have individual faces. He slides up to a small group, waiting their turn to buy hot pasties from a barrow at the curbside. For once their excited talk may turn out to mean something . . .

A rattle of voices, approximately African, in noisy conversation.

1st ALEXANDRIAN WORKER. The patriarch said –

2nd ALEXANDRIAN WORKER. No the patriarch never said –

3rd ALEXANDRIAN WORKER. Damn patriarch can say whatever he want, man: I tell you the big fellow stand no nonsense now nor never!

There is general agreement at this.

KYBELE (*as narrator, coming in over the conversation*). So who can the 'big fellow' be, if not Arius? Jaxartes buys his own pasty, puts his question.

JAXARTES (*diffidently*). I'm looking for the Christ-church where Arius is preaching tonight –?

The conversation suddenly stops.

JAXARTES (*to himself*). Did I say the wrong thing? Hand on dagger, under my cloak . . . No: they're all smiling.

3rd ALEXANDRIAN WORKER (*expansively and rather contemptuously*). Church? Arius don't use no church. Not any more: Jesus Christ lives and walks on the streets of this city and that's where you'll hear him or nowhere. The big fellow told us, to hell with the incense-houses, to hell with these damn books: he go where the people go, bring the people their own flesh and blood!

Fade out street noises.

Scene Four

Interior: a library with hushed voices and cautious movement of PEOPLE *among book-stacks. Fade in slowly behind* NARRATOR).

KYBELE (*as narrator*). To hell with books? Nobody would tell them that, if he had not first been reading books. [Secret policemen always know: in the beginning is the word, but before it can be spread it must be written down.] Jaxartes has a man in the Great Library here: Alpha-secundus his code-number for the organisation. They meet between crowded book-shelves and pretend to be looking together for a volume . . .

ALPHA-SECUNDUS (*a fussy scholar's voice*). We have very few specifically Christian works here: for them you should go to the Catechetical School. (*He lowers his voice.*) Of course we do have some, I've already carried out a degree of research as you requested and sent the results to the Emperor: but not about Arius. *He* seems to have got all his material from Antioch. He went there on a visit and when he came back he had this totally new doctrine. Oh, the patriarch was in here and everyone else was here, pulling the shelves to pieces to find out how to refute it – they were looking up Philo, Plato, Cleanthes of Assos, Posidonius of Apamea, every philosopher who ever published: attempting to prove by means of non-Christians that official Christianity is the only possible truth . . .!

JAXARTES (*also in a low voice*). Why do you think he went to Antioch?

ALPHA-SECUNDUS. He came from there in the first place. He was taught in the school of Lucian, a martyr of the persecution. The Alexandrian clergy think that Lucian was far too close to Judaism.

JAXARTES (*he has a clue*). Judaism? *Was* he?

ALPHA-SECUNDUS. It's not exactly my field. Too recent, you understand. And his papers after his death were kept in Antioch: we had hoped for them for our collection, but, alas, the Antioch scholars – very jealous of their local documents. Though mind you, I wouldn't know how much of value they'd contain – all Christian records edited after the fall of Jerusalem have been to some extent doctored.

JAXARTES (*this is new to him*). Have they? How so?

ALPHA-SECUNDUS. It's what I said, Judaism. There's a great deal of church history the church doesn't want us to know, you know.

JAXARTES (*to himself*). In terms of security, Judaism can only mean – subversion. If the books and papers of Lucian, doctored or not, should prove to be the key to it – (*Aloud, decisive, excited:*) Antioch! I can be there, must be there, by the end of the week . . .!

Scene Five

Interior.

HOSIUS (*pathetically*). Oh foolish, foolish women –

KYBELE (*as narrator*). Bishop Hosius seeks consolation: Eumolpus, his trusted consultant.

EUMOLPUS. Lean back in your chair – let me rub some oil and herbs into the spring of your neck – I often think my imprisonment, even in that appalling Antioch gaol, was a far lighter burden than all the complexities of official recognition. For example, Nicomedia: I mean the bishop, not the town – it was a letter from *him* set this tiresome matter afoot, yes?

HOSIUS. A letter from Physcon the baker, which he countersigned.

EUMOLPUS. Yes, I know: but *why* did he?:

HOSIUS (*caught by* EUMOLPUS' *significant tone*). Why . . .? Are you suggesting Nicomedia put the baker up to it? I never thought of that, I must be losing my touch. I'm losing it everywhere. I've already offended the Emperor by failing to settle this unnecessary dispute in Alexandria . . . We have letters to write about that, Eumolpus, let us waste no more time, pick up your tablets, write direct to the cadaverous Arius, he exceeds beyond all bounds, why, even the Bishop of Nicomedia is openly supporting him –

EUMOLPUS (*again significantly*). Yes, he is.

HOSIUS. Yes, he is . . . So *that's* what it's all about! Nicomedia knows the Arius matter will have to be brought up at the Council of Nicaea: and that I will be influencing the Emperor to turn the council against Arius: and so, he must discredit me. And so – go on, go on – what else should I infer?

EUMOLPUS (*soothingly*). Wise as a serpent, letting not the left hand know what the right hand doeth –

HOSIUS (*who appreciates* EUMOLPUS' *subtlety*). Aha –?

EUMOLPUS. – we lay out as it were on a table all conceivable ramifications, starting with the fact that, technically speaking, the Emperor not yet baptised, the Imperial Household is heathen.

HOSIUS. Well?

EUMOLPUS. But the Empress and *her* household are Christian. Nicomedia has entrapped you into giving her advice upon her Christian domestic affairs. And that advice may bring you into conflict with the Emperor, because it is Christian advice, and he is not a Christian.

HOSIUS. Oh nonsense, Nicomedia can't make anything of that.

EUMOLPUS. He can: if he brings into it the substance of some of these rumours –

HOSIUS (*alarmed*). Rumours? What rumours?

EUMOLPUS. The black woman Melantho and her child, low-class cult-magic at the inn of the Salutation. Melantho was associated with Mary the Companion who . . .

HOSIUS. I drove her away. Not my fault if she's here in Nicomedia.

EUMOLPUS. So whose fault is it? She must have a licence to perform in that bawdy-house: the police wouldn't have given her one if the local bishop vetoed it. He may support Arius but surely he has no taste for witchcraft? So why *didn't* he veto it?

HOSIUS (*gloomily accepting the logic*). Because he wanted her here. He will discredit me by pointing to her . . . You say, rumours, already . . .?

EUMOLPUS. The putting-together of names, that's all, nothing positive, just that you, me, and Melantho, were travelling together in Gaul, and Melantho's child has no apparent father, and –

HOSIUS. – and therefore I am mixed up in the most salacious kind of neo-heathenism and through my contacts with the royal ladies I am mixing *them* into it as well! Eumolpus, this is monstrous. I suppose the next thing will be that Physcon the baker wants to rescue the Empress's slave-woman from a high-society den of ritual prostitution?

EUMOLPUS. They haven't called it that yet.

HOSIUS. But they will – if I give Fausta the help she is looking for, if I write on her behalf to say 'no' to the letter Nicomedia counter-signed.

EUMOLPUS. Nicomedia supports Arius. Who else does – in this palace . . .?

HOSIUS (*after a moment's thought*). Constantia, the Emperor's sister . . .?

EUMOLPUS (*it is the answer he was looking for*). Very friendly with Nicomedia. And Constantia and Fausta have hardly a word to say to one another. This looks like a church feud: but it could become a palace feud, and a palace feud between the women – to capture the Emperor. He is pulled towards Arius: or he is pulled towards . . .? Where does Helen come in?

HOSIUS. She hates Fausta the daughter of Herculius. She hates Constantia whose mother was Herculian. 'Bad blood' . . .

EUMOLPUS. So Helen is a third force: Helen is for *us*.

HOSIUS. For the true church, oh yes, she will build a shrine for the African relics – it is *her* we must work upon.

KYBELE (*as narrator*). Women feuds, palace feuds, church feuds – out of the innocent bewilderment of one entangled slave-woman, so vast an entanglement bewildering these subtle men with all its potential consequence. Had they thought first of Physcon the baker and looked into his simple motives – greed, pride, perhaps lechery – how simple a business they could have made of it. To be fair to Bishop Hosius, he does try to keep it simple.

HOSIUS (*trying to keep it simple*). In the matter of Fausta's hairdresser – nothing further must be done. Nicomedia must have what he asks for – otherwise he will get what he wants . . . And we must discover once and for all, what is the connection with Melantho and her child. Myself, I cannot think there is anything in it, cannot think so, cannot think so . . .

He is on his way out, muttering: and then he stops.

HOSIUS. Eumolpus, if there *is*, the whole church is in danger, we will have exposed ourselves before the Emperor: and the Emperor will never be baptised! Eumolpus, I trust you: but tact, my dear fellow, tact above all, and discretion . . .

He goes out and shuts the door.

EUMOLPUS (*to himself, very vindictively*). Oh discretion – but I do not forget, it was the mother of Melantho, the great Jezebel of heathen Antioch, who brought me into the gaol, brought me into the torture-room! If her daughter is in Nicomedia, Eumolpus at length will find for her and all her associate women, *whoever they may be*, an equal and commensurate agony. But, no – I do not hate women: merely seek out their weaknesses to bring to God's grace Constantine, the greatest man in all the world . . .

> Wild-fowlers now and then
> To take a flying cock-bird, catch first a sitting hen:
> The hen cries out, trapped in the fowler's snare,
> The cock will hear her, high up in the air,
> And down he comes: and then he flies no more . . .

Scene Six

KYBELE (*as narrator*). 'From Crispus, Caesar and General, son of Constantine Augustus, to his deceased tutor Lactantius – or should it be to Lactantius reincarnate as the Goddess Kybele? Goddess or nymph,' he wrote to me, 'you have enticed me . . .' And because he wrote, I wrote again: an initial rash impulse became an entire delicious sequence of indiscreet belles-lettres. Quite out of my normal style I found myself mutating into Ovid and Sappho rolled up into one. A great deal of gossip for the young prince on the distant frontier, how his father's forthcoming jubilee was affecting even Naples, all manner of ceremonious preparation, distinguished foreign visitors to make links with, and to glorify, revived empire from beyond the remotest ocean; even Hibernians were expected with a very particular tribute – a leash of wolfhounds as a gift for the guardians of Virgil's tomb. It appeared that Virgil was one of their own, his name more properly Feargall, he was a Cisalpine Celt and therefore kin to a ruling caste among the Irish. I had never heard this before, Lactantius cannot have known it: I was sure it would astonish Crispus.

I told him how I had made acquaintance with the House of the True Way in Naples, a community of kind and motherly Christian women who invited me – I don't know why – to their regular monthly soirées, to contemplate eternal truths held in common by both the old and the new religion. Had they heard about the Imperial seal on the letters delivered to my summer-house . . .? They proved most anxious to make the Christ-cult human to me. Such a straightforward Homeric beauty in the stories which they clung to – 'a baby born in a manger because there was no room at the inn . . .' Oh yes, their hearts went out to the simple mother of such a child, they too might have given birth to a little saviour in the straw. All the more moving because of what had in fact happened to so many of them in the days when their god was illegal. One – a widow, lamed and half-blinded by Herculius's troopers: another – a mother who had seen her two daughters burned alive. How could I refuse when they invited me to travel with them to the council at Nicaea? I told this to Crispus: but let him ponder for himself, who was converting whom . . .

Scene Seven

Exterior: On a ship at sea, in rough weather getting rougher. The STONE-MASONS' *song is coarsely performed by five or six voices, one* SINGER *giving the verses and the others coming in on the refrain, marking time with handclaps and slapping their mallets on the deck.*

STONE-MASON (*singing*).

> One in three and three in one
> When a bishop's on his throne
> We all can see what he has done
> To keep our Lord for himself alone –
>
> *Refrain:*
> Oh aloney loney loney loney
> Spiritual body ain't got no boney –

KYBELE (*as narrator: speaking with the refrain going on behind, repeated as much as need be*). Jaxartes, on the ship for Antioch: he's not been aboard half-an-hour when he finds himself face-to-face with the practical results, the practical dangers even, of the popular preachings of Arius. The song has been written by Arius, the singers are Arius's people – a conscripted gang of Egyptian building-workmen, specialists in underwater harbour construction, travelling under guard to repair the docks at Seleucia. They are singing out to provoke the anger of a well-dressed group of clerics who sit under the lee of the stern-cabin, sipping spiced wine, nibbling discreet olives, hoping they won't be sick . . .

JAXARTES (*to himself*). Anywhere else these priests would already retaliate – thank the gods they've the sense to see an overladen deck is no place for a brawl.

STONE-MASON (*taking up the verse again as the refrain beats itself out*).

> Human beings, you and me,
> Bow your knee to the one in three
> To the three in one hold up your hand:
> God is far too abstract for you to understand –
>
> *Refrain:*
> Ab-stracty tracty tracty heavenly god
> Spiritual body ain't got no good red blood –

KYBELE (*as narrator – as the refrain once again is repeated*). The weather is getting worse, the water at every roll pouring in over the gunwales. The soldiers on the fo'c'sle are beginning to take notice – wondering should they come aft to try and preserve order –

As the refrain comes to its ragged end, the SINGER *moves aft – i.e., his voice increases.*

STONE-MASON (*speaking angrily, not singing*).

> Abstract, what d'you call abstract –?
> Yes sir no sir
> Three bags of roaring fart
> A living man like Jesus
> 'd trample 'em into the dirt!

JAXARTES (*alarmed, to himself*). God, one of the priests has pulled a bludgeon out of his luggage! I'm getting below out of this –

KYBELE (*as narrator*). He's too late, the whole crowd of stone-masons has now moved between him and the hatchway. The ship's master beside the steering oars is as jumpy as a dog in a farmyard –

SHIPMASTER (*bellowing*). Belay that there – lay forrad where you belong – sergeant, control those hooligans, damn you – where's the bosun? – bosun, some of your men with belaying-pins, the soldiers need help –?

STONE-MASON.   A living man like Jesus
                     'd trample 'em into the dirt!

Oh yeah but according to *you*, he came out of heaven and he flew back into heaven and while he was down here he neither ate drank nor went to the shithouse, and *that's* what we're supposed to imitate! Go imitate a bloody crocodile.

This final obscenity does it: there is a confused furious roar from all involved and the sound of immediate violence. Cross-fade.

Scene Eight

Exterior: on board ship: but the noise of the fighting and of the storm has died down.

JAXARTES (*to himself*). He had caught my attention before the fight began, an old man like a broken Hercules, sitting up in the bow, crippled leg, blind eyes, leaning on a staff as thick and knotty as his own wrist: a coarse leather bag was all his luggage, [his clothes were seven or eight layers of leather and sheepskin.] One of the crew had had to help him to a safe place on the deck. How was it then, in the very whirlpool of violence and rage, he was able to rise, slip forward like an eel, knowing exactly where he moved to, catch with his left hand the elbow of an angry black-skinned labourer and whisper two words in his ear? Two words: and in one instant all the fighting was over. So: here we are. It's all over as quick as it began. Not only that, but the squall of wind has hurtled past us, and now we sail in bright sunshine on a level blue sea as carefree and sportive as a dolphin. The old man, unaccountably, is once again sitting up in the bow: he peers toward the sky, at nothing. I ask the master who he is?

SHIPMASTER (*rudely*). Don't you know who he is? Everyone knows who he is. John the Reader who lived in prison for the glory of Christ thirty-five years: he was in the copper-mines and the marble-quarries, he broke stones on every road between Damascus and the Red Sea.

JAXARTES. Where's he going?

SHIPMASTER. How should *I* know where he's going? A man like that goes where the wind carries him: or maybe the wind carries him wherever he chooses to go. If he hadn't paid his passage he wouldn't be on board. What more d'you want to ask?

We hear him walk away: calling orders to the crew forward).

SHIPMASTER. Bosun, have the hands take a reef out of the foresail – lively now – jump to it –!

JAXARTES (*to himself as the* SHIPMASTER *gives these orders*). Oh but I want to ask a very great deal more. How came a blind man so quickly so firmly to establish his control upon such a dangerous mob? Can he be some kind of leader: a captain, for example, in a secret society? It is however clear from the tone of the shipmaster's voice, further questions will be far from prudent . . . Make a note.

KYBELE (*as narrator*). And so, to Seleucia, and then by fast carriage to Antioch. Jaxartes expected an immediate rendezvous with his highly professional chief-of-station: but – as often happens when the secret service tries to be secret – a certain lack of clarity: they missed one another. Jaxartes took a gamble – went straight unaccompanied to the new basilica being built to the memory of blessed Lucian.

Scene Ten

Exterior: a street adjoining a building-site. Wagon-wheels, cranes, the sound of MASONS' *hammers, and cries of* WORKMEN *to their fellows. These effects have been coming up behind the narration.*

JAXARTES (*to himself*). The apartment-house where Lucian lived . . . his undercover divinity-school would have been in the back garden . . . the Bishop of Antioch's pulled it all down . . . and this huge pretentious construction will in due course replace it – church, college, library, elaborate shrine for the martyr's bones . . .

KYBELE (*as narrator*). He prowls around the outside of the building-site: wondering where the books and papers have their temporary storage. And wondering whom to ask about it. He has heard the present bishop is totally unsympathetic to Arius: so there may be some small difficulty. He has also heard the brother of the present bishop is a highly corrupt building-contractor who used his relationship to steal a march on his business rivals . . . which might have something to do with –

JAXARTES (*to himself, overlapping* KYBELE). – with all these ruffians standing around, rusty cutlasses gripped in their fists – church-porch militia yet again – but from whom do they need to protect what . . .?

GUARD (*a sudden shout, followed by a run of feet and clatter of weapons*). That's the man – get him –!

KYBELE (*as narrator – to sounds of a scuffle*). A sudden rush: and before he can even so much as grope for his dagger, he is grabbed, held, and thrown to the ground by a large force of bricklaying bully-boys.

Sounds of a scuffle.

JAXARTES (*outraged, but assuming a meek demeanour*). Gentlemen, please, let me explain, I am a pilgrim, I am a tourist, I am a very harmless student of apologetic divinity. The reputation of blessed Lucian has already –

GUARD. I don't care if his reputation's got to Atlantis, you're not coming in here. It's the orders of the bishop. Those codices are highly fragile and precious antiquities, we can't allow –

JAXARTES. Then they *have* been preserved?

GUARD. Of course they've been preserved. If you want to get a look at 'em, apply to the bishop. But he's not going to let you. We can't allow every rag-tag and bloody bobtail to come messing among packing-cases in the middle of all this work!

JAXARTES. So how do I find the bishop?

GUARD. You don't. He's in Nicomedia. Put your feet on the street – *move*!

JAXARTES *moves away.*

KYBELE (*as narrator*). What was it all about? Of course when there is construction there is always scope for pilfering, and security on an important site is cardinal, Jaxartes well understands that. But something not quite straight in the eye of the guard when he mentioned the books, something –

JAXARTES (*as he walks*). Something damnably shifty.

Fade.

Scene Eleven

Interior.

CHIEF OF STATION (*an underbred policeman's voice – he is a 'local', but bear in mind there was no specifically 'Roman' type at this period: all citizens were 'Romans': the concept of an 'occupying army' has long since dissolved in the wash as it were . . .*). You were seen this morning by one of my people, in and around the Lucian basilica –?

JAXARTES (*to himself*). Of course, no apologies. My highly professional chief-of-station, who should have made the rendezvous on my arrival, seems to think it was all my fault. I won't comment.

CHIEF OF STATION. It would have been better had you talked with me first. We have a stake-out in progress down there, it could have been difficult. I have here the paperwork you asked for.

Documents handed over.

JAXARTES (*riffling through them*). Good, you've done well. (*to himself:*) I'm revising my opinion of him. (*Aloud:*) You said 'stake-out'?

CHIEF OF STATION. Er – if I may so so, sir –?

JAXARTES (*to himself*). He's going to be awkward, perhaps I shouldn't revise my opinion. (*Aloud:*) No you may *not* say so: I want to know what's going on. Well? *The* CHIEF OF STATION *coughs, very embarrassed, and then comes out with it.*

CHIEF OF STATION. It *is* extremely delicate, considering who's involved, sir – the Lucian archive, the religious codices – they appear to have disappeared, and the bishop is playing it very very close to his chest.

JAXARTES. What exactly do you suspect?

CHIEF OF STATION. A couple of possibilities. One: that the bishop has stolen them himself, in pursuance of some financial fraud.

JAXARTES (*after a sceptical grunt*). And number two?

CHIEF OF STATION. Caesarea has got them. That's Caesarea in Palestine. The library there was founded by Origen, an Egyptian theologian who quarrelled with a former patriarch of Alexandria –

JAXARTES. Just like Arius.

CHIEF OF STATION. Not quite, not doctrinal. A question of jurisdiction. He was irregularly ordained in Palestine, and as a result he had to live in Palestine till the day of his death. His doctrine, however, has been attacked: and Bishop Eusebius of Caesarea has defended it. Eusebius might also think he can defend the books of Lucian, if someone could get hold of them for him. He hates and despises our Antioch bishop.

KYBELE (*as narrator*). Jaxartes listens with half an ear. Eusebius is important, he's a friend of the Emperor, he's already in trouble with his fellow-bishops because of the Arius trouble, but that's not *quite* the point at issue . . . Caesarea . . .?

JAXARTES (*to himself*). . . . there was something in Christian scripture about Caesarea . . . To be sure, the Apostle Peter! He refused to go to Caesarea to baptise a Roman soldier, saying Christ was for the Jews alone – no, that can't be right: he *did* go to Caesarea, because God sent him a vision, showing clearly he must not call any man unclean. Ah, but when was the story written? After the fall of Jerusalem? A doctored text? Was Peter really quite so easily brought under a gentile roof? Is this, or is it not, the nub of the problem? Greek, Jew, Paul, Peter, loyalty to Empire, or bigoted conspiracy . . .? Caesarea, I can be there, must be there, by the end of the week –!

Scene Twelve

Exterior: Dockyard noises, building up behind narration.

KYBELE (*as narrator*). A ship is leaving that very night but Jaxartes is too late: when he arrives at the port, she is already casting her warps. And then, of a sudden, appearing out of nowhere from among all the dockyard clutter – Blind John the Reader, moving forward at great speed, his staff outstretched arm's length, two fingers of his other hand thrust into his mouth –

A shrill whistle.

KYBELE. Just behind him, a small boy, laden with packages – all of them wrapped and stitched in waterproof tarpaulin. The sailors on the ship have seen them, the mooring-cables are hauled taut again, and the old man with amazing deftness heaves himself onto the poop. His bundles are sent up after him, the small boy scuttles off like a rat into a hole.

JAXARTES (*to himself, urgently*). The size, the weight, the careful covering – if *I* had valuable books to convey, just so would I parcel them up. I *have* to be on this ship, no matter how I get there – (*Shouting aloud*). Ahoy, hold that vessel! Government Officer, official journey, lower a gangway, Captain, I'm coming aboard!

Scene Thirteen

KYBELE (*as narrator*). The ship-master assumes as a matter of course that Jaxartes is a revenue inspector investigating smuggling. As a result he is most obsequious, and insists, with adhesive courtesy, that his last-minute passenger should berth with him in the cabin. Jaxartes can't refuse, it would look very odd, but it means there is no way he can get close to the blind man. The captain is an Arabian, name of Haroun, much more civil than the surly brute on the ship from Alexandria, but no more usefully informative. All through supper he keeps talking of his adventures in the eastern ocean – he wants Jaxartes to understand that though he *has* been a smuggler, he was a smuggler for imperial advantage –

Scene Fourteen

Interior: the cabin of a ship at sea. JAXARTES *and* HAROUN *are eating a meal; the* STEWARD, *at intervals, clears plates etc., and moves about the cabin.*

HAROUN (*an ingratiating middle-aged man*). – the Indians for the most part control the traffic in the middle ocean: and then in furthest east it belongs to the men of China – have you ever seen a man of China? Take a look at my steward, excellence, when he comes to clear the dishes – take a look at him *now* – another bottle of wine, Chung, we have a very great lordship at cabin-table tonight.

There is an indeterminate, approximately human, noise.

(*With a showman's chuckle.*) He has, you see, no tongue, so he just makes his noise. It was cut out by the Persians, the time he saved my life on what we call the silk-run.

KYBELE (*as narrator*). It seems a good opportunity for Jaxartes to study his newly-acquired documents.

There is a rustle of papers as JAXARTES *opens his portfolio.*

HAROUN. To avoid the Persian customs-revenue, no other way with silk but by sea across the gulf –

He rambles on engagingly, while JAXARTES *reads the papers.*

JAXARTES (*to himself*). 'Upholders in Antioch of the Arius doctrine largely to be found amongst those factions originally heathen, and supportive of the late co-emperor Maximin Daza and after him Licinius. Maximin Daza had projected a new universal pan-oriental cult, bringing in Persian power as a counter-balance to the Roman west . . .! Eventual goal, the severance from the west of all our eastern provinces. A new empire centred upon Tigris-Euphrates basin, from which an ultimate subjugation of the west . . .'

HAROUN. You are asking me, yes, how is it after such prosperity, I relinquish the eastern ocean for these moderate inland waters? Not hard, excellence, to explain – I am now a man with a wife, with many children, I am begged by them, 'O, Haroun, love of my life, do not venture any more toward the perilous gulf, let the men of China, men of India, take all the danger for you!' For does not the King of Persia have my name in his black book –?

KYBELE (*as narrator*). The fantasies of secret agents become very much reality once they can convince their masters that they believe them themselves and therefore they are worthy of belief. Jaxartes is already convinced.

JAXARTES (*to himself, much troubled*). Subjugation of the west . . .!

HAROUN. I said, excellence, in your opinion, do you not think so?

JAXARTES. What? Eh? I beg your pardon, I wasn't exactly listening . . .

HAROUN. Ah, excellence, your official papers, no, I must not disturb you. But I did wish to enquire, excellence, do you think, for a seafaring man, it is absolutely requisite I adopt an official religion? I ask you as imperial officer for gratuitous and kindly advice?

JAXARTES (*pompously*). I always take the view, my friend, religion is civic duty. Civic duty means, present yourself as your emperor presents himself.

HAROUN. Ah, but, you see, how *does* he present himself? To take alone the Christ-god. Arius says one way, the patriarch says the other, and the Emperor has not yet spoken. In ports of Egypt, for a seafarer, this will become most crucial. My wife and my children implore me, for my own benefit, I must make up my mind: if Jesus was a god, there is one god three-folded, his name is Father-Son-Spirit, and that is one great thing: good. But if he was a man? Then what do we say? There is but one god, and Jesus is his prophet?

JAXARTES (*grimly, making his own meaning*). There is but one god, and *Arius* is his prophet? The man who'd have that said of him would be the greatest man in the world . . .

HAROUN (*enjoying the fantasy*). Do you know what my wife said? 'O love of my life,' she said, 'there is for me but one god, and my husband is his prophet'! Ha ha ha, she is a very witty woman, excellence, as well as most beautiful . . .

Scene Fifteen

Exterior: behind KYBELE, *an eastern town at siesta: the odd dog barking, birds perhaps. Also footsteps and the blind man's stick, where indicated in the narrative.*

KYBELE (*as narrator*). At Caesarea, as though by magic, Blind John was off the ship and Jaxartes got never a sight of him. Disappointed, he determines to go straight to the library: and there – on the portico – the blind man coming out, he hasn't got his books –

JAXARTES (*to himself*). – oh never mind his books, here is a *man* to be followed –!

KYBELE (*as narrator*). Follow him one street, follow him two. He is hot, he is tired, he is searching for a piece of shade. Down an alleyway, into a courtyard. He sits down. Jaxartes stands, ten feet away from him, watching him.

Should he question him? He *must* question him. But what is he to ask? To be sure, the Roman empire is a hedge-maze of subversion, but choose the wrong entry-point, your path is blocked by brambles, you've got nowhere, found out nothing . . . Jaxartes, most unusually, is, for the moment, *not quite sure* . . .

JOHN (*suddenly*). Come into the archway, brother: or the sun will make your head sick. Or is it Jesus makes you sick? Or Arius the preacher . . .? You saw him on shipboard.

JAXARTES (*to himself, disconcerted*). Of course, they say a blind man can recognise anyone by the sound of footsteps. That's how he knows, of course . . .

He moves towards JOHN, *and speaks to him.*

JAXARTES. Arius? He wasn't there?

JOHN. Maybe you didn't see him. *I* saw him because I have no eyes. You *heard* him, don't tell me you didn't.

JAXARTES (*puzzled, but groping at it*). You mean the words of the song?

JOHN. I mean the song and I mean the singers. I mean the naked hungry men, who must dive into the deep waters to plant the freestone, for foundations of empire: and nobody asks of them, do they do it of their own choice? They were fighting: and they might have killed. If they had, you would call them criminal.

And Arius brings Jesus back to them, in their own image, a strong brown-skinned man, all the anger and pain in his bones, stripped for labour under the hot sun, stripped for death upon the criminal's cross. Oh yes, there are criminals – have been criminals – who were emperors as well. But when was an emperor ever nailed up between two pickpockets? There you are, you see, the difference: their Jesus: yours.

JAXARTES (*feeling the way into the conversation, a little out of his depth*). You talk in the terms of prophecy – those who have ears to hear let them hear? These hungry men, they had their ears, and they were prepared to hear . . . how were they prepared?

JOHN (*with a chuckle*). You mean, who's behind Arius? You want names, places, dates, sources of information, outside-agitators – to write it down, and write it again, and yet a third time – and get it wrong?

JAXARTES (*to himself*). He couldn't have found *this* from my footsteps?

JOHN. Did no one ever tell you, you should never believe all that is written? You said, the terms of prophecy. Let's *look* at the terms of prophecy.

Peter on the day of Pentecost came running into the street: hundreds and hundreds to hear him, who were choked like a kettle with steam from belly to the top of their brain – it had never been released: and all the glory of their vision was stifled. What did he tell them? He said – 'you too!' Not only to the great and learned the vision of truth: but 'you too,' he said, '*you*!' 'Save yourselves,' he said, 'from this crooked age, your sons and your daughters shall prophesy, your young men shall see visions, your old men dream dreams, even slaves, both men *and* women – I will pour out upon *everyone* a portion of my spirit!' [And so it happened. And it happened again, in the gaols and the labour-camps: and I tell you it still happens, and once again it will happen again.] Don't fidget, hear the word. If I tell you a lie: then you prove it, and I'll shut my mouth for ever. If I tell you the truth, you have a choice: either accept it, or you walk away. There was a rich young man and Jesus said to him, 'give all that you have to the poor' – and *he* went away, didn't he? [He didn't prove that Jesus lied: he knew the truth, and he turned his back.] Let me tell you something: our man Jesus was very glad he turned his back . . .

JAXARTES (*to himself, in some distress*). He grabs hold of the lap of my cloak, pulls my face right up against his own sightless face – I don't want to question this man, all I want to do is *go* –

JOHN (*in a hoarse whisper*). There was also a rich young emperor . . .

He now starts to sing in a dirge-like atonal manner, quite quiet to begin with, but building up after a few lines into a strong ballad delivery.

JOHN (*singing*).

> There was a rich young emperor
> And O he dreamed a dream –

JAXARTES (*to himself*). What . . .? I can't hear him . . . He's buzzing in my ear like an elusive mosquito . . . does he *mean* me to hear him . . .?

JOHN (*singing*).

> He dreamed a dream of Jesus
> Bright as the sunshine beam.
>
> He rose up in the morning
> And he told us what he'd heard
> Our prison doors were broken down
> By the glory of that word.

JAXARTES (*to himself*). Why, he sings about Constantine's vision – I must not try to get away now – god, but the smell of his breath, and the strength of his hand on my shoulder –!

JOHN [(*singing*).

> Oh we had had our vision
> And the emperor had one too
> And the world was a world of freedom
> And what were we to do?]

[In the prison-camps we had bent our broken bodies to the hard labour. In the free world we still bend our broken bodies to the hard labour. And the Christian men that put us to it – they too had had their vision.]

> They dreamed a dream of Jesus
> In silver and gold and power
> He called them lords and bishops
> And he set them on a tower
>
> [To view the world and measure it
> And take from it more and more
> And the emperor freely gave to them
> Of all his wealthy store.]

You see, when they dreamed, they called it Jesus, but when Jesus himself in the days that he walked the wilderness, when he had the same dream – he knew that it was Satan. He knew it and we know it: and you know it, my small and fearful brother. Names, dates, and places, you think you can take them and measure them like learned men on a high proud tower –

> Can you know can you tell
> Are they false are they true
> If a name was given to you
> Of a criminal emperor
> What would you do –?
> Would you nail him on the cross so high
> While the sun turned round in the turning sky
> That day that day all the world would be over
> And the kingdom come for ever and ever . . .

Whose kingdom? (*He utters this last question with a sudden terrifying lunge of his voice.*)

JAXARTES (*an immediate response: swift and simple.*) THIS ONE!

A jerking movement, one body against the other: a gasping grunt from JOHN. *Fall of a body.*

JAXARTES (*to himself, as though amazed at himself*). And my dagger came out, in my hand, from under my cloak: and I put it between his ribs . . .?

JOHN (*with a laugh*). Oh there you had your kettle, and it boils . . . (*He laughs again: but it turns into a death-gurgle*).

KYBELE (*as narrator*). Does Jaxartes know why he killed the old man?

JAXARTES (*to himself*). He was – ambiguous. I – was – *not quite sure*. Now he is dead, his subversion has been proved: for if he was not subversive, why would I have killed him? No one has seen me – the city's asleep . . .?

His hurrying feet.

Scene Sixteen

KYBELE (*as narrator*). He turns his back upon the sprawling corpse, goes direct to the library; he tells the curator – with his fullest assurance – he has come, [as no doubt was expected,] to catalogue the new books from Antioch.
   [The curator, who was expecting nobody, believes himself to be at fault: with his own fullest assurance he shows Jaxartes in, opens the bundles for him, and leaves him to his research.] What he finds, as he reads, makes him hiss with excitement: he begins there and then to write out an urgent message –

JAXARTES. Place all Arius followers under surveillance. Make ready emergency search-and-arrest warrants. Despatch to Caesarea fullest archival details of Blind John of Antioch, alias John the Reader. Most immediate top secret, in cipher: to section-controllers, chiefs-of-station, provincial, metropolitan. Authority for action: Director-in-Chief, Imperial Secret Service . . .

The last words of this message re-echo in diminishing repetition as though travelling through the Empire. Mix with galloping horses. Fade out.

Scene Seventeen

Exterior: a palace corridor. MARY*'s feet in hasty transit: met by* SEMIRAMIS, *who stops her, furtively.*

SEMIRAMIS. Mary – hist, Mary – the love-feast this evening at the House of the True Way – I'm not able to come, I have to help attire the Empress, full formal regalia –

MARY. But Semiramis, they are expecting you, it's your turn to serve: and what about Physcon the baker? His claim to be your lawful Christian husband was to be discussed by our membership tonight. You do know he is back in Nicomedia and is staying with the bishop?

SEMIRAMIS (*shocked*). No! Sweet Mother, what is happening! No word from the Empress, no word from Hosius, no word from the Lady Helen – and oh, no word from Joachim!

MARY. No word from anyone except the baker – he is boasting his rights of possession all over the town.

SEMIRAMIS. We cannot rely upon anyone else's help – you must tell them at the House that *they* must reach Joachim! I am his bride-in-Christ and he must come and declare it –! Oh, Mary, let the word fly to Joachim –!

Scene Eighteen

Interior: a large room in the palace.

KYBELE (*as narrator*). Constantine's half-sister, Constantia, lived in the palace. It was said no woman influenced him as closely as she did. She was about the same age as Fausta, and related to Fausta through the Herculian side of the family.

Sounds of several feet entering the room. They stop: FAUSTA's *feet continue to approach, nervous haste.*

CONSTANTIA (*to herself: cold, self-restrained*). An unexpected visit from Fausta to my apartments, two hours before midday. She brings her five children and all of her walking-servants: a formal presentation.

FAUSTA. If I could, most noble sister-in-law, a word with you alone . . .

FAUSTA *and* CONSTANTIA's *feet, as they withdraw a little.*

FAUSTA. My husband the Emperor, a request, an invitation, will you dine, with him, and with me, at his great table tonight – exceedingly anxious he, I, both of us, your company, dear Constantia – I –

CONSTANTIA (*to herself, as* FAUSTA *chatters on*). If I were married to my brother, I would not be white in the face, would not stammer and stutter and fail to say what I wanted to say – ah, she is trying again –

FAUSTA. Nothing in the palace is as it should be, don't you see? How can I tell what it is? Uneasiness, disquiet – even my servants are laughing and whispering. Constantia, have you heard anything? You see, I must ask you –

CONSTANTIA (*to herself as* FAUSTA *continues*). I give her no answer because I don't know what is the question. My sources have told me that Arius is to be arrested, the Bishop of Nicomedia to be arrested. Is this invitation the way Constantine would let me know my own support of Arius has outlived its usefulness to him? That the council at Nicaea will be a heavy new weight thrown into an old balance: and I must swing myself accordingly?

FAUSTA. She has been my slave for years, she has been so loyal, I gave her my promise – I must be loyal to her –

CONSTANTIA (*to herself as* FAUSTA *continues*). *My* loyalty – the Empire of Constantine. I tell everything to him – or almost all but everything. And in his own way in his own time, he tells me everything: if it may be deemed by him to have application to me. He told me to become a Christian and then to become the wife of the grey-haired and devious Licinius, and I did, because the Empire of Constantine needed it. The great men behind Licinius turned Christian also, because of my example: the Bishop of Nicomedia baptised them and became my friend: the Empire of Constantine needed it. And then only last year the Empire had a new need: my husband must be killed by my brother. And it was done.

FAUSTA. They are whispering I only keep my hairdresser as my slave because of my vanity, Constantia –

CONSTANTIA (*to herself as* FAUSTA *continues*). Constantine is not a Christian, he is not free to be a Christian, because he is of the west and the west is in large part still heathen. He did not obtain the loyalty of the great men behind Licinius. Licinius being dead, they were loyal to my little son. They would have wished *him* to be the Christian emperor of the Christian east – and maybe of the west too – and

I told this to Constantine. So the Empire of Constantine needed a dead child. And received one. *My* child. Or rather, the child of Licinius.

FAUSTA. It is important for me I should not be involved in intrigue which would only upset Constantine –

CONSTANTIA (*to herself as* FAUSTA *continues*). They were loyal to the child, and now they are loyal to me. I am loyal to Constantine, so their loyalty is held by me for the Empire of Constantine. No other way for the emperor of the west to rule both west and east. I have therefore been friends with the Bishop of Nicomedia and with Arius who has become his client. I do not trust Nicomedia.

FAUSTA. I come to you because you are experienced and you know what should be done for the best –

CONSTANTIA (*to herself as* FAUSTA *continues*). The sole purpose of the bishop's work is that eastern Christianity should dominate and control the Emperor: if Constantine will not serve this purpose, then an eastern emperor, *against* Constantine. I am flesh and blood of Constantine and his need is my need. Here is his wife: the only loyalty she seems to know is to the woman who adorns her hair . . .? Ah, she's coming to the point.

FAUSTA. I went to the Bishop Hosius and asked him to tell the Bishop of Nicomedia but since then nothing has happened. Would not you go to the Bishop of Nicomedia –? If you, as his friend, were to impress upon him, as a friend –

CONSTANTIA (*to herself*). How can she be so ignorant? (*Aloud: and sharply*:) You're aware of the word, Fausta, 'render unto Caesar that which is –

FAUSTA. 'And unto God that which is God's' – yes, of course, but I thought –

CONSTANTIA (*with great scorn*). What in the name of God has God got to do with your hairdresser? Your slave is your own: and yours only: to keep, or to set free.

Fade.

Scene Nineteen

Interior: the banquet hall. A subdued hum of many PEOPLE *eating more or less in total silence, with some light music softly playing.*

CONSTANTIA (*to herself*). And so, in the evening, to my brother's great table and all his great men who surround him. He is dull and thinks his thoughts – eats his meal in silence: therefore we are all silent.

Footfalls of a MAN *coming up to the table.*

CONSTANTIA. In the middle of the fourteenth course, when a chamberlain brings him a letter, the silence is deeper than ever.

The footfalls go away again and we hear the letter being opened. The MUSICIANS *stop playing.*

CONSTANTIA. No, we are not to be told what it is that the Emperor is reading – no doubt in his own time it will at length be revealed – by word of mouth, or else by stroke of sword.

CONSTANTINE (*to himself, as the music recommences*). From Government House, Caesarea, under seal and cipher of Director-in-Chief, Imperial Secret Service, for hand of Emperor only: Josephus the historian has written that the rebellion of Judaea –

CONSTANTINE/JAXARTES (*together – fading across each other*). – of Judaea against Rome was the greatest war ever known upon earth. Once again the same threat and –

JAXARTES (*as from a distance, he is not at the dinner table*). – and they are lurking all over the empire. They wait only for the King of Persia to assemble his forces and then when he does, Judas Maccabaeus, Joshua, David the blood-stained star, will re-enter their usurped inheritance. We must all be on our guard: the famished Lion of Judah wears today a new face, it is the face –

CONSTANTINE (*his voice coming in again to finish*). – it is the face of Jesus Christ.

The music evolves into ominous drum-beats.

6
NICAEA

Scene One

Opening music.

KYBELE (*as narrator*). The Council of Nicaea, 325 AD, made Christianity in the Empire what it now is, and what it will be when it moves outside the Empire. A day or two before the Council, Constantine went into private conference with Bishop Hosius. His Secret Service had alarmed him with an enigmatic message: 'The famished lion of Judah wears today a new face, it is the face of Jesus Christ . . .'

Scene Two

Interior.

CONSTANTINE (*talking quietly and earnestly, an intimate voice*). It is not an easy thing for an Emperor to make friends. I've been thinking of Diocletian. [He spent all his early life among friends, his comrades of the regiments; he made them his co-emperors. But, in the end,] he died alone, of his own choice and desperation. [I made up my mind I would have no co-Emperors, I would refuse the enormous disappointment that killed Diocletian, killed him even before he was dead . . . I'd say the very worst possible of all forms of death.]

HOSIUS (*consolatory*). Diocletian despaired because he was not the friend of Christ –

CONSTANTINE. He despaired because of me: his last available comrade: I did not let him know that I was about to make friends with Christ. But anyone can make friends with a god: it is when we turn to human beings that we find out we have broken, in some other place, a human heart. For surely my one true friend, in this life, is not Christ, but the man who brought me to Christ . . .

HOSIUS (*very pleased, but deprecatory*). Your Majesty is too kind –

CONSTANTINE. You were the one that was kind. You, who found a rash bloody-minded young soldier in search nonetheless – it seems a paradox? – of peace and good order humane government, harmony. You were a man of harmony and love, you brought me a word. Paradox again, because what was the word? 'I come not to bring peace but a sword.' Christ was a mystery. With such great skill you inducted me into it. With even greater skill you made the mystery so mysterious that I failed to see what it truly contained.

HOSIUS (*disturbed by an enigmatic new edge to* CONSTANTINE's *words*). Your Majesty's train of thought is a little in advance of mine. If, perhaps –

CONSTANTINE (*still quietly and intimately: but with a growth of obscure menace*). Wait: you will understand. I did not understand. Now that I do, I am unable to discern all my weaknesses, my flawed judgement, the mistakes I inevitably made through so many years of blundering cross-purpose. Discerning them, I can correct them: correcting them, I am at last one sole Emperor who knows himself and therefore needs no friends. I am at last a free man: and because you have brought me to this unhoped-for but most welcome freedom: are you not even more my friend than ever you were?

HOSIUS (*seriously alarmed*). Is it conceivable Your Majesty regards me as having in some way betrayed your trust?

CONSTANTINE (*still without any heat*). I said friendship, not trust. There can never have been trust. Look at it: it's a matter of history – we do not have the same history. Yours starts with Adam, Eve, the serpent. And from then on, humanity is nothing, until the remedy for the serpent arrives: Jesus. And from then on again, three hundred years, you are bringing together, at Nicaea, for the Council, from all over the world, the broadcast word of Jesus, incarnate in his blessed churchmen.

That's you. Whereas my history, from long before the birth of Jesus: Romulus and Remus, the milk-giving wolf, the building of Rome, the growth of Rome, the worth of all Roman humanity – the rulers, the law-givers, the brave soldiers who went to war year after year to protect and extend the city.

Rome made friends with Jesus when I made friends with you; our two strands of human history became entangled together, touching at various points, separated at various points. Separation means lack of knowledge, lack of understanding, and therefore lack of trust: so you see why I said, only friendship. But how long can friendship last if trust is not there too? I have in mind one episode, very crucial in my history. Maybe not in yours; at least, you led me to believe not. The great rebellion in Judaea –

HOSIUS (*seeing at last where all this is tending*). Ah –

CONSTANTINE (*overriding his ejaculation*). Two rebellions in fact, one after the other, finally put down a couple of centuries ago. And finished with. Or not finished with? Because here is the problem. If your history is also the history of this rebellious nation, which never was able to accommodate itself to my history; not alone can there be no trust, but there can also be no more friendship. I am left waiting for you to rise and strike; Hosius, you know me: I am the one who strikes first.

The menace is now unmistakable. HOSIUS *is determined not to be panicked.*

HOSIUS (*as though the question were too ridiculous to contemplate*). You believe I am a secret Jew.

CONSTANTINE (*still quietly*). Not only believe it, I can prove it. This man Arius in Egypt with his uncontrolled preachings, which you pretend to deprecate, has in fact revealed your secret. There is but one God and Jesus is his prophet: and Arius is his prophet . . . If Arius is right, if Jesus was the Son of Man – then he can come again and again, each time with a different name, each time he can say, 'I am at last the true Christ, the previous ones brought only half the message, I have the correct message! My kingdom after all is of this earth, and we shall overthrow the Empire.' Arius begins by stirring up the hungry and naked against the powers of good government. I have it written down –

Shuffling of a large pile of documents.

This very large pile of reports: my history – not yours. Physical, not spiritual. Though the persons who researched it for me made good use of your spiritual archives. When I looked at what they sent me, I put into practice all the patience, the contemplation, I had observed in your character: this was a quest for the ultimate truth. At last at last, old friend, I am teaching you . . .

Rustling of documents.

Arius learned his opinions from Lucian of Antioch. Lucian's life-work was the editing and perhaps also the revision – the doctoring, shall we say? – of four of your gospel-books.

Rustling of documents.

Lucian derived his method from Origen of Caesarea. Origen's life-work was the editing, revision, doctoring, of certain other sacred books. Not the books of Christ, but the books of the Jews before Christ. And how did he do it? He took the Greek text, which you are always quoting to me, and he compared it, verse for verse, against the Hebrew text, which I didn't even know existed. The Hebrew text told him that Christ, when he came, would not be a god but a human man, and a conqueror, and a king. Here, I have some specimens of it –

Rustling of documents.

Isaiah the prophet, expecting what all the Jews ever since have expected, and which you the peaceful Christians now tell me is to be fulfilled:

> The Lord hath loved him, he will do his pleasure on Babylon,
> and his arm shall be on the Chaldeans.

Babylon is Rome, the Chaldeans are my army.

> Break forth into joy, sing together, ye waste places of
> Jerusalem, for the Lord hath redeemed Jerusalem.

Jerusalem, I am informed, means nothing but Jerusalem. And then – I have the passage marked:

Rustling of documents.

> Behold I have given him for a witness to the people, a leader
> and commander to the people.

That is not a divine spirit: that is a very successful General, a guerrilla chief, a terrorist. If I can see this, Origen saw it; because Origen was collating all these passages in Caesarea, which is in Palestine, which had been called Judaea only three generations before. The name was changed by the Emperor Hadrian, because Hadrian had obliterated, or thought he obliterated, by edict of law, every single trace of Jewish culture beyond all hope of revival. Nine hundred and fifty eight Jewish towns utterly destroyed, five hundred and eighty thousand Jewish men killed. Women and children . . . I have no figures. Jerusalem, as the book says, indeed a waste place . . . You forget I was brought up in the army. You forget that the army has never forgotten the wildfire of terror that ran through the regiments when an enemy came against them wholly devoted to the implacable ideological vengeance of one huge punitive God. Therefore, at the hands of Hadrian: a necessary and complete genocide. Take out the Jews, put in the Romans and Greeks. But Origen made a discovery: the people of Israel had survived, in disguise, in another language.

They looked Roman, they talked Greek: but their thoughts and their prayers were Hebrew. They brought Origen their Hebrew books – he was their survival – he made them into his books – and now they are yours. You are Origen, I am Hadrian. Your history is the Jews' history, despite all your denials, for I now believe Arius to be the only honest Christian. The Jews' history is blood and death to the order of Rome. I am tangling yet again with the unmerciful nightmare serpent of ever-lasting rebellion. Friendship, how can there be friendship? Your coils are about my throat . . .!

Scene Three

Exterior: an eastern bazaar: crowds of people, animals, etc. and snatches of music. Growing out of this, a group of MALE VOICES *chanting the Beatitudes to an oriental musical setting – it is as though a delegation of priests in the street is providing a foretaste of the vocal harmonies of the Council of Nicaea.*

SINGERS.
> Blessed are the poor in spirit for theirs is the kingdom of
>   heaven
> Blessed are they that mourn, for they shall be comforted.
> Blessed are the meek, for they shall inherit the earth . . .
> (*Etc.*)

The sound effects fade out behind the singing, and then the singing fades down behind KYBELE's *speech.*

KYBELE (*as narrator*). Strange experience to arrive among thousands of Christians with my new friends the Christian women. I felt both outsider and insider; and yet no discomfort – between us all there was trust. We pushed our way into Nicaea, each holding up our little flags with the colours of Naples, we must not be separated in the mob, we must not lose sight of the Bishop of Naples, who had met us in perspiring panic to bring us through to our accommodations.

BISHOP OF NAPLES (*huffing and puffing*). This way, dear sisters, this way – no, not that way – *this* –!

KYBELE (*as narrator*). He would brook no correction, although our leader Theoclymene had found exactly where to go . . . At last, *she* led *him* to the doors of our allotted boarding-house.

BISHOP OF NAPLES (*decisively*). Ladies, stay in the porch, in your group, I will arrange for your dormitories with the clerk.

They have entered into a portico which is open to the street, so the street noises diminish, but only slightly.

KYBELE (*as narrator*). But the clerk made a difficulty. The Bishop's face went very red, he beckoned Theoclymene, whispered to her, they looked at me. She came over to me, biting her lip.
    This, the woman who had seen her two daughters burned alive at the orders of Herculius: she was incomparably brave. And yet now, a face of fear: and what she told me was not true.

THEOCLYMENE (*elderly, nervous, refined*). I am sorry, in this house, they – they will only take baptised Christians . . .

KYBELE (*aloud: with bitterness*). And behold, there was no room at the inn . . . Why can't I know the real reason?

THEOCLYMENE (*very disconcerted*). But I – I don't – you must understand –

BISHOP OF NAPLES (*bearing down on them to rescue* THEOCLYMENE: *he speaks with affronted anger*). Who are you to question the honesty of this most holy woman of Christ? I will tell you who you are, a subversive heathen agitator, or why else did the Secret Police come around here this morning to put a mark against your name on the list?

KYBELE (*as narrator: with sound effects appropriate to what she describes*). So that was the reason! They turned their heads away from me, gathered away their skirts, their terror and my terror became at once indignant fury. I swept into the street –

We hear exclamations from the WOMEN – 'agitator?' – disgraceful' – 'an insult to the community' – *etc.*

– borrowed a drum from a little minstrel-boy, and – defying the danger – I shouted out amongst the hubbub against the great lie of Nicaea, where Christian mothers were in fear of a Christian father who in turn was in such fear of a so-called Christian Emperor, more appalling to him even than Herculius.

She beats a little tabor in time to her slogans.

KYBELE (*shouting out in the street*). Kybele says: boo to the Emperor. Kybele says: boo to the Bishops. And boo to the freedom for this new religion! Kybele beats her drum and says: let us have freedom from religion! Let us have freedom for infinity of human adventure and impose no horizon . . . No horizon, no – boo to the lot of you!

She concludes with a flourish on her drum. The street noises and the clerical singing continue as before. Her only reception has been a moment of silence and some dismissive laughter from BYSTANDERS. *Fade out street noises again.*

Scene Four

Interior: inside a coach travelling at speed.

HOSIUS (*very worried*). Eumolpus – he has not said that the Council is cancelled.

EUMOLPUS. Act as though all were normal, dear Bishop. Continue with arrangements. All these schedules to be completed.

He rustles documents. From now, EUMOLPUS *talks in a continuous stream, not paying attention to* HOSIUS.

Accommodation . . . 310 Bishops already accepted. This list, and this one, provisional acceptances only . . .

HOSIUS. He may not cancel. He may postpone . . .?

EUMOLPUS. In the new caravanserai, at least 500 people. Billets in town for another thousand . . .

HOSIUS. On the other hand, I am seriously afraid he will allow us to proceed: but without him. I don't want him present if he comes as Supreme Pontiff. But . . .

EUMOLPUS. If married Bishops bring families, attendant clerics eat elsewhere . . . Or families eat elsewhere. Query, will they agree to that . . .?

HOSIUS. If he remains absent after promising to come . . . a clear sign of displeasure . . .

EUMOLPUS. Will the Council last longer than two months? Check food supplies already collected. Sufficient warehouses requisitioned . . .? Laundry facilities . . .?

HOSIUS. At sight of his displeasure the hostile mobs could take revenge upon us: the Emperor could then say – driven by public opinion – a new persecution!

EUMOLPUS. Stabling arrangements . . . Eastern Bishops arrive by camel caravan . . .

HOSIUS (*suddenly*). Eumolpus, I have to tell them: have to tell them what I was told today!

EUMOLPUS (*roused from his papers*). Do you really think that prudent?

HOSIUS. They have become, we have become, far too complacent: and here are the fruits of disunity! Here, I will tell them, are the –

EUMOLPUS. They'll all blame each other. Never themselves.

HOISIUS. [You despise them Eumolpus, you have been too long in the court.] Many of these good men, blinded, mutilated, by persecutors. Bound to agree to anything to prevent such another horror.

EUMOLPUS. Agree to anything? Agree to what? Division between factions immeasurable. Did you not tell me the supporters of Arius –

HOSIUS. No more than seventeen are fully committed to him. If only more of the western Bishops had been able to attend!

EUMOLPUS. Willing to attend. You overestimate the interest of the West in theology. You should have said to them: political.

HOSIUS. Exactly what I wrote to the Bishop of Rome: and exactly his reason for refusing to come! To the See of Peter, he said, supremacy always but he would not lower himself to argue it in front of a room full of Greeks. God help us, what can we do with them . . .? (*Suddenly getting an idea.*) Jason the Argonaut! he had to plant dragon's teeth in the furrows he had so painfully ploughed, and from them sprang up armed warriors ready to kill him. Eumolpus – I am Jason! [Where is the Medaea who will teach me the way of escape?

EUMOLPUS. Medaea was a heathen witch.

HOSIUS. And you're a philosopher. Can you not allegorise even so barbarous a fable? Under Medaea's instruction,] Jason hurled a great boulder in among the warriors. [They thereupon fought each other until none of them were left. Heathen witch or not: Medaea did foreshadow the inward working of the Holy Spirit. All I need is the right boulder and to have her point it out to me.]

The coach is slowing down. The bazaar noises come up loudly behind the sound of the wheels, as though they are moving through the narrow streets.

HOSIUS. The Emperor's threat will be my boulder.

Crossfade to:

Scene Five

Exterior: bazaar, with coach sound effects as described in narration: bazaar diminishes abruptly at the entrance into the caravanserai. Here there is a buzz of a crowd of people: occasional noises as of workers on the building-scaffold, and horse, ass, camel sounds from the open stabling-arcade.

KYBELE (*as narrator*). I watched as the carriage forced its way into the crowded town: Hosius and Eumolpus swung themselves to the ground, pushed through the throng, towards the gate of the caravanserai. The building was not even finished, men and women on scaffolding, putting the last touches of plaster and whitewash – in the middle of the courtyard a great fire, all the Bishops around it, anxiously expecting Hosius.

A burst of applause from the BISHOPS, *as* HOSIUS *goes to meet them. Cross-fade to suggest short passage of time.*

(*as narrator*). He stood before them under the moonlight: he gave them words of a total disaster –

HOSIUS (*the conclusion of a short speech*). . . . he has said we are secret Jews, he has said that our proclamation of the Coming of the Prince of Peace is no more than a cloak for military rebellion, he has said that the kingdom of Christ is the kingdom of this earth and we are blood and death to the order of Rome!

There is a brief and horrified silence.

BISHOP OF ANTIOCH (*suddenly erupting: a stand-no-nonsense managerial voice, coarse and bullying*). Deliberate political trick, divide East against West, impose secular power over all of us –!

His intervention breaks the stunned sense of impasse and many voices all start shouting at once:

BISHOP OF NAPLES. We should welcome it, it proves that he knows how much power we have.

A PEDANTIC BISHOP. We should resist it, it proves that we were always right to suspect western Imperial authority –

BISHOP OF NICOMEDIA. Not Imperial, not secular, it is the intrigue of the Bishop of Rome –

FANATICAL BISHOP. A sign from God, God desires us to cut ourselves loose from the handclasp of Caesar, the manacles of Mammon –

BISHOP OF ANTIOCH. If it hadn't been for that damned Arius, we wouldn't be in this fix –

BISHOP OF NICOMEDIA. Arius has given us our own eastern identity –

FANATICAL BISHOP. Arius has blasphemed: the Emperor has blasphemed: cast out the brood of Satan –

General confusion of shouting about ARIUS – '*Arius yes, Arius no, death to the heretic Arius, Arius is a saint of God*' – etc.

KYBELE (*as narrator*). The Bishop of Antioch was just able to impose some sort of order.

BISHOP OF ANTIOCH. No, I am speaking! It's all the fault of all you who refuse to accept orders from Antioch or Alexandria. Bishop of Rome's not made our mistake, Bishop of Rome imposes discipline, and that's why Rome is a threat!

Cross-fade to suggest lapse of time.

KYBELE (*as narrator*). He spoke at length: and after him, they all gave vent.

What follows is snatches of a noisy debate that in reality would have gone on a considerable time.

PEDANTIC BISHOP. It is all the fault of those of you who –

BISHOP OF NICOMEDIA. No, I am speaking! It's all the fault of those who condemn all manner of heresies and then simply leave it at that.
　　Half those expelled have not even been told why – so of course they suspect that personal feud and intrigue are at the bottom of it and why wouldn't they –?

Cross-fade to suggest lapse of time.

PEDANTIC BISHOP. It's all the fault of those of you who have displayed such total ignorance indeed illiteracy that you –

FANATIC BISHOP. No, I am speaking, though not so much my carnal self as the Lord God who sits on my tongue, cowards, traitors, dissemblers, when the persecutors demanded you paid incense to abomination, how many of you withstood in the glory of martyrdom? Christ, were he still amongst us, would kick you into the ditch!

Cross-fade to suggest lapse of time.

PEDANTIC BISHOP. I repeat it is all the fault of the most culpable negligence, whereby the deepest researches of sacred scholarship have been cast on one side for –

BISHOP OF NAPLES (*against a growing clamour of scandalized disagreement*). No, I am speaking on the profoundest moral question – corruption of the system itself – how can we set an example to the heathen if (a) Bishops can move at will from diocese to diocese, trying on, as it were, the comparative revenues for size; (b) if no one consecrates them except one debauched drinking-companion half-an-hour after midnight – oh I name no names but he knows who he is! (c) if an acknowledged heathen who happens to have accrued wealth can be baptised and a Bishop all in the one same day because it suits his political ambition; (d) if a known sectarian expelled from the church in one city re-appears in another one not only as an ordained priest but the Bishop's assistant, and within a year becomes the Bishop himself – once again I name no names! (e) if there are eunuch-bishops, fornicators, adulterers, usurers, oh yes, you know not only what I mean but who I mean – the very tumult you are making has proven my case conclusively!

Cross-fade to suggest lapse of time.

PEDANTIC BISHOP. It is all the faul tof those who cannot agree the date of Easter! The most important of all dates in the calendar of the church and –

BISHOP OF ANTIOCH. No, I am speaking! It's all the fault of those of you who refuse to accept orders, wherever they may come from.

They all start talking at once again.

PEDANTIC BISHOP. It is essential to remember that the Jewish reckoning of the original date of Passover is not at all conclusive when considered against –

BISHOP OF NAPLES. No, I am speaking! There are no less than twenty convicted criminals at present in episcopal office –

BISHOP OF NICOMEDIA. No, I am speaking! The excommunicate followers of Paul of Samosata who have been received again into the church have not in every case been re-baptised, whereas those of the Novationists –

FANATIC BISHOP. No, I am speaking, who dares to utter against me is the instrument of Anti-Christ –

PEDANTIC BISHOP (*his voice rising out of the hubbub*). No, I am speaking, and nobody nobody nobody has been listening to one word I have said –!

IRENE *suddenly gives an extraordinary cock-crow, which silences everyone. She gives a second cock-crow.*

KYBELE (*as narrator*). A tall muscular woman, in the garb of a mountain shepherd, all of a sudden out of the darkness, between the Bishops and the blazing fire.

IRENE (*a strong young rustic voice – she is about 18*). Before the cock crows twice, you will have denied me thrice.

BISHOP OF ANTIOCH (*the only one capable of speech*). Who are you to say that?

CYPRIOT BISHOP (*an old man, tremulous but determined rustic voice*). And who are you to ask her?

We hear him limping down across the courtyard.

KYBELE (*as narrator*). The old Bishop beside her, lame in one leg, lacking an eye, also in shepherd's clothes, the rugged crook in his hand no ornament but the well-used tool of his trade –

CYPRIOT BISHOP. – she's Irene the Presbyter, my daughter, from the island of Cyprus: you give ear to what she tells you, because God knows you have need of it.

IRENE (*impatient with him: a well-practised bit of backchat*). And God knows I can tell it myself, I don't have need of you –

CYPRIOT BISHOP (*not abashed, to the others*). Not o' my voice she don't, that's certain: maybe when she's finished, we'll find two sticks are better nor one. Go on, then, tell 'em the tale.

The BISHOPS *are murmuring in a disconcerted and scandalised way, now the murmurs become clarified into a series of repetitions of the word 'Authority' – 'Where is her authority?'.*

IRENE (*firmly*). I was in prison and condemned to death, about to become a martyr of Christ, whereby the keys of the binding and loosing were bestowed upon all confessors.

CYPRIOT BISHOP. Would you call that enough authority?

BISHOPS (*generally not shouting but speaking in agitation among themselves*). No, we would not – she cannot be a presbyter – who made her a presbyter? (*Etc.*)

HOSIUS (*achieving silence*). Wait, wait, gentlemen, please, she has stated her authority, we must let her justify it before we reject it –

FANATIC BISHOP. Nothing can justify that a woman should speak. Does not Apostle Paul in his letter to –

IRENE (*firing up*). In his letter to Galatians Apostle Paul says it straight: 'Neither Jew nor Greek, slave nor free, male nor female, for in Christ you are all one person'! So far your first denial. Your second one: Paul again: Corinthians, the words of love: 'Unless you have love you are sounding brass and a tinkling cymbal.' [I've stood amongst you all these hours: I'm all but deaf with the roar of your brasswork.] When Paul came to Cyprus, to the very house where we live now, he was as heathen as you are and as loveless and greedy as you are.

CYPRIOT BISHOP. But the word of Christ struck him blind.

IRENE. And after that he changed his tune.

This unorthodox statement causes a noisy flurry among the BISHOPS.

He used to be Saul, but because he was in the service of the Roman Governor Paulus, he gained the citizenship, didn't he, changed his name, to the same name as his patron. The Apostle Mary, mother of John Mark, was a woman from Cyprus.

Her words give rise to episcopal expostulation: but HOSIUS *hushes it swiftly. As* IRENE *continues there are similar objections from her* AUDIENCE: *but she continues regardless (and none of the interruptions must be so loud that any of her words are lost).* HOSIUS *keeps a firm check on the would-be hecklers.*

She had a house in Jerusalem where Jesus and his friends ate and drank the Last Supper: and where the Spirit in the shape of a fire-breathing woman seven weeks later came in at the smoke-hole and blew a glow out of all of their heads, till they ran into the street crying 'Christ Risen!' – she was the first out onto her own doorstep, with Mary, the mother of Jesus, and Mary, the sister of Martha – all of them Apostles, don't forget there were twelve women Apostles as well as twelve men – they were dancing and laughing and beating their tambourines. And after that time, with John Mark and Barnabas her brother, she brought Christ Risen back home to Cyprus.

IRENE *breaks into song: a simple rural ballad-air.*

IRENE. And Paul was in Cyprus. (*Singing.*)
>And in Cyprus he sought out
>Christ's flock to persecute:
>He laid his hand on Barnabas
>And hauled him into court.
>But the eyes of Paul were blinded
>Before the Governor's chair,
>And the heart of Paul converted was
>Like a burning coal of fire.

It was Mary the Apostle who healed him and baptised him. And when her friend Priscilla, the travelling tent-maker, passed through Cyprus, she took Paul, who'd once been of the same trade, to go on his travels with her. And so he preached: and made his letters in his own hand-of-write . . .

This is received in silence: followed by a growing turbulence of indignant speech among the BISHOPS.

KYBELE (*as narrator*). Nothing that she said made any sense to them at all. According to their story, Damascus was where Paul went blind – if Christians on Cyprus were still telling one another what she told –

PEDANTIC BISHOP. – they must also believe that Paul must have falsified his own history in order to –

BISHOP OF NICOMEDIA. – to give himself pre-eminence among travelling Apostles, which by right she claims belongs to –

FANATIC BISHOP. – to any name at all from the intolerable perversion of these shameful old wives' tales –

IRENE. And why not old wives' tales? We keep sheep on Cyprus, our family have kept them there through generation of generations: at our house where three roads meet is the only well which did not fail in the years of drought that have consumed Cyprus: and who else but the old wives would come together under our roof and take hold of all our history?

CYPRIOT BISHOP. We have the very bodkin Paul made use of for his tent-making when his eyesight came back to him, it hangs over the door in the room where we hold our love-feasts.

IRENE. Right beside the pointing finger of the statue of Aphrodite who first made Cyprus a holy place, so we call her not only the Mother of the island but also the Mother of Jesus, she herself being no more than an old wife, what's wrong with

that? [– some of you are not too old to have old wives still around what you choose
to call mother –]

This really arouses the BISHOPS, *who start calling out in fury – 'Heathenism,
apostacy, heresy, blasphemy –!' etc.*

CYPRIOT BISHOP (*trying to stem the rage*). Oh my good brothers, if indeed you are
my brothers, have respect for the simple people who make their own way in the
words of Christ without any need of book-learning! I say to you, stand back: she is
a priest and a virgin of Christ –!

A roar of mob-anger and they rush at him. Cries of 'Whore of Babylon –!'

KYBELE (*as narrator*). She rose up from amongst their fury, cast the dust off the sole
of her boot –

IRENE. For the third time: denial.

KYBELE (*as narrator*). – and walked out of the courtyard. They would have pursued
her, but the building-workers on the scaffold, shouting out a song from the muse of
Arius, jumped down into their path and held them back –

Nicaean workers, female as well as male, sing:

NICAEAN WORKERS.
> One in three and three in one
> Once a Bishop's on his throne
> We all can see what he has done
> To keep our Lord for himself alone –
> > Oh aloney loney loney loney
> > Spiritual body ain't got no boney –

The great noise diminishes as the BISHOPS *are withstood. A cock-crow (genuine).
Fade.*

KYBELE (*as narrator*). And then, the cock crew, a real cock: and it was morning.

Scene Six

*Exterior: in the caravanserai still. There is now a small buzz of conversation, and the
odd animal noises, as before: but quietly, behind* HOSIUS's *speech.*

HOSIUS. When the cock crew for Simon Peter he went out into the dawn and wept.
It crows for me, Eumolpus, and I rejoice. There has been no denial. We have seen
a complete church – if only for one moment – united against falsehood. The old
Greek heathen falsehood. Now for the greatest danger. Heathen and Jew have this
much in common, they came first, they shall be last. And the ruin of Judah began
before the rebellion: it began with a man on a donkey, who was not only a man but
God, riding in at the east gate, branches of palm, 'Hosanna!', behold the withered
fig-tree of the super-annuated Old Testament! Not only a man but God: not only a
god but Man. If we say he is God only, who for a time pretended to be man: then
Aphrodite is his mother, and we might as well call him Cupid. If we say, with
Arius, he was a man who was taken up from the grave to live with God as though
he were God, then we rebuild the temple of Israel; we are no more than a Jewish
sect, we might as well call him Enoch, Moses, Elijah: cut off our foreskins, and
accept the hatred of Rome. How can it be this is not yet understood? The Emperor
understands; he is a soldier, who imposed upon his army an oath of allegiance.
Statement of whom they served, statement of how long they were serving – 'for
Lord Constantine and all his fortune, until it shall be achieved.' Definition of Lord
Constantine – 'Augustus of the West, in pursuance of his just claim to be Augustus
of the whole Empire.' If they did not take the oath, no place for them in the army:
if they took it and then broke it, they were drummed out of the ranks. And that's

how he won, and that is how we shall win. All our future fortune, all our just claim, is greater, far far greater, than anything he could conceive: the lordship of Christ is the lordship of entire creation, living and dead. The oath-breaker out of our ranks goes straight into eternal fire. I will draft such an oath and therewith we shall purge our battalions. Let the Emperor look at it, let him read it as though it were a soldier's oath, let him – as a soldier – have the privilege of deciding what is to be done to those who refuse it. (*He speaks aloud.*) Eumolpus, your tablets!

EUMOLPUS. Statement, definition, allegiance, a final credo of belief – is it possible for three hundred years not one of us saw the necessity?

HOSIUS.

> Little cock so white and red
> Was he sent by God to thrust his head
> And crow upon the guest-house wall
> And none but Hosius aroused
> To the truth of his clear bugle call . . .?

Very well, arouse the others. Where is the Bishop of Aelia Capitolina . . .? My dear friend –

He moves decisively through the groups of chattering BISHOPS.

KYBELE (*as narrator*). Hosius was concerned to find support for a creed which must inevitably exclude Arius. He had inducements to offer. For instance, the Bishop of Aelia, which is also called Jerusalem, was promised a new importance for his See. He was not of course told that Hosius had no authority for such a promise. Nonetheless, vote number one to Hosius. The first shall be last and the last first. Jerusalem had always felt his just historic claims to be most unfairly overlooked . . .

HOSIUS. Next, Alexandria – do I see the Patriarch there? My dear friend –

KYBELE (*as narrator*). Alexandria is warned that the oath of allegiance must include a definition of the Son of God not quite so ethereal as his theologians would have preferred. There have to be some concessions for those Bishops who at present support Arius. But Vote number two to Hosius.

HOSIUS. Oh, by the way – the Emperor is disturbed that your church porch gang-bosses control so many export warehouses on the Alexandria waterfront – it is cordially expected that the corn supply to Italy will be continuously maintained as a result of this arrangement . . . Antioch – where is Antioch –?

KYBELE (*as narrator*). No problem with Antioch: except his suspicion that a creed which can satisfy Nicomedia and Caesarea is bound to have something wrong with it. Hosius points out that in the quarrel over supremacy Jerusalem must inevitably suspersede Caesarea, and Nicomedia will lose all importance once the New Rome of Greater Byzantium is established . . . Vote number three . . .

HOSIUS. The Bishop of Rome's two representatives, if you please –

KYBELE (*as narrator*). Vote number four is a foregone conclusion once Hosius again mentions the transfer to the New Rome, after which the Bishop of Old Rome will have no rivals in his own city. Except for the ancient nobility. And the Emperor no longer concedes anything to the ancient nobility. This again a promise of most doubtful authority . . .

HOSIUS. Carthage –

KYBELE (*as narrator*). He has his next vote, number five, very easily from Carthage. Carthage needs Hosius to defend him against the Donatists . . .

HOSIUS. Now, where is Nicomedia –?

KYBELE (*as narrator*). Nicomedia, a serious problem: close to the Emperor, but just how close? A vociferous supporter of Arius.

BISHOP OF NICOMEDIA. My house has been watched, my servants have been tampered with, my carriage was stopped three times on the road from Nicomedia –

HOSIUS. Sh – not in public! There have been assassination threats, apparently from heathen elements: you cannot blame the Emperor for taking good care of our safety –

As he speaks, he is drawing the BISHOP OF NICOMEDIA *under an archway adjacent to the main courtyard. The sound effects alter as a result – they are away from the mass of people, and closer to the stalled transport animals.*

BISHOP OF NICOMEDIA. I do not blame the Emperor, I blame you. And I do not see how our safety can possibly be improved by hauling out onto the road the aged doctor Arius and subjecting him to a bodily search!

HOSIUS. He was travelling with you?

BISHOP OF NICOMEDIA. Of course he was. If he'd come here by himself he'd be in a dungeon by now!

HOSIUS (*ignoring* NICOMEDIA's *anger: and speaking quietly and significantly*). When he speaks at the Council, you will defend his doctrine.
    The Patriarch of Alexandria has brought the Deacon Athanasius: he will refute your defence. Athanasius is a formidable polemicist. I suspect he will carry the meeting.

BISHOP OF NICOMEDIA (*knowingly and contemptuously*). You are trying to find out how many votes I can secure.

HOSIUS. Not enough to win, but sufficient to ensure a decisive and disastrous split. Did you not hear what I announced about the Emperor and the Jewish threat? Continued support for Arius has become a political act. The security services are not going to distinguish between nuances of doctrine. Don't you see, we are all implicated?

BISHOP OF NICOMEDIA (*after a slight pause*). You have a solution. That paper in the fold of your sleeve is not there for nothing.

HOSIUS (*as he draws out the paper*). This paper is what we vote upon, first. Theologically speaking, you ought to be able to sign it.

We hear him pass the paper to NICOMEDIA.

BISHOP OF NICOMEDIA (*studying it*). A new credo? How new? 'We believe in one God only', yes . . . 'One Lord only, Jesus Christ, the Son of God', yes . . . 'the only begotten of the Father, that is from the essence of the Father, true God from true God' . . . How d'you define 'essence'? I detect ambiguity.

HOSIUS (*calmly*). You are meant to. Go on.

BISHOP OF NICOMEDIA. 'Begotten, not made, of the same substance with the Father, by whom were made all things' . . . Not quite so ambiguous. I would find this easier to sign if it said, 'of *similar* substance'. I would find it a great deal easier to sign if it was written in Greek. Do you translate 'of the same substance' by 'homo-ousios' or 'homoi-ousios'?

HOSIUS. You're the Greek-speaker. Make your choice.

BISHOP OF NICOMEDIA. The two words to the ear are practically the same: but they have to be written down . . . Hosius, this is a fudge, and you know it is a fudge.

HOSIUS. Never mind whether it's a fudge or not. Can you or can you not sign?

BISHOP OF NICOMEDIA (*speaking very slowly*). If I heard it read out, I could, probably, give a vocal assent. But if it were presented to me on paper . . .

HOSIUS (*also very slowly*). It need not be presented on paper.

BISHOP OF NICOMEDIA (*after a pause*). Arius will want it on paper. Arius will refuse to sign.

HOSIUS. In which case he will be the solitary victim of his own egocentric integrity.

BISHOP OF NICOMEDIA (*again after a pause, with a chuckle*). 'Egocentric' is good. (*He stops chuckling.*) I suppose you think *our* integrity –

HOSIUS (*blandly*). Collective responsibility.

BISHOP OF NICOMEDIA (*no chuckling*). Even better. Eusebius of Caesarea will understand that very well . . . If I can persuade him, he can persuade the others . . . oh yes, you'll get your signatures. Your voices, I should say. Provided, I should say, that we are allowed at least the appearance of a full and fair debate . . .? Oh yes, just one thing. How is this creed any different from the shorter ones we already have? In practical terms, I mean: what do we do with it that makes it so special?

HOSIUS. All the earlier creeds vary from one place to another, one Bishop to another, and they do not even pretend to define the Son of God, they merely announce his existence, his birth, death, resurrection, and that's it. This document is a test: the first, final, and fundamental test of what is or is not a heretic. And so we tell the Emperor –

> He builds his new wall around his new city.
> We too have built ours. And no one need take pity
> Upon those who will not come in. Their own choice, once it is
>   made
> They have proved themselves wolves and brigands: they are
>   outside
> Both our law, and his. He promised his toleration.
> To Recognised Religion. Withdraw recognition,
> They are seen to belong to neither Jehovah nor Jupiter nor
>   Christ.

Fade.

Scene Seven

Exterior: the same, after a lapse of time.

KYBELE (*as narrator*). Thereupon, immediate return for Hosius to the Emperor in Nicomedia, leaving behind him Eumolpus. Eumolpus made it his business to deal with the old Cypriot Bishop.

Footfalls of several MEN, *including the* CYPRIOT BISHOP'*s limp, in an echoing colonnade.*

EUMOLPUS (*severely but not harshly*). The Bishop of Antioch is your ultimate superior: the Bishops of Salamis and Paphos in Cyprus will also consider your case . . .

BISHOP OF ANTIOCH (*bluntly accusatory*). Not a case: it's a downright sin. You brought amongst us the Prince of Darkness to tell lies, downright lies.

The footfalls stop. The BISHOPS OF SALAMIS AND PAPHOS *make little judicial murmurs: and continue to do so throughout the scene, every time* EUMOLPUS *or the* BISHOP OF ANTIOCH *offer comments.*

CYPRIOT BISHOP (*his pugnacity has left him and he is grievously upset*). Oh my brothers, I gave the sight of my right eye for the honour of Lord Jesus – do not tell me my darkness is eternal complete darkness – the Prince of Darkness? No – but my own daughter – you have seen her – she is not the –

BISHOP OF ANTIOCH. Anthony the hermit says even his own mother: she came to him in the desert, and yet she was the Devil.

CYPRIOT BISHOP. We're only here because our people have had no water for twelve years, and our own well, that my daughter spoke of, is beginning to dry up – and so we thought –

EUMOLPUS. You thought this sacred Council had been called to provide your people with material benefit? Who put that thought in your mind?

CYPRIOT BISHOP. She and I together, because she knows I go all asunder among so many mighty lordships, we could have a word with the great Emperor to beg him from his regiments sappers and miners with science that could teach us how to dig –

EUMOLPUS (*with apparent sympathy*). All the people night and day praying and fasting for an end to the drought? And your daughter is always there?

CYPRIOT BISHOP. She is. She is the priest.

EUMOLPUS (*gently enough*). For twelve years, since her imprisonment, your daughter has been the priest. For twelve years you have had no water. For twelve years in public she has described the Apostle Paul as a liar?

BISHOP OF SALAMIS. Does he not read the scripture?

BISHOP OF PAPHOS. He can't read the scripture.

BISHOP OF ANTIOCH (*brutal and jocular*). So he doesn't even know he's supposed to leave his father, mother, daughter, son, to follow the Lord Jesus . . . Old friend, you have been rolling in unthinking carnal pleasure in the very middle of your huge family, and now you wonder why God supposes you're no more than a pack of heathens . . .!

CYPRIOT BISHOP. God forgive me – what must I do? Oh tell me, brother, tell me – I repent on my bended knees –

He shuffles to his knees.

BISHOP OF ANTIOCH. Here's a list of the requirements –

Rustle of paper.

CYPRIOT BISHOP. Let me hear them: I shall obey.

BISHOP OF ANTIOCH. I'm going to despatch a pair of Deacons straight to your village: they will instruct all the men there in the content of scripture – and only of written scripture, take note. The men of the village thereafter will discipline the women. No functions for women – and particularly not your daughter – except as dutiful worshippers. You will not waste the Emperor's time with any nonsense about waterworks.

The drought will only be broken when it's manifest to all your people you've driven out the Prince of Darkness. And we start to drive him out when your daughter comes to me and humbly submits herself for officially-imposed penance. And then she's to be out of Nicaea by midday. And all the rest of your family as well.

CYPRIOT BISHOP. But without my family to help me, how am I going to travel home?

BISHOP OF ANTIOCH. You'll travel with my two Deacons. I'll fix the expenses-dockets with the Emperor's finance-office. And when you get home, you'll take a solemn and public vow: complete sexual abstinence for the rest of your life.

CYPRIOT BISHOP. My wife to be punished as well? But the sin has been mine, not hers, why should she have taken away from her the consolation of our love together?

EUMOLPUS (*sincerely*). If your wife is a true Christian, she will rejoice in her deliverance from the eternal curse of fallen womanhood. What greater gift of love can there be from you to her?

Scene Eight

Exterior: the same, after a lapse of time. EUMOLPUS *and the* BISHOP OF
ANTIOCH *are pacing the colonnade.*

EUMOLPUS. But still he remains an accredited Bishop, and with a heathen idol
   prominent in his place of worship?

BISHOP OF ANTIOCH. Never mind about his idol. You interfere with these
   backwoods images, you've got riots on your hands. I can't go replacing him. Who
   can I find at short notice to do duty in a dead-and-alive hole like that?

EUMOLPUS. But his interpretation of the Apostle Paul –

BISHOP OF ANTIOCH. One of these days you theologians will come up with some
   practical sense: until you do, you'd better realise I am metropolitan Bishop and I
   make the decisions. He can believe what he wants about Paul, so long as he does
   what he's told. When he does what he's told, I can tell him what to believe.

KYBELE (*as narrator*). As I watched the poor old shepherd carry the verdict to his
   family, a snatch of rhyme from a street-game of my childhood came unbidden into
   my mouth.

*The buzz of the caravanserai continues behind her as she sings, quietly to begin with,
to herself, tapping her drum.*

(*Singing.*)   'A story, a story, come listen to my story:
                   A story, a story, can *I* be in your story . . .?

(*With a sudden burst of savage emphasis on the last line:*)

                   Oh no one's in my story, unless you all obey . . .!

As narrator:

The crowd of Bishops' servants at the gate of the caravanserai were staring at me in
a kind of horror, it was as if they all knew the police had my name, it was as if they
all knew that very shortly I should be . . . (*She breaks off for an instant with a
shudder.*) I gave them back stare for stare, I gave them the poet Lucretius on the
subject of imminent death – (*Aloud again:*)

                   'Rotting flesh, and fast-dissolving soul,
                   Old life makes new: and all within this world.'

I was not, I was, I am not, I do not fear . . .

Scene Nine

Exterior.

CONSTANTINE (*grimly*). The other creed you read to me twelve years ago was half
   the length and twice as cogent. Hosius: we are not to be persuaded by accumulation
   of new words.

HOSIUS (*speaking in this scene with refreshed confidence*). If words do not persuade,
   then all laws and oaths are meaningless. Majesty, you live by words –

CONSTANTINE. No, by the sword.

HOSIUS. Only when the words have failed. These words will not fail. The first creed,
   the Apostles' Creed, identified the church in the broadest possible manner against
   the Jews and the heathen. This one – more precise – identifies the true church
   against the false, against philosophical errors from both heathen and Jew. I am
   asking you, as the Imperial purple personified, to recognise our identity expressed
   in these words. Our oath of allegiance.

CONSTANTINE. Allegiance to the purple?

HOSIUS. No: to the one true God. To whom you too have declared an allegiance.
You can measure against this document –

Rustle of the document, here and where else needed in the scene.

HOSIUS. – all that the church will in the future do or say. You can also measure
against it any more of these reports you may receive from your agents in far-distant
libraries.

CONSTANTINE (*formal and unforthcoming*). Upon that we will advise ourself. We
have the utmost trust in our Security Service.

HOSIUS. Once the Bishops in Council give assent to this oath, we will be your
Security Service. And once the purple, present in Council, with all your oath-bound
Bishops, has heard and pronounced upon –

CONSTANTINE. Hosius, I have told you: we are about to advise ourself. If you wish
to assist, explain each clause as I read it out. These words must benefit Empire as
much as they benefit you: the purple robe against the white. Prepare yourself with
words to make words seem important. We leave the sword, for the time being,
where it hangs upon the wall. Hosius, I am looking at it. It is just above your head.
And so I read, the voice of the purple:
        'We believe in one God only, the Father . . .'

HOSIUS. The voice of the white robe. There is no mother, no possibility for the cult
of the female to subvert the natural order. No secondary godheads with specialised
priesthoods to quarrel over precedence, and provide focus for rebellion.

CONSTANTINE. And so I read:
        '– the Father, omnipotent maker of all things, visible and
            invisible . . .'

HOSIUS. No private cults purporting to expound some fabricated mystery of what
happened before the beginning, and thereby to confuse our minds about all that has
happened since. All this effectually to outlaw the old religion of the heathen. The
old religion of the Jew will be outlawed by what comes next.

CONSTANTINE. So I read:
        'And in one Lord only, Jesus Christ, the Son of God . . .'

HOSIUS. A Greek could believe that God might have a son: a Jew could never
believe it. But the Greek could not believe that the Father is one God only.

CONSTANTINE. So I read:
        'The Son of God, the only begotten of the Father, that is from
            the essence of the Father, God from God, light from light,
            true God from true God, begotten not made, of the same
            substance with the Father, by whom were made all things
            whether in heaven or earth . . .

Why have you underlined 'of the same substance'?

HOSIUS. Because Arius will not accept it. I am informed that his friends will. That
clause will crush Arius. The proletariat of Alexandria, if they still support him, will
cease to be accounted Christian. There will then be no danger that their popular
leaders can seize the bishopric, defy you, and cut off your grain-supply. Nor can the
eastern church join together with the Jews – and with the Persians – to overthrow
the Empire.

CONSTANTINE. You have written in the margin 'of similar substance' and put a
cross against it. Why?

HOSIUS. Some Bishops might suggest we use that phrase instead. If we do, it is the
Trojan horse by which Arius will recapture the citadel: it must not be permitted.

CONSTANTINE. But the difference is minute. The proletariat of Alexandria are not
going to –

HOSIUS. The proletariat of Alexandria are not going to understand any of it. Neither will three-quarters of the Bishops. In the very middle of the creed we present an almost incomprehensible mystery: the inter-communication of spirit and flesh, John the Evangelist calls it the Word. 'In the beginning was the Word.'

CONSTANTINE. Word of the white robe.

HOSIUS. Of the grey robe as well. The heathen philosophers who debated this endlessly and came to no conclusion. Those among your Bishops who are open to the Holy Spirit have accepted the Holy Spirit and through faith and through prayer these are the words of their experience. The faith and the prayer belong to every Christian. These words will ensure they are directed where they need to go.

CONSTANTINE. Where the white robe needs them to go. I thought we were talking about the needs of the purple.

HOSIUS. The white depends upon the purple for its very existence.

CONSTANTINE. To say nothing of our generous subsidies.

HOSIUS. The instructed, thoughtful Bishops, with this creed, will control the thoughtless Bishops, who will control the subordinate clergy, who will thus control the people. The purple has never been able to control the people. Not their minds and thoughts. Only their actions.

CONSTANTINE. But can the purple control the minds and thoughts of the white?

HOSIUS. You can hold us to our oath: when you hear us take the oath you will be able to –

CONSTANTINE (*reverting to his unforthcoming stance again*). If we hear you. If . . . So I read:

> 'Who for us men and for our salvation came down, was made flesh, became man, suffered, rose the third day, went up into heaven, and will come to judge the living and the dead . . .'

HOSIUS. That is a synopsis of the four authoritative gospels.

CONSTANTINE. There are more gospels than four.

HOSIUS. It eliminates all the rest.

CONSTANTINE. Are they not then as true as the four?

HOSIUS. Sir, I do not know. I was not there when they were written. They contradict, that is the point. They are therefore eliminated: and no one will read them again. Will you note, please, the last phrase, 'come to judge'. That judgement, we are told, will take place in Jerusalem.

CONSTANTINE. Who has told us?

HOSIUS. John the Divine, his Revelation: as authoritative as his Gospel. 'On Mount Zion,' he writes, 'stood the Lamb: the hour of his judgement has come!'

CONSTANTINE (*with a sudden access of controlled rage*). Jerusalem three hundred years is a bone in our throat. Oblige me by calling it Aelia Capitolina: as laid down by Hadrian. He decreed it was high treason to use the Hebrew name. Hosius, be careful.

HOSIUS (*starting again*). In the city of Aelia – (*He breaks off and takes courage.*) No – I will risk high treason, I committed it every day against the persecuting Emperors, so why should I fear a benevolent one? The city of Jerusalem – (*He pauses briefly to see if he is to be arrested.*)

CONSTANTINE (*growls*). Make your point.

HOSIUS (*emboldened*). Jerusalem was chosen by God the Father for the death of his Son. The death of his Son makes it our city, no one else's. The death of his Son makes fixed for all time the name of the city as Jesus himself knew it. 'Aelia

Capitolina' serves only the advantage of the discredited heathen persecutors. And as for the Jews –

CONSTANTINE (*in a sort of panic*). If we talk about Jerusalem they will think they can get it back! No sophisticated argument can overcome that fact, it is a police fact: I have the files! There are Jews in my Empire, there are even more Jews in the Persian Empire, they communicate in secret, they have set up cells, they distribute literature, they make use of their scriptures as a code for conspiracy –

HOSIUS. And out of their own scriptures we will confound them! But we have to know their scriptures even better than they do – Origen of Caesarea knew them very very well –

CONSTANTINE. You wish me to believe that Origen used the Jews to confound the Jews. Why, you talk like my own Secret Service: who always maintain that the most obvious motive is never the true motive. Nonsense!

HOSIUS. Did your informant tell you of the Book of Daniel, ninth chapter? 'There will be an abomination of desolation in the holy place until the end of time?' And if he did, did he remind you that Jesus himself repeats those words in the authoritative Gospel of Matthew? Once the temple has been destroyed by the armies of Rome, it is never to be restored, never: until the Lamb of Judgement.

CONSTANTINE. So therefore, you say, Jerusalem, under that name, once again a holy city – but a Christian holy city – I am to reverse the policy of Hadrian, of every Emperor since Hadrian, a decision that should concern only the Security Services: for the sake of the words of a soothsayer and a Hebrew one at that? The army will never stand for it, the Secret Police will transfer their allegiance: good God you are putting me in peril of a coup!

HOSIUS (*taking it calmly*). I know there was a time when it seemed as though all the Empire would eventually turn Jew and thereby abolish the purple but the Apostle Paul prevented that – he offered salvation without circumcision – so simple a remedy – but it worked! Those who wished to convert, converted to Christ. Not any more to Jehovah. What I am suggesting is equally simple. Popular opinion is highly susceptible to soothsayers. Popular opinion will protect the purple against the ignorant fears of the army. Mind you, we must be careful: not of the Jews, but of the heathen philosophers. I refer you to Porphyry – who alleged that Daniel did not in fact prophesy, he merely recorded what he saw, the temporary desecration of the Jerusalem temple by Greeks, five hundred years ago.

CONSTANTINE. Which totally destroys your argument. If people believe Porphyry –

HOSIUS. Ah, but they won't. Because we bring a stronger argument: the strongest of all. Possession is nine tenths of the law. We not only restore the name, we restore the city. Basilicas, shrines, thousands of pilgrims, a whole new Christian population –

CONSTANTINE (*irritably*). I am dealing already with one new Christian city, I cannot possibly afford two –

HOSIUS. Allocate the money from the security budget, put it all in the hands of your Secretary for Defence. That way you get the army to understand and accept it. And then, the final statement: no question where you stand in relation to the Jews, no question where we stand in relation to the Jews: you tell the world you have done all this to let the whole world know it was the Jews who murdered Christ!

CONSTANTINE (*simply*). But they didn't. It was without doubt a Roman prosecution. I have the documents in my archive, filed under 'The Deeds of Tiberius'.

HOSIUS (*to whom this is totally unexpected and very troubling*). Your – your archive – but – Majesty –

CONSTANTINE. I am looking at the creed: and I read the last clause. 'We believe in the Holy Spirit'. Well?

HOSIUS (*a little confused, but trying to collect himself*). The Holy Spirit, yes, that is as much as to say, the collective considered wisdom of the better class of Bishop, as passed down from the first Apostles by the laying-on of hands. From now on we are going to take the strictest precautions about the consecration of Bishops. Oh, and also, the Holy Spirit, it completes the Ineffable Trinity. The Trinity, being Ineffable, requires the aid of the Holy Spirit in the mortal brain of man to be properly understood, and as the Holy Spirit is part of the Trinity –

CONSTANTINE. – the white robe once again secures all power to the Bishops. You are stumbling in your speech. You are still thinking of the Deeds of Tiberius. Don't. We are reassured: the Jews from now on are a deicide nation: they will find no friends anywhere.

HOSIUS (*with great relief*). Ah, Majesty – you mean – you have accepted the efficacy of the creed?

CONSTANTINE. I mean I understand that the creed does not depend upon what did or did not happen in Galilee or Jerusalem or anywhere else in Palestine in the reign of Tiberius. Taken by itself, we can see that it will never set the peasants on the march to claim redistribution of the land or death to all tax-gatherers. To that extent it does fulfil the requirements of the purple. But on its own it is not sufficient to persuade us to come to Nicaea. We need further reassurance. Proposals of Canon Law?

HOSIUS. Church-discipline, jurisdiction, all these will be agreed.

CONSTANTINE. Unanimously?

HOSIUS. Some minor points will be contested.

CONSTANTINE (*tetchily*). If the purple is to take the chair, we need to know which. We cannot preside over anarchy.

HOSIUS. Majesty, there will be no anarchy . . . (*He realises this is a crunch-point. He stumbles a little and then takes the bull by the horns:*) Likewise, Majesty, likewise . . . Majesty, forgive me: the white robe cannot accept the Presidency of the purple. The Supreme Pontiff of the heathen observances has no role in the church of Christ.

CONSTANTINE (*after an appalling pause*). We have read your words. We have patiently heard your words. We have not for one moment cast a glance at the sword, where it still hangs above your head. We sit quietly, a little child, to receive your considered instruction. If the Imperial purple is not required to preside at Nicaea, then what – in the name of the Unconquered Sun, Hosius – have you come to Nicomedia to persuade the purple to do!?

HOSIUS (*very carefully*). To attend our deliberations as sovereign protector of the whole realm and of the Christian people contained in it: and also, as you say, as a little child of Christ.

CONSTANTINE. Protector – and child? I cannot be both.

HOSIUS (*encouraging*). No Emperor was ever both. You will be the first! Nothing that is to be done today will ever have been done before. The white robe asks the purple to sit at this Council, not in the chair, but as a child, to one side –

CONSTANTINE (*sourly*). – in a mute and humble posture –

HOSIUS. – and holding in your hand the sword of your protection.

CONSTANTINE. A child with a sword will terrify nobody.

HOSIUS. David with his sling was laughed at by Goliath. We don't ask you to bring a sling. This creed will be the sling. We want you to keep your sword to do with it what David did: when the huge giant fell down he cut off his head. Nobody was laughing then.

CONSTANTINE. Yes, I think we understand. Arius and his friends refuse the new creed, as put to them by the white: you will then ask the purple to – kill them? I think not.

HOSIUS. Not kill. Banish. Send the excommunicates hundreds of miles away from their areas of support.

CONSTANTINE. We don't have the power.

HOSIUS. Arbitrary decree.

CONSTANTINE. That would be to act as Supreme Pontiff: a rank we are denied. Anything else would be unprecedented.

HOSIUS. Majesty, not so. Precedent number one: you banished recalcitrant Donatists.

CONSTANTINE. A threat to public order: their doctrine was not in question.

HOSIUS. Precedent number two: the late Emperor Aurelian evicted heretics from church-property at the request of local Bishops.

CONSTANTINE. But he was a persecutor.

HOSIUS. It was a matter of law. The property had not been confiscated: therefore it belonged to the Bishops, whether Aurelian approved of them or not. If Arius is excommunicated, he will try to hold on to his pulpit. The case is strictly similar.

CONSTANTINE. First you say, arbitrary decree: next you say, legal precedent. It cannot be both. No other religion has ever asked me to –

HOSIUS. No other religion has ever imposed a precise doctrine of belief. We are concerned with the souls of men, not with their outward actions. We are unprecedented; Christ is unprecedented: therefore –

CONSTANTINE. – therefore you must have the purple as a persecutor. You would be better off electing your own Supreme Pontiff. Which Bishop is to be your procedural convenor for this Council? You could make the office permanent. Put all the odium onto the white robe for a change.

HOSIUS. Even if we did, he would not have the power of banishment. But we did not choose our convenor because we thought he would be supreme. A simple question of practicality. Rome is not here; Alexandria is presenting his case against Arius from the floor; Jerusalem is too feeble: so the convenor will be Antioch.

CONSTANTINE. Antioch is a boor.

HOSIUS. He will make a strong convenor: but for permanent responsibility, quite unacceptable. Besides: no Syrian Bishop would gain the support of the West.

CONSTANTINE. Do you suggest Rome would gain the support of the East?

HOSIUS. He might: if he had your support, from your new city, in the East . . .

CONSTANTINE. But he would not support me, if I continue to observe traditional ceremonies in Rome . . . You ask me to protect you, and yet you ask me to repudiate my protection of my non-Christian subjects.
    You determine the posthumous repudiation of great Hadrian, and ask me to take all the risk and the expense. You determine heresy and ask me to punish it. How many heresies? We have talked about Arius. There are also the Novationists. Will you excommunicate them as well?

HOSIUS. Their quarrel is with the orthodox doctrine of repentance. It is more a problem of the Canon Law than the creed. I am quite sure that they –

CONSTANTINE (*laying it down firmly*). I am quite sure that they are not going to be troubled by you. One set of outlaws at one time, if you please.

HOSIUS (*exultantly*). So Arius *is* an outlaw –?

CONSTANTINE (*cooling him down*). If he is – and I promise nothing – I only say, if – if we banish Arius, why?

HOSIUS. Because he rejects the Holy Spirit as vouchsafed to assembled –

CONSTANTINE. Not good enough. The traditional believers, to say nothing of the Jews, will describe me as your creature and make a mock of the purple for ever. If Arius is guilty, it must be of something that will strike to the heart of non-Christians as well as your false Christians. Is he a Jew?

HOSIUS. Not exactly, but tending –

CONSTANTINE. Is he a heathen?

HOSIUS. The same answer.

CONSTANTINE. You said we must be careful of Porphyry. Porphyry was no Jew but his satire inclined that way. Why should not Arius be described as a 'Porphyrian'? Diocletian was a Porphyrian: and he was a persecutor. If we are to seem to persecute, there must be no mistake. No one to be able to say we are Diocletian. But supposing – don't interrupt, the purple is about to lay down its own terms – supposing Arius is banished. The man has written books. We can't banish those.

HOSIUS. Make an edict and confiscate. When you confiscate, burn.

CONSTANTINE. [Diocletian did that too.] If they still keep their books . . . the death penalty?

HOSIUS. Of course. You have an edict, it must be obeyed. Death for disobedience not for forbidden thoughts. The white robe gives you security by defining forbidden thoughts, but God alone disposes their chastisement.

CONSTANTINE (*to himself*). God alone knows what Diocletian will say, where he lies in his mausoleum . . .

HOSIUS. [Majesty –?

CONSTANTINE (*to himself*). . . . he took his own life because we left him all alone . . . the great temples he built, the statues he erected . . . empty and meaningless, an age that is gone and past . . .]

HOSIUS. Majesty, you were about to lay down certain terms –

CONSTANTINE (*suddenly as grim as he was at the beginning of the scene*). We were thinking of ourself, on a small stool, holding a sword, waiting for permission to use it, while the white robe takes over the Empire. We were thinking this is not quite how Eusebius of Caesarea had discerned the God-given power of our office. You insulted him a year ago: but he alone among all of you knows the history of your faith. Are you aware he has been writing it? He sent me the final chapters the day before yesterday. Be so good as to read to me the passages I have marked.

Sound of a volume being opened.

HOSIUS (*reading, after a deprecatory cough*). 'Let me now obediently sing aloud the new song: how a day bright and radiant, with no cloud overshadowing it, shone down with shaft of heavenly light on the churches of Christ throughout the world.'

CONSTANTINE. Who has been building those churches?

HOSIUS. Majesty, you have.

CONSTANTINE. Continue: read Eusebius.

HOSIUS (*reads*). 'There are in these cathedrals thrones for all the souls on which rest the flames of fire of the Holy Spirit, just as in olden time they appeared to the Holy Apostles –'

CONSTANTINE (*he is making an important statement*). Stop. Today is Pentecost. Pentecost is flames of fire. Pentecost is twelve Apostles, in a narrow upper room.

Pentecost is three hundred-odd Bishops, under my roof, amid columns of gold. You claim that your Bishops are descended from the Apostles. If I am to come among them, how can I be any less? And I do not ask a throne. If you can grant me, in some form of words, just so much equality, I am content with the lowest stool: and I will banish Arius to the region of the Danube.

HOSIUS (*overjoyed: if these are the 'terms' they are just what he hoped for*). Clothed in the purple – and yet with the white robe over it –! – there were twelve Apostles – and now –

CONSTANTINE. – now there are thirteen. That is my status and title! You are Apostles to those who accepted Christ: I am Apostle to those who have not yet found him!

And in order to bring them in, the lame, the halt, the blind, I am preparing their wedding-garment – I build churches, I build cathedrals, I distribute largesse to make beautiful the house of Christ – read again from Eusebius – the beauty of the house of Christ, in Rome, in Jerusalem, in the New Rome I have yet to construct – read, Hosius, read –!

CONSTANTINE *joins in – he has already got this bit by heart.*

HOSIUS. '– the towering walls that reach for the sky, the costly cedars of Lebanon that form the ceiling, the great gate with its brazen leaves, of breathtaking loveliness –'

HOSIUS   )(*reading*). '– its dazzling proportions, the incredible vastness, the
CONSTANTINE   )brilliant appearance of the workmanship –'

Scene Ten

The voice of KYBELE *comes up over the last passage of Eusebius: she is singing her ditty to her little drum.*

KYBELE (*sings*).   'A story a story, come listen to my story
A story a story, a mystery is my story
A story a story, am *I* in your story?
Oh no one's in my story, unless you all are saved.

'A story a story, a whisper in the dark
A story a story, a flicker and a spark
A story a story, can I *not* be in your story?
Oh no one's in my story: unless you all obey!'

(*She speaks, in a low but by no means childish voice.*) The Lady Kybele, Epicurean philosopher whispers to humanity a message that was written centuries before the Christ-message: 'Live and let live: eat, drink, and remember – your highest duty is to secure the happiness of this world, for there is no other . . .'

Closing music.

7

AN EYE FOR AN 'I'

Scene One

Opening music. Exterior: noises of excited CROWD *in the streets of Nicaea, building up behind narrative.*

KYBELE (*as narrator*). 325 AD. the Council of Nicaea, where the bishops put together a compulsory creed and those who refused to swear to it were banished by the Emperor Constantine. Three hundred and sixteen accepted, three refused. The priest Arius refused. He denied that Jesus Christ was of the same substance with the Father, homo-ousios in Greek. Some were later to say it ought to have read homoi-ousos, of similar substance, and that this little letter 'i' might have accommodated Arius's doctrine. But it didn't, he was expelled, and all his books were burnt. From now on, Christ was king and the king was Christ: the eye of the king was everywhere: and Jesus the Peacemaker was paying the Imperial police. I was in front of the council hall when Arius came out: and I saw the police.

A great gong has started to clang: there are shouts (from within the hall) of 'Anathema! Anathema! Let them be cast out!' The shouts suddenly are louder as though a throng has issued onto the street: and a general chorus of groans and jeers from the waiting CROWD.

Swords drawn, closing in on him, hustling him through the crowds to the military wagon that would take him into exile. You'd think Arius was a ruined man . . . so why was he smiling . . .?

The CROWD*'s groans and jeers have died away now* ARIUS *and* COLLEAGUES *have been removed. The gong continues: but its beat is now accompanied by a whole chorus of gongs and bells from all over the town. The* CROWD *starts to cheer.*

Then out came the bishops who had voted against him, inspired by the Holy Spirit, sure of eternal reward. The Emperor, whom they had hailed as the Thirteenth Apostle, was about to announce through his herald a more immediate earthly benefit –

The CROWD *has fallen silent to hear the* HERALD.

HERALD. Tomorrow, in Nicomedia, in the Imperial palace, a celebratory episcopal banquet, the like of which has not been seen since Solomon the Wise feasted the whole of Israel for seven days and seven nights upon the consecration of his holy temple!

More cheers.

God has triumphed, not the Emperor!

Cries of 'Hosanna!'

GUARD. Stand back, please, stand back! Give way for the Dowager Empress!

KYBELE (*as narrator*). Here was a surprise, no one had expected Lady Helen to be present. She had not been seen in public before: it was scandalously whispered she was too rude, she was too British, she was a drunkard, her invitation to court was a terrible mistake. Yet here she had been, in the council-hall all this time, and no one had known! How could they have known?

A murmur of curiosity and surprise through the CROWD.

Would you believe she was walking in the middle of the ladies from Naples, a big strong hearty old creature, dressed no better than a henwife, her great hand clamped on the shoulder of an odd-looking crook-backed young woman. When Helen saw her coach waiting, she avoided it with a laugh.

HELEN (*at large*). Lord Jesus knows I walked hundreds of miles after the regiments, looking out for my tall young officer: so don't you buggers tell me I need a coffin with wheels on it to get to Nicomedia to have dinner with his son!

This gets great public applause.

KYBELE (*as narrator*). She had a lump of bread in her fist, and she munched, and strode out of the town. As she passed through the people, she blessed them, and she kissed them, and she laughed and they laughed. It was all the police could do to stop them following her in a cheering mob . . .

HELEN*'s demagogic departure puts an end to all the cheering etc. Pause. A growing noise of dogs and* MEN, *a confused shouting, beating of staves on the flagstones,* PEOPLE *running to get out of the way, all coming nearer.*

And then: I saw soldiers with staves – and deacons with huge dogs. There were no longer any Christians in the crowd. Only heretics and unbelievers: church and state between them were evicting us from Nicaea, for half the township, stone and mortar, turned out to be church property and we were trespassers; we had no choice but to go!

Cries of 'cast them out!' etc., into cross-fade to next scene:

Scene Two

Exterior: A horse galloping on a paved road.

CONSTANTINE (*to himself, as he rides*). God triumphs, we don't: God's Bishops triumph: his Emperor, the Thirteenth Apostle, becomes a mere mortal man, to slip out incognito to freedom on his favourite black mare – galloping between my twelve invisible colleagues – Simon Peter, Andrew, James and John – all of them. And they choose my road – to the seashore, to my boat, across the water to Byzantium! Where I make my new Rome at behest of these twelve – and they give me the needful omen . . .

Cross-fade.

Scene Three

Exterior. The horse hooves now in the distance, getting nearer as HELEN *speaks. The sound of stones being dragged and dropped onto a heap.*

HELEN (*to herself*). In a place where three roads meet, hard by the base of the mountain, I, Helen and my holy-woman, Mary the Companion, my doll Baba; and a pile of stones –

The galloping suddenly right on top of her. A clattering and plunging as the horse narrowly avoids running her down.

(*She shouts angrily.*) Whoa, whoa, you furious bucko, where do you go!

The horse comes to a stand. Her tone changes as she sees who it is.

Why, it's my son, the Emperor-apostle! You would ride right over your mother! Begotten not made, and he has forgotten the body from which he came!

CONSTANTINE (*astonished*). Mother . . . (*To himself, bewildered:*) She has been in my court for over a year and yet I have scarcely spoken to her, and here she is, my mother, by night upon the road-side, breaking stones . . .? And smiling. How to account for this molten flow and heat of emotion through all my bowels? As though I were no more than five years old: and there was nothing in all the world beyond her and me, and her arms outstretched to gather me into her warmth. (*Aloud, and annoyed:*) Mother, what are you doing here?

HELEN (*to herself*). Oh yes he was so big, crowded inside me for ten full months, and then one day the waters broke, he rushed out with such furious curious speed even the midwife took alarm. Already a huge white tooth in his great ruffian head to break out blood from my nipple. (*Aloud:*) My son, the Emperor . . .

CONSTANTINE. I said, what are you doing here?

HELEN (*harshly*). What your bishops should be doing instead of grunting at your banquet-table; making myself useful, dragging down the old gods and building up the new. Bad blood to be driven out. And that way, son, I save your Empire, don't I?

CONSTANTINE (*embarrassed and therefore bureaucratic*). Are you authorised to – to pull down this shrine and to – to turn it into a –

HELEN. Into Golgotha! The cross of Christ at the cross-road. Authorised? I paid the occupier. One dirty old heathen priest, with no belief in anything. But those who pass here now shall both remember and believe. Truth of suffering for all time.

She starts working again, shifting stones. We hear the clank of a chain. Effects continue behind:

CONSTANTINE (*to himself*). A grim cross of timber lying on the broken ground, the younger woman shuffles toward it – bends to lift it, has not the strength, her arms give way and it falls, trapping her under its weight. I am suddenly aware she is girded with iron chains. Without word of complaint, she drags her whole body underneath the heavy beam, heaves herself upward: bears up the cross upon her own back: until at last it stands vertical, and at last my mother helps her: between the pair of them, they make this Golgotha. And its shadow in the moonlight strikes right against my head . . .

Banging of stone against stone, as they pack the base of the upright.

HELEN. Hold it straight, you idle bitch, I said straight. Oh and how much better is my son without his nonsense, in his own hair and human clothes! You should stay like this always, don't let those bloody bishops make a god of you in the name of God: because I know and you know that you're nothing of the sort.

More banging of stones.

CONSTANTINE (*to himself, angry*). Diocletian was quite right; my father was quite right, to get rid of her when he was told!

HELEN (*to* MARY). Hand me the mallet –

CONSTANTINE (*sharply*). Why is that woman in chains? Why do you treat her like – ? God, but I know who she is! She is Mary the Companion, Bishop Hosius recommended her – she is a recognized minister of Christ – she –

HELEN (*bleakly*). She is the runaway adopted child of a land-bound Spanish serf: and that is her legal status.

CONSTANTINE (*indignantly*). We have a duty to observe her independent religious dignity –

HELEN. We have a duty to pay tax upon her head and I have paid it. I work for the service of Jesus and she works as my equal beside me. If she wears her chains for penance, what is that to you? Would you rather I kept her in indolent luxury like your wife and her bad-blood nephews, draining the life out of the land, corrupting your own soul? (*She addresses* MARY, the better to taunt him:) Why, Mary, he has no knowledge of what's been happening behind his back: Empress Fausta the child of witchcraft running off with his own slave-woman Semiramis toward God knows what unnatural fulfilment of desire: and you, my holy serf, who helped her to do it!

CONSTANTINE (*totally bewildered*). Slave-woman, what slave-woman?

HELEN. He doesn't even know the shameless hairdresser is his own property! And yet by his code of law every citizen is responsible for the property he holds. Are we surprised that the people are calling Constantine the Second Nero?

The stone-banging comes to an end.

So: it is finished. Mary, we have more to do. Pick up Baba, give her to me. Come with me, trudge!

We move off with MARY *and* HELEN, *the chain clanking. As they walk, the odd impatient clopping of the standing horse fades out behind them: But* CONSTANTINE *calls:*

CONSTANTINE. Mother, Mother.

HELEN (*to* MARY, *as they walk*). Oh, Mary, must you still protect her, and the slave she ran away with? Don't drag those chains, girl, pick them up, I can't hear myself speak! (*She changes her tone to one of almost pathetic persuasion:*) All you need do, my dear, is just whisper it, in my ear, all this burden and bitterness will be lifted away from you, once again you shall recount the Book of God to an old woman . . . Oh, Mary, we were such good friends – can we not, once again –?

MARY (*dull endurance*). I have told you I know nothing. I do not know where they are. Neither Fausta nor Semiramis.

HELEN (*furious*). Ungrateful girl, must I beat it from you with the weight of your own chain!

She beats MARY *with the end of the chain.* MARY *moans a little, an animal-like stifled noise. As* HELEN *hits her, she goes on speaking, in what is her own personal fear and agony.*

You are making me ridiculous! I put my name to an official royal document, declaring Semiramis to be a slave of the household and in no way the personal property of Fausta: and making her over to Physcon the baker. And unless we can find her, there is going to be enquiry made! And my son will ask his mother by what right did I make use of the Imperial seal: and if I cannot answer him, by his own law he is empowered to torture me to death! And not only me but you, and not only you but Hosius, the only bishop among all of them who truly breathes the Holy Spirit . . .!

She has stopped the beating.

(*Breathes heavily.*) I know what to do: I shall give you to Hosius: he caused all this trouble, let him make you talk: he is responsible, Hosius, yes . . .

Scene Four

Exterior: CONSTANTINE *still on his stationary horse.*

CONSTANTINE (*to himself, brooding, disquieted*). Dear heaven, she called me Nero. Nero who killed his mother, or Nero invited to slide into his mother's promiscuous bed? (*calling:*) Mother! I am Constantine and I will have been Emperor for twenty years and undefeated! Next summer in Rome I invite you as Dowager Empress to preside over my Jubilee: oh, Mother, I will build you a monument! (*To himself, after a short silence:*) The dark shadow of the high mountain swallowed the pair of them up . . .

His horse shies suddenly, and he controls her with an angry exclamation.

What was it had frightened my mare? Ah: and I saw it! Look – a white face, grinning up at me, flat on the ground, broken marble, broken on purpose, mutilated with blows of a chisel – I saw the face of the ancient goddess whose image at this crossroad had stood unscathed nine hundred years . . .! Why did my mother talk such nonsense about my wife . . .?

His horse moves carefully forward and then increases speed.

Scene Five

Exterior: A large column of PEOPLE *being herded forward by shouting* GUARDS, *they are muttering, talking, singing.*

GUARDS (*passim throughout the sequence*). Come on, keep it moving, no straggling away from the edge of the road – we want none of you undesirables slipping back into town through the underbrush – keep to the road, dammit – keep to the road – move –! (*Etc.*)

1st DISSIDENT (*in angry triumph*). We are the devil in the parable, expelled from the haunted house –

2nd DISSIDENT. Nicaea will be swept and garnished, and then we return sevenfold!

General laughter.

KYBELE (*as narrator*). And so there we were, old, young, men, women, children, with bundles and handcarts, stumbling under guard through the dark towards a ruined abandoned township where we could stay, they told us, twenty-four hours: and then, after that, out of the province for ever.

Cross-fade to indicate lapse of time.

This could not have been spontaneous, it was arranged at least a week in advance, names noted, lists prepared – was it happening all over the Empire? And how many were going to survive?

A group of DISSIDENTS *is singing:*

DISSIDENTS (*sing*).

> One in three and three in one
> When a bishop's on his throne
> We all can see what he has done
> To keep our Lord for himself alone –
>
> *Refrain:*
>
> Oh aloney loney loney loney
> Spiritual body ain't got no boney –
>
> Human beings, you and me,
> Bow your knee to the one in three
> To the three in one hold up your hand:
> God is far too abstract for you to understand –
>
> *Refrain:*
>
> Ab-stracty tracty tracty heavenly god
> Spiritual body ain't got no good red blood

3rd DISSIDENT (*a woman: talking as the singing goes on*). I was sitting with my friends in came the deacons, found a book by the man Arius: out on the street and get moving! Hardly gave me time to put the baby on my back.

We can hear the BABY *crying: She tries to hush it.*

1st DISSIDENT. Them tenements by the cattle-market, they cleared everybody out –

The song continues with great vigour.

3rd DISSIDENT. Where's the rest of our lot? Haven't we got anything to sing?

She starts another song, which is taken up by a lot of voices near her, and drowns out the first song. It is a psalm-like chant.

DISSIDENTS (*sing*).

> Weep weep Jerusalem
> How solitary lies the city

> Like a forsaken woman
> The princess of all the peoples is desolate
> Like a forsaken woman
> Like a woman hurt and forsaken
> By her husband
> All her palaces and walls
> Are like a barren woman
> And like a sheltered woman
> All her paths.
> Like a woman of bitterness
> All her daughters are like women
> Mourning for their husbands
> Like women deprived of their only children.
> Weep weep Jerusalem
> Her tears flow upon her cheeks
> Because of her sons . . .

KYBELE (*as narrator*). The Arians were not the only heretics: there were Ebionites, the Jewish Christians, with their lament for Jerusalem fallen . . .

A pause, as the Ebionite song continues.

Cross-fade to show lapse of time.

2ND DISSIDENT. Hey, you with your placard, I can't read it, what does it say?

4TH DISSIDENT. 'Here is Christ of the Land of Phrygia, here and now: watch out!' Montanus the Prophet, who had been a prophet of Kybele the Great Mother, said that from her Phrygian womb Christ would return to judge the world and where is Nicaea but in Phrygia? (*Wildly.*) Evoe evoe Kybele, Christ is the son of Kybele!

KYBELE (*as narrator*). My own name being Kybele, I wondered was this an omen. I was in most desperate need of one. Those crying out for the goddess Kybele marched maybe twenty paces ahead of me.

JAXARTES (*venomously, close to her; not loudly*). Kybele, evoe Kybele . . .

KYBELE (*as narrator*). But the voice of one man who picked up the name from them was immediately at my back: and he spoke it as though he meant it for me. I turned, I saw his face, and his eyes looked straight at me, they said to me: 'Old woman, I've never seen you before. I never want, ever, to see you again: but be certain I'll never forget you.' (*There is a tremble of fear in her voice as she tells this.*) And then he began to chant, not for Kybele, not for Arius, not for Jerusalem, but all of a sudden a form of words to make rebellion the priority above all specific doctrine.

JAXARTES (*commencing a regular repetition*). No Rome, Christ alone! Con-stan-tine of Nero's line!

KYBELE (*as narrator, still with fear*). And those on either side of him began to shout with his shout, forgetting their own slogans, all merging together against the Empire itself.

JAXARTES' *chant becomes general.*

KYBELE. All the time he kept looking at me, I tried hard to move away but he was still there close behind me.

GUARDS (*suddenly running up and pushing people aside*). Clear the road – shut your mouths, damn you – clear the road – into the ditch, into the ditch – move –!

The chant falls away into a confusion of protesting cries. Trampling of a horse's hooves and PEOPLE *yelling as they are knocked about.*

KYBELE (*as narrator*). We did not know who the horseman was who came pressing from behind so violently through the confusion of our ranks.

CONSTANTINE (*to himself as his horse clatters forward*). I am the father of my country and I was riding down my own children as I had ridden down my mother: Who was so stupid to allow these disorderly elements to come all together in the one place . . .? The name of Nero was in their mouths!

As he pushes clear of the thickest part of the throng, the chanting re-establishes itself.

JAXARTES (*his voice coming out on top of the others, very close*). No Rome, Christ alone! Con-stan-tine of Nero's line!

CONSTANTINE (*to himself*). He was shouting louder than all of them, I took a great swing at him with my riding-crop. After I passed him, it came to me, I knew his voice! Was it possible? Jaxartes of my secret service could be here among this rabblement?

The chanting dies away behind him as he clatters on. He rides on for a while. Cross fade.

Scene Six

Exterior: One horse, moving uphill.

CONSTANTINE. I thought I left Nicaea with my twelve sacred colleagues, what illusion was this, there was now another one at my side . . .?

The clatter of another horse seems to join his own.

(*To himself:*) And then – I was over the ridge –

He breaks into a gallop as the gradient changes: the other horse now clearly with him.

– no longer the angry multitude: and with me there was riding but one man, that was all. Out of the corner of my eye – if I looked at him directly, he was not there – I asked him who he was – (*Aloud:*) Who – ?

'PAUL OF TARSUS' (*speaking swiftly and urgently with a thin needle-like, insidious quality*). Wherefore seeing we also are compassed about with so great a cloud of witnesses –

The sound of the horses fades away slightly as though this conversation does not really belong to the realistic setting. The voice of PAUL *appears to come from inside* CONSTANTINE: *a projection of his alter ego.*

CONSTANTINE (*to himself*). His voice, quite distinctly, the hooves of his horse, there at my flank and a little to the rear.

'PAUL OF TARSUS'. – let us lay aside every weight, and the sin which doth so easily beset us, and let us run with patience the race that is set before us.

> Oh speed yourself spur yourself
> Gallop like the wind,
> The twelve dumb fools who set out with you
> Are already left behind . . .

The galloping, which had suddenly speeded up extremely, now slows down to a walk: but still not quite a realistic sound-effect.

CONSTANTINE (*to himself*). There at my flank always, and a little to the rear. (*Aloud:*) You are not an apostle?

'PAUL OF TARSUS'.

> Oh that's what they said
> And the eyes in my head
> Were made blind by the rage of their hate.
> Yet the last shall be first
> And they knew it to be true:

>   Had it not been for me,
>   There would have been nothing for you.

CONSTANTINE. Blind? An apostle, and yet not an apostle? You can be none other than the man of Tarsus.

'PAUL OF TARSUS'. In nothing am I behind the very chiefest apostles.

CONSTANTINE. Yet you did not know him the man of Nazareth, see him, touch him in this world of flesh –

One horse only, and its pace shifts again into a gallop.

(*Speaks to himself.*) At which point he seemed to leave me: until later, on board the boat that sped me across the Bosporus – his voice in the wind once again . . .

Cross-fade.

Scene Seven

Exterior: On board ship, brisk windy weather.

'PAUL OF TARSUS'.
>   World of flesh is good for nothing
>   But to drive in the thorn of pain.
>   I choose you, as he chose me,
>   All on your own alone.
>   She or he that will confound us
>   We remorselessly strike down.

CONSTANTINE (*in a sort of angry frenzy*).

>   You must have known him, must have
>   seen him,
>   Must be able to say at least
>   What kind of species he was,
>   God, man, or fabulous beast –
>   No one for certain
>   Has ever told me for certain –
>   There must be some truth at the root
>   of it,
>   Some root of truth – incontrovertibly
>   true –?

'PAUL OF TARSUS' (*gives a sardonic chuckle which fades away on the breeze*).

CONSTANTINE (*to himself*). But the wind blew: and all else silence. He was gone with the sunrise.

Scene Eight

Exterior: A great crowd of PEOPLE *in a wide space, behaving as described in the dialogue, with the barking of dogs intermittently throughout the episode.*

KYBELE (*as narrator*). In this ramshackle market-place of the ruined town in the gap of the mountains, I found myself with the jostling crowd queuing up and quarrelling for a miserable dole of slops served out by a public slave under guard from the military.

1st DISSIDENT. This is filth – it's not soup –

2nd DISSIDENT. Don't touch it, they want to poison us –

3RD DISSIDENT. What d'you mean, don't touch it, we've got to eat something!

4TH DISSIDENT. Hey, get outta that, I was here in front of you –!

General dispute.

GUARD. Keep it orderly, keep in line, or I'll break your bloody head off!

A sudden burst of music, tambourines and flutes. The CROWD *falls silent, after a gasp of surprise.*

KYBELE (*as narrator*). The music was so unexpected that it silenced the entire tumult. Upon the steps of the old temple in the middle of the square stood a dark-faced woman, tall and gaunt, as tense as a bowstring, dressed in the robes of the desert-people – she came out and down amongst us: behind her, a kind of litter, carried by young women: standing upon it, a strange dark child in white, garlands of flowers all over her.

The tambourines cease: a slow march played on a drum.

They moved slowly round the square.

2ND DISSIDENT (*whisper*). Why, it's the Flying Angel, the magic child from Nicomedia –

3RD DISSIDENT (*whisper*). From the Inn of the Salutation – have they cast her out as well?

2ND DISSIDENT (*whisper*). This is witchcraft, protect yourself, Lord Jesus have mercy upon us, Lord Jesus have mercy upon us . . .

KYBELE (*as narrator*). Finally: a funeral bier . . . Whose? The corpse was female, sharp Persian profile, rigid and pale as an ivory-carving. Behind the bier, another woman, heavily veiled, bowed head.

The drum beat continues, and then stops. A dead silence for a moment: then a dog howls. The drum takes up again, a faster, more complex rhythm.

At the end of the square, against the base of a broken fountain, the litter with the angel-child suddenly and most deftly converted into a theatrical stage. In front of it they laid the bier. A cluster of brilliant emeralds aross the dead body's folded hands. The gleam of the cooking fires made them sparkle unendurably. The tall dark woman spoke.

The drum beat stops.

MELANTHO (*some distance away*). I am Melantho, daughter of Oenothea, who serves the divine mother of Babylon, bringing life upon earth to all created things. Constantine, Emperor, has renegued upon his service to her: so tonight all we have is death.

Scene Nine

Exterior: a windy building site. WORKMEN *are hammering, digging, pushing wheelbarrows etc., calling now and then to each other.* CONSTANTINE *and his* ARCHITECT *moving about on inspection.*

CONSTANTINE (*to himself*). All the work, at first sight, upon my new city, enlarged Byzantium, appears in good shape. Until the date, yet to be named, of official inauguration, my visits, matter-of-policy, are anonymous: although the Chief Architect knows who I am. (*Aloud to* ARCHITECT:) Any problems?

ARCHITECT (*middle-aged, self-confident, briskly respecting the incognito*). The boundary-wall. You tell me you cannot determine the exact line until you hold the ceremony?

CONSTANTINE (*irritably: he has been through this before*). It is the ceremony itself which will determine. A solemn religious rite, there may well be a divine revelation.

ARCHITECT (*no less irritable*). In which case we must have a date.

CONSTANTINE (*standing no nonsense*). Not before the church of the Twelve Apostles is complete, to contain my own – the Emperor's tomb, as well as theirs.

ARCHITECT (*not prepared to quarrel over this*). No problem as to the structure. Foundations are very strong: the crypt of an old Mithras-temple. This way, over here . . . I am short of good goldsmiths. Possibilities among the Christian refugees out of Persia – that is if you don't object to the oriental style – anyway, my labour-contractor is looking into it, a most competent man from the south of Italy, he's worked wonders with the food supply – ah, there he is! Physcon!

PHYSCON (*from a distance*). Hello?

He comes running.

ARCHITECT. About those Persians, I wonder could you explain to – to this gentleman from the Board of Works –

The conversation is interrupted by a sudden thunderous noise a little way off, followed by confused cries of pain and fear and the sound of running feet.

CRIES. Earthquake, earthquake! Out of the trenches, earthquake – emergency, earthquake – Mithras is cursing us! – the anger of Lord Mithras –! (*Etc.*)

ARCHITECT. Good God, it's the Apostles' church!

PHYSCON. That wasn't an earthquake – I didn't feel a thing.

ARCHITECT. No. but something's come down – hurry – what has happened?

They run towards the confusion. The FOREMAN*'s voice emerges from the tumult, which falls silent to let him speak.*

FOREMAN (*hard and angry*). The retaining wall fell in under the base of the Emperor's tomb. There's ten of 'em trapped in there, I think they're all dead. Stretcher-bearers, quick! Oh they say it's the curse of Mithras: but I know better. We have warned you these last two weeks, the revetments to that trench are totally inadequate: we lost two yesterday, four injured the day before, and now this morning, ten. The people are weakened with short rations, there's been no delivery of food contracted to be supplied. We're pulling out of the job until we are given what we was pledged.

A general growl of agreement from the WORKERS *(male and female).*

PHYSCON (*very angry*). Back to your work, all of you! (*He raises his voice.*) Security! I want the guards! Quick! Over here! Quick!

Rapid arrival of booted military feet.

Sergeant, if this crowd is not back on the job again when I count three, a spear in every man, every woman, who refuses!

ARCHITECT (*desperate to avert an incident with the* EMPEROR *on the site*). Wait wait wait – this is no way to do it! D'you want to have 'em downing tools from one end of the site to the other – !

The creaking of an ass-and-cart fills the tense silence.

CONSTANTINE (to himself). In the middle of all the commotion: a little man with a cart, piled up with painted sculptures, he was driving it away as though nothing had happened at all . . . (*Aloud to* ARCHITECT.) If you've injured to take care of, you're going to need a pair of wheels – you: stop! Unload it!

The cart stops, and we hear the statues being pulled off.

Just a moment, what is all this? Discarded statues of Lord Mithras and the

Guardians? I thought there was a rule about preservation of religious relics. Where are you going with them?

DRIVER (*defensive and aggressive all at once*). Nowhere but where I was told, according to Commissioner Physcon.

PHYSCON (*blustering*). How dare you say I told you to take these images anywhere! He's running a bloody racket, that's what he's doing. Extensive site-pilferage of the gravest description. Sergeant, put this carter under arrest – and that trouble-maker as well!

Angry protests from both the CARTER *and the* FOREMAN *as the* SECURITY-GUARDS *secure them.*

(*adopting a confidential tone toward* CONSTANTINE). Fact is, sir, and I'd be glad if you'd pass it on to the Department, we're dealing here with a constant pattern of sabotage from irreconcilable heathen elements in the workforce. That big chap in the handcuffs there, he was the ringleader. Take him to the penal barracks.

The WORKERS *give a savage growl expressive of resistance: 'no arrest! Let 'em go!' Etc.*

GUARD. Stand back! Back, when you're told!

CONSTANTINE (*to himself*). At that very tense moment, a heart-stopping discovery.

The noises of confrontation suddenly cease, and there are gasps of awe and alarm.

ARCHITECT (*quiet voice, disturbed*). They found this, in the base of the trench, underneath the dead bodies. One of them must have uncovered it, just before the wall fell in . . .

CONSTANTINE (*to himself*). An ancient bronze slave-collar, very large, very heavy, very ominous . . . How to tell them it is not a most dangerous portent? (*He clears his throat for attention: and receives it.*) Ah, good people: this collar is a sign of – of the old slavery of the old world from which, by Christ, by your Christian emperor, we all of us, now, are liberated. As for the accident: an Imperial donation for all those injured and dependants of those killed. Funeral rites, Christian and old-religion, to be celebrated at your Emperor's expense. He is always glad to honour the endurance and courage of his faithful servants. Release the prisoners. May God protect Lord Constantine!

General applause. One of the WORKERS *starts a hymn and the* OTHERS *join in.*

WORKERS (*sing*).
>God, for Lord Constantine,
>Stretch out your long plumb-line,
>Make straight this city and its golden shrine:
>   Hallelujah!'

ARCHITECT (*genially*). All right, everyone, back to work!

PHYSCON (*astonished*). And by God, they're going! (*To* CONSTANTINE, *confidential again: as they move away.*) Sir, if I may say so, a most powerful piece of oratory. Quite changed what could have been a very nasty situation. Pity we can't have the likes of you as our Emperor. It's not the man himself, of course, causes all the discontent: but the family, oh dear. D'you know, only last week I paid good money down for a strong female slave, a Christian; the household was selling her, all open and above-board. When I go to Nicomedia to collect her, what do they tell me? She can't be found. Somebody somewhere inside that palace is running a bloody racket, don't you tell me . . .

Fade out.

Scene Ten

Exterior: the ruined town again. A tense silence, as MELANTHO *orates.*

MELANTHO (*not rodomontade: she is slowly getting hold of her theme and audience*).
This dead woman was Semiramis . . .

KYBELE (*as narrator: as* MELANTHO *continues*). Melantho spoke to us, phrase by
phrase, of how Semiramis, daughter of an enslaved daughter of a great family of
Palmyra, had turned Christian in Gaul through her friendship with the women of
the House of the True Way . . .

MELANTHO. . . . she had loved a Christian soldier, and their marriage was of
Christ . . .

KYBELE (*as narrator*). She was sold by the palace to a baker who made bad bread
for the workers upon the new city. Melantho told how Queen Zenobia declared
Palmyra independent of Empire, how her city had been destroyed and all her
people put in chains, how the Emperor's new city was a new Christian insult to the
memory of Palmyra; and finally how Semiramis, having heard . . .

MELANTHO. . . . having heard that she was to be handed over to the baker, this
woman died for love.

KYBELE (*as narrator*). The death of Palmyra, the death of Semiramis, slavery,
coercion, Imperial Christianity, all drawn together into the discourse: she was
listened to in complete silence, even the guards seemed over-awed.

A flute begins to play: a plaintive and repetitive series of notes, over and over again.

Melantho told us that the Great Mother, before whom nothing was, and after whom
nothing would be, had made death irrelevant. What we saw upon the bier was only
a pretence of death: the Mother for a space had taken Semiramis, and because of
her great love, would return her to those who had loved her; and all of us would
see it happen. There would be a sign.

MELANTHO. All in the sky together, a few short hours and you shall see them: the
sun and the moon and the morning star!

KYBELE (*as narrator*). We would all be the witnesses, even the Empress would be a
witness . . . were we to believe the woman in the veil was indeed the Lady Fausta?

MELANTHO. At the coming of the Divine Wisdom, no more death, no more
slavery, no more serfdom, no more taxation, no more warfare, no more starvation,
no more . . .

KYBELE (*as narrator*). The constant repetition of one tune upon the flute, rising
higher and higher, was affecting our brains, I think . . .

There is a murmur among the PEOPLE.

The crowd seemed to twist itself, agony of religious ecstasy: and I – I was tempted –
exhilarated, yet ashamed, my heart turned over – why, I was, I was yearning – for
some sort of salvation . . . I no longer knew whether I could credit what I saw . . .

MELANTHO (*a strong, clear announcement: almost sung*). With this emerald the
Lady Fausta saved the life of my child. And when you see the sign, my child will
restore the life of the Lady Fausta's beloved slave . . .!

KYBELE (*to herself: as the flute music wanders up out of hearing*). I think they all
saw what I saw, and yet it could not have been there. Between the curtains of the
stage, just above the angel-child, the rough-hewn planks of a phantom gallows-
cross, and a nailed, naked, bleeding man. Melantho said he was Christ, and yet that
he was not Christ; because the Mother does not demand any human-being be
tortured to death to save the world. Melantho said we saw this so we would know
the Prince of Darkness and never again be seduced by him. But one man, just in
front of me, the dark man with the unearthly eyes who had called out my name on
the march, he did seem to be seduced . . .

The murmurs of the CROWD *are growing, turning into ecstatic and anguished cries and groans.*

JAXARTES (*to himself, transported*). See how his eyes are calling me, his body stretched out to me – sweet pain into my body, I float, I stretch out my soul . . .

KYBELE (*to herself*). His limbs were whirling and threshing, soundless words out of his lips . . .

JAXARTES (*to himself*). Am I not Jaxartes, secret soul of the Emperor, to protect him from the East – and out of the East she has propelled this vision – am I to denounce it or to love it with my life? And why is the face upon the cross the face of the son of the Emperor – ? Crispus and not Christos, or rather Crispus who is Christos, first to die in all his beauty and then to rise again and who shall rise with him – ?

KYBELE (*as narrator*). His soundless words became one word, Crispus, Crispus, Crispus –

JAXARTES (*aloud*). – Crispus, Crispus – and who shall rise with him but me – ?

KYBELE (*as narrator*). He tore off his clothes from the red-hot glow of his outlandish turgid yard and thrust it forward toward the burdened cross – did no one else see him? But he saw that I'd seen him. From the look that he gave me I knew suddenly I had seen my death, but there was nothing I could do, the music, the vision, was fixing me to the ground. And then, the angel flew.

As she speaks the music has come back, excited tom-tom drums: this reaches a climax, and suddenly is stopped, to be replaced by a swooping string-music, harps or lyres, behind her next lines.

Oh many times had I seen a flying-ballet at the theatre: but there one was aware there were cords and a crane. I repeat: this angel flew. Like a fish in brilliant water, and we all swam alongside her . . . Only the veiled woman stood still: the stillness of a royal personage enduring hours of public protocol.

FAUSTA (*to herself*).
>In the time of the night when I was no
>   longer Empress
>But a desolate small woman, unrobed, alone,
>   and going to bed.
>Movement behind the hangings: I thought
>   it was a bird
>Caught there, rattling its wings to tell
>   me its distress –
>Let it free for pity's sake – !
>No bird but Semiramis: she trembled and shook,
>Held out to me a paper, not able to speak.
>Physcon the baker had been granted what
>   he sought:
>Next morning – Imperial order – he would
>   be there for her at the gate,
>She must be ready for him: her life was
>   at an end.
>She who had loved me when I was a child
>She who had loved me when Constantine
>   loved me
>She who had loved me even when Constantine
>Took out his eyes and put in the eyes of Christ:
>She was the last and she had been the first.
>I had given her my word and now I was foresworn.
>Oh I was wicked Eve, stripped in my shame,
>Not knowing which way to turn,

> How to hide from the spying eye of the
> > Emperor-god in the gloom
> Of the cold dark garden? How to hide
> From my only love who fluttered down dead
> > at my bed side . . .?

The drum-beat has returned and is added to the string-music. Cries, yelps, screams.

KYBELE (*as narrator*). Orgy, it became an orgy, heaven knows what we were celebrating, discarded garments tossed into the air, onto the ground, bare limbs hurtling through bonfires . . . Kybele, Kybele, were you part of all this or outside of it, which . . .?

The raucous drumming and audience-responses die away. In the silence, the song comes clear, pure, and sweet:

HELEN-FAUSTA (*singing*).
> > O Mary of Bethlehem, Mary of Bethany,
> > And all the other Marys and Magdalene Mary,
> > They came swinging incense and standing
> > > no nonsense
> > To claim the dead corpse of the true love
> > > of women.
>
> > From the very beginning when there was
> > > no beginning
> > To the ultimate finish when there is to
> > > be no finish
> > The boat on the water sails forward on
> > > the water
> > O is it a boat or is it a fish . . .?
>
> > O Mary of Bethlehem . . .! (*Etc.*)

The first verse is repeated and fades away as KYBELE *speaks:*

KYBELE (*to herself*). The gentle rainfall of the music lulled me quite asleep . . .

> *Cross-fade.*

Scene Eleven

Exterior: The same scene, after a lapse of time. Silence broken by murmurs, grunts, little movements, as though the PEOPLE *are all more or less asleep, but not quite.*

JAXARTES (*to himself, rousing himself*). Awake, awake, Jaxartes, the hypnosis is over . . .

KYBELE (*as narrator*). The hypnosis was over. Or so it seemed to be over. My rational mind, at least was refusing captivity. Not so with everyone else, a great garden of dead souls in the grey pale light before dawn . . . except for the man from whom the name of Kybele, from whom the name of Crispus, had stuttered forth like successive omens: a crouched vulture upon a battlefield, he moved among the stupefied people.

JAXARTES (*to himself, moving through the* CROWD). I am on duty, provocative agent, awake and on duty: and my duty is clear, no Crispus, Constantine: and Constantine's wife is a self-exposed catspaw for eastern conspiracy, for Persian conspiracy, and the Persian conspiracy is co-ordinating a coup – ! Where are my men – where – ?

He finds one of his MEN *and addresses him in a sharp whisper.*

JAXARTES. You there, awake awake – cock-a-doodle-doo –

AGENT (*dopily coming to his senses*). Eh – ? Ah – ? Sir! Receiving orders, as per order, sir – !

JAXARTES (*hissing at him, and then whispering again*). Ssh! All our men together, wake 'em up, move – !

AGENT (*not totally comprehending*). But don't we have to wait – the sun and the moon and the morning star, she said 'wait' – ?

JAXARTES (*with intensity*). She is no longer in control of you: nor of me, nor of me – I am in control, and when I blow my whistle –

AGENT (*repeating as by rote*). When the Colonel blows his whistle, move in and arrest everyone.

JAXARTES. Everyone, everyone: and one in particular, grey gown of a philosopher, and the eyes of a lecherous rabbit, impossible to miss her, she is to be killed, Kybele to be killed.

AGENT (*still as by rote*). Kybele to be killed.

KYBELE (*as narrator*). His bleared underling came stumbling through the mist in my direction, stumbling right past me, repeating his orders, Kybele to be killed.

AGENT. Kybele, killed, killed . . .

KYBELE (*as narrator*). Impossible just then to escape unnoticed, I must wait upon events and choose my moment.

Cross-fade.

Scene Twelve

Exterior: The same, after a short lapse of time. PEOPLE *waking up.*

MELANTHO (*speaking in a low level voice*). Between night and day the silence, between night and day the moment of choice. Empress Fausta made her choice when she gave the sign to Constantine –
    The Cross of light against the sky
    To burn his head and dazzle out his eye –
And he took it and stole it for his own, saying, I am the jealous god: if there be any other, let it appear.

JAXARTES (*as narrator*). I saw and I heard. Total enveloping silence, and then: such a pale thin light of dawn, pale and thin the horned moon, pale yellow the uncertain sun: and also, one pale pinprick of light, neither moon nor sun, but –

MELANTHO. The morning star!

JAXARTES (*as narrator*). The emeralds upon the corpse glowed, gleamed and dazzled, the angel-child stretched out her finger –

HELEN-FAUSTA. The Lady of Wisdom, who is the mother of all things living, stretched forth her finger and put light into matter and life into the clay of death –

There is a cry as of a NEW-BORN BABY. *Then a great gasp from the* CROWD.

JAXARTES (*as narrator*). I heard and I saw: a whole thousand of weary people lift up their sudden voices and cry for Fausta, Empress! The veiled woman threw back her veil: all could see that she was who she was . . .

The gasp of the CROWD *has turned into a cry, which becomes a rhythmic acclamation:* 'Faust-A, Faust-A, Fausta imperatrix!'

JAXARTES (*speaking to himself*). Now is the moment, *now* - !

He blows a blast on his whistle. There is a rush of booted feet, cries, yells, screams, PEOPLE *falling over each other, running away, roaring in agony.*

Scene Thirteen

Exterior: the same. The sound effects fade away behind KYBELE*'s speech, gradually, as a sound of rising wind grows up, and then flames.*

KYBELE (*as narrator*). Today in Hibernia I am accused of false pretences when I call myself philosopher. If ever that has been true, it was true upon that strange sunrise when the whistle blew, the armed guards came surging into the market-place, spears out, swords out, people hemmed against barricades: God knows how the fire started, but the thatch of a hutment was burning, the wind blew the blazing straw, all around us a wall of flame, the soldiers lost their discipline, sword-blades no longer a threat but a bloody fact – oh calm-hearted Epicurus, where was our acceptance of death? Did your disciple Kybele sit down and gently contemplate the reintegration of natural atomic structure? Did she even try to save the lives of any of those on either side of her? Or did she think only that all this horror had been commanded by one who had read her letters and so pursued her to the ends of the earth?

No sound now but the wind; and her feet running through rough country, her breath gasping.

Scorched, torn, blinded, I got out, I don't know how far, to a little slope beyond the ridge of hills, collapsed upon my knees, vomited like a dog (*She retches.*)

Then silence, save for the wind.

DION (*his voice travelling from a considerable distance; he is hysterical*). Homoi-ousios, homo-ousios, homo-homoi, iota, 'i', one small vowel of all the alphabet and the blood is on the swords and the fire is in the rooftree, and those of us who spoke the word abroad open to all the world are now to be driven into gutter-pipes into warrens into catacombs once again, look at me, look at me, I had to burrow my way out and every inch of my skin is bleeding.

KYBELE (*as narrator*). Even at a distance I knew who it was. Dion of Antioch, long time ago my fellow-student, until he turned Christian and adhered to the school of Arius. He was down below me in a valley at the edge of a main road where a long line of farm-carts was waiting to be passed-on to Nicaea through a military check-point. Behind them, a government carriage, bearing the monograms of the Province of Britain and the Christian church. Dion's words were to its passenger, white robes – yet another bishop? – who sat on a tussock of grass, tenderly wiping the face of a third man, half-conscious, sprawled across his knees. I moved carefully down towards them: Christians . . .? No, I could not trust . . .

She moves slowly among the undergrowth, nearing the BISHOP*'s voice.*

BISHOP OF LONDON (*a youngish, warm-voiced man, with a 'Welsh' accent*) If all this has happened, only one thing I can do, turn my horses right about here and now! Heaven above, I myself would have been part of this vindictive council had I got to Nicaea in time, had the storms along the seacoast of Gaul abated a few days sooner.

We are now close enough to hear the groans of the wounded MAN, *and the fidgeting of the coach-horses.*

And who can say for whom I'd have voted? Lord Jesus I don't know more than two words of Greek, homoi-ousios isn't one of 'em, I can tell you. If Imperial theology means nothing but murder, high time the Bishop of London returned to his original scripture, and for preference among his own people. This poor devil is Hibernian, I can tell from his embroidered coat. Whatever he's doing here, my job is to see him home again. And yourself, where are you going?

DION (*wildly*). Outer darkness, wherever else? Don't you know: I am anathema?

BISHOP (*reassuringly*). Not in my coach: I have a travel-warrant. Don't I tell you, I don't speak Greek? Here, help me lift him in, unfortunate stranger, that he ever set his foot into this ill-omened empire.

They lift the man into the coach.

KYBELE (*as narrator*). No, I could not trust: but I had no choice but take the risk. I moved cautiously towards him –

Her steps running the last few yards.

(*She calls aloud.*) Dion, Dion, don't you know me? – Dion, help me – get me out of here – !

BISHOP. Do you know her?

DION (*dully*). Yes I do.

BISHOP (*resignedly*). Must we take her?

DION. I think we have to.

BISHOP (*quirkily*). Do I remember the Good Samaritan? Or do I remember I am more Briton than Roman? Whichever, and be damned to all of 'em, in the name of Our Saviour, she can come.

They get her into the coach, the door slams, the horses start up. Sounds of coach hurrying on behind KYBELE'*s speech.*

KYBELE (*as narrator*). Nightmare journey, fever, delirium, day after day, no knowledge how long it took, odd shifting passages of argument in and out of my comprehension, between Dion and Bishop, Dion maintaining religious doctrine had nothing to do with it, persecution now directed against all forms of rational thought –

DION (*still highly excited, as the coach speeds along*). They will exterminate us all, you, me, her, even this wild heathen here that has not a word of our language –

BISHOP OF LONDON (*nearly as excited*). No no, you forget I have very many words of his, if he and the lady were in fit condition, we could all by interpretation learn so much of his country.

The HIBERNIAN *groans now and then, and mutters unintelligibly.*

I would never call Hibernia wild: traditional, that is all; out-of-Empire, that is all – by God they are to be envied for it! [And I tell you these police-dealings are by no means indiscriminate. Consolidation of central power: by intelligent calculation they have to be resisted! You allow them to drive you mad – why, man, you are as big a fool as they would wish you, think of that!]

KYBELE (*as narrator: as sound effects shift to illustrate her statement*). And then at some customs-house high up in Macedonia, Dion was struggling to get out of the coach, and the Bishop held him back –

The coach has stopped. The two MEN *are struggling.*

BISHOP (*urgently but not loudly*). No no no, this is not a safe place, will you look at all the soldiers – !

DION (*also urgently, not quite so discreetly quiet*). That road to the north leads to Arius in his exile, I must follow it, I must join with him –

He is free, and out of the coach onto the ground: he slams the door and the DRIVER *starts the horses up again, slowly.*

DION. – farewell – !

KYBELE (*as narrator*). We saw him in dispute with the Corporal of the guard, saw him try to run –

An angry cry from the CORPORAL – *at some distance.*

– saw at once a hurled javelin that struck him between the shoulder-blades.

DION (*gives a scream*).

The COACHMAN *immediately whips up the horses to a gallop.*

KYBELE. After that, onward, onward, and the Hibernian crying out – as the Bishop explained to me – that his brother was dead in the massacre, all his powers were departed, and where were his beautiful wolf hounds, he had left them at Naples for the dead poet and the poet had eaten them –

The HIBERNIAN *is gibbering too fast even for his language to be made out by us.*

All he wanted to do was to go alone into a forest to heal himself from this curse [and why would not the Bishop permit it – ?

The gibbering slows down to an odd moan at intervals. The coach is now travelling more slowly as well.

BISHOP OF LONDON (*in a more reflective tone than earlier*). In Britain I would: but here his life depends on my being close beside him. I cannot assist his sorceries, however well-intended.] Mind you, he's a potent man, Chief Druid of Armagh, if I can help him home, our few Christian among the Irish will assuredly reap the benefit. Between Britain and Ireland we bridge the bound of Empire: we have our own Christianity, not yet tainted by coercion. Pelagians, they call us, meaning 'Christians-beyond-the-sea': [arguably our remoteness, our nearness to nature, to certain ancient wisdoms, makes us that much more receptive. No accident that Nero Caesar tried to kill every druid in the island . . .]

The noise of the rolling coach fades away: and we hear the wind in tree-tops and birds singing.

KYBELE (*as narrator*). In northern Gaul the Bishop of London left us: he had clergymen to consult. He told me Hibernia was my best hope of safe refuge, gave me a letter to his friends there: and the druid saw me take it. [he saw me: he ground his teeth at me: and then he and I made our way to the woodland hermitage of two old women, Irish Christians, upon the seacoast. the Bishop told us they knew every discreet shipmaster trading out into the western ocean . . .] From then on I had no part in Constantine's empire. For what happened near Nicaea just after my escape, and for all the deadly consequence, I can only make assumption. Let us assume that Jaxartes went at once to meet his master . . .

Scene Fourteen

Exterior: wind blowing. A galloping horse approaching from far away.

JAXARTES (*to himself*). He rode out alone, he'll ride back alone. On the edge of the road, wait for him, leap out upon him, stop him –

The horse comes nearer and nearer. JAXARTES *shouts to halt it.*

JAXARTES. Emperor!

The horse is pulled up, violently.

CONSTANTINE (*astonished and alarmed*). You . . .! Jaxartes?

JAXARTES. Who else?

CONSTANTINE (*shaken for a moment, but recovering himself*). I thought for a moment, you were – you were –

JAXARTES (*to himself*). So I tell him, tell him all of it . . . How we search and we search in the ashes and ruins, and among all the corpses not one corpse that we want. No conceivable escape from the catastrophe of that town, and yet they have vanished. I might have been talking to his face upon the coinage. (*Aloud: very urgently.*) Emperor, there is only one place they could possibly flee to. Persia. Emperor, bring her back, we have to bring her back, She has with her the flying child: she says, her child.

CONSTANTINE (*confused*). Who says? Whose child?

JAXARTES. Sir I have explained, it was the –

CONSTANTINE (*contemptuously*). The woman in the veil whose face you did not see for more than a moment. And so you don't know who she was.

JAXARTES (*insisting*). Emperor, the name of the child.

CONSTANTINE. Ah yes, it had a name.

JAXARTES. Helen-Fausta.

CONSTANTINE (*brooding*). So you said. It had a name. And: 'The Anointed One': it had that name.

JAXARTES. So what are my orders?

CONSTANTINE (*cold*). For you, there are no orders. For your successor, there will be. No doubt. Without doubt.

JAXARTES (*taken aback*). My successor? You mean – ?

CONSTANTINE (*savage*). Yes: you are abolished. And if you, or any of your men, dare speak to anyone about this – this hallucination, you will also be dead.

He urges his horse and gallops swiftly away.

JAXARTES (*bitterly, to himself*). Constantine Emperor, from this day, *you* are dead. I am not abolished, my service is not complete. Christos, my lord and my love, conveys me now to – Crispus, Caesar and General . . . Begotten and not made, of like substance with the father . . .

Scene Fifteen

Exterior: the horse galloping.

CONSTANTINE (*to himself as he rides*). They grapple with me, throat chokes, huge python serpent, python of Delphi put to death by Phoebus Apollo, cold clinging stifling as a slave-collar of antique bronze . . .

'PAUL OF TARSUS'. Don't let it stifle your voice. Yours is the voice. The world waits for it.

Suggestion of a second horse, as in earlier sequence.

CONSTANTINE: I ride in company? Yet again? Yet again?

'PAUL OF TARSUS'. Enmity, enmity, from serpent and woman, to seed of the serpent and seed of the woman . . .

CONSTANTINE. Seed?

'PAUL OF TARSUS'. Search diligently for the young child, and when ye have found her, bring me word again . . .

CONSTANTINE. Word? That I may come and worship her also . . .? In Rama a voice heard, Rachel weeping for her children, and would not be comforted, because they –

'PAUL OF TARSUS'. Because they were not, because they were not, because they were not . . .

Scene Sixteen

Interior: CONSTANTINE *striding through corridors and rooms, flinging open one door after another: a scurry of* PEOPLE *in his wake.*

CONSTANTINE (*to himself*). They were not in the palace, they were not in the court of the palace, they were not in the rooms of the palace, they were not in the corridors – (*Aloud to the attendants, in a frenzy:*) Where, where, where is the Lady Fausta?

SLAVE-WOMAN. Lord, she is in her bath-house, she is alone –

CONSTANTINE. Alone – ?

SLAVE-WOMAN. She prepares for the grand banquet –

CONSTANTINE. Bath-house –

He strides on, flinging more doors open until he comes to the bath-house. He shuts this one behind him.

Bath-house – filled with steam – and in the steam – no one – except – who is that? Fausta, is that you?

'PAUL OF TARSUS'. No, but under the water. She is a fish, she is a water-snake, she dives down deep.

A troubling of the water in the pool followed by the sound of a body emerging from it, though not actually getting out of the pool itself.

CONSTANTINE (*after a pause*). Where is your slave Semiramis?

FAUSTA (*deadpan, from in the water*). While you were at Christ's great council, she fell ill and she died.

CONSTANTINE. She died? She died dead?

FAUSTA. Dead: and she is buried.

The water stirs again as if FAUSTA *is swimming away.*

CONSTANTINE. Then where is the flying child – ?

FAUSTA (*moving away*). Who? Where is who?

Her last word is cut off as she goes under the surface.

'PAUL OF TARSUS'. If you would seek an angel, look first for the water that is troubled in the pool: for an angel gone down deep or a demon gone down deep will never come up any more . . .

A troubling of the water.

Fade.

Closing music.

8

INTERROGATIONS

Scene One

Opening music

KYBELE* (*as narrator*). The Druid and I were both half-mad when we came to the old women's cottage in Gaul. Understand, they were Christians, daughters of an Irish chieftain by his slave-woman; so slaves themselves. A refugee into Hibernia, from persecution in Egypt, had caused them to give their souls to Christ: a gift which the druids denounced as robbing the slave-owner of the souls of his people. Violation of custom. They must be forced to give up their god, or be sold overseas. They chose exile. They were bought by a Christian farmer in Gaul, who in his old age offered them their freedom. They said, freedom for one is nothing, unless it is freedom for all: and they refused. Just so the Empress Fausta offered freedom to her slave, and the slave refused. And therefore Fausta, amid all the contortions of the new Christianity, interrogations, trial – who owns Fausta? – passions of heart in conflict with systems of law: her husband who so yearned for her nonetheless had her confined, in a secret set of rooms in his palace of Nicomedia . . .

Scene Two

Interior: a small room with a dull echo.

FAUSTA. I am not to see my children. I am not to know where I am. Nor how long I am kept here, behind windows so closely shuttered, with no one but deaf-mutes. And why, when you come, do you just ask me the same question? Suppose this time I ask it for you? 'Fausta, your slave Semiramis; where is she?' And so I answer: 'Emperor, I have told you, she is dead, and she is buried. Your baker cannot have her, however much he makes a fool of you.' And now, you will go, until next week?

CONSTANTINE (*after a lengthy pause*). Semiramis is not buried.

KYBELE (*as narrator*). Semiramis was safe . . . With Melantho and the child Helen-Fausta, she had crossed into the disputed province beyond the Euphrates. The great trade-fair at Batnae: they were met by Melantho's mother, Oenothea, the priestess, who now lived in Ur of the Chaldees, under protection of the King of Persia.

Scene Three

Exterior: A crowded bazaar with all appropriate sounds, brought up behind KYBELE's narrative.

OENOTHEA. For Semiramis, her man Joachim has been found. Deep in the Arabian desert in the service of his god. A caravan of pilgrims is going there tomorrow. The camel-master has been notified you are to be of the party. Leave the child with me – she will be safe. When you return, you will know the shape of your future . . .

Fade out bazaar effects.

KYBELE (*as narrator*). [Perhaps she did: but let me tell you, when I and the Druid came into Gaul we did not at all know the shape of ours. Although the two old women spoke the Druid's language, none of us belonged to each other.]
    Grimonia and Proba healed the pains of our bodies, they held and comforted me, [even though I was cautious to give my trust yet again to women of their religion.] They made Christian prayers for Dion, which was natural; for the Druid's brother,

---

* This speech was condensed for recording.

which was generous [and gratuitous:] and for myself they lit a candle; when I said it was for Epicurus they did not refute it. They accepted him as it were a saint of their own god. All my hardness disappeared: and the Druid's increased. I lay in my sickbed and watched him. I could see that he hated us: he should have had his own observances, alone, in the forest; but impossible, he said a curse was fetched onto him by the women, in that they were Hibernian, and they were Christian, and they were slaves. And then by me, in that I was day by day succumbing to their gentle kindness and receiving them as friends, [though even to me their self-retained slavery was a very great confusion]. And then the day came that I rose from my bed and joined in the women's prayers; I did not believe, but I joined. Also I showed them a letter, from the British Bishop to his Hibernian friends; did not think to tell the Druid what it said, nor that he was a philosopher to whom respect of all letters was due. Next day I went out into the forest. When I returned, Proba and Grimonia were dead. Their fragile little bodies head down in the cauldron of simmering herbs upon the fire. The Druid was gone. And I did nothing, but run run run to the seacoast, and there was the Hibernian ship that Proba and Grimonia had told me to expect, and here I am in Hibernia; [and here, twelve years afterwards, is the Druid to make his claim against me. Oh, I beg you, before you decide, let me tell you what happened to Fausta . . .]

Scene Four

Interior: as Scene Two.

CONSTANTINE. Fausta, we have opened the grave: the slave is not there.

FAUSTA. You are the Emperor, you make the laws, you know all the laws, where is the law tells me that the mistress of the slave is responsible for the slave's dead body?

CONSTANTINE (*speaking heavily, in an attempt to be persuasive*). I do not extort confession. All I want is the truth. You alone can give ease to my mind. Don't you remember, you were twelve years old, in the residency in Gaul, such great danger lurking and you put a name to it. Herculius, your father, you told me he sought my life; he was the one that died. You betrayed him for love of me. And once again you gave me life, you prepared me for the vision of the Cross, before it came: I was ready for it, understood it, and so I was sole Emperor.

Fausta, it can not be possible you mean to take away the life you gave? Fausta, for the love of whom? My mother says you ran away with your slave out of sapphic lust: Physcon the baker says that your slave was his: Colonel Jaxartes, state-security, he says – says – I can only believe that the Colonel was unhinged by – by the horror of a sudden bloodshed . . .

FAUSTA. So you believe him. Your own mind, unhinged, tilts helplessly toward horror. Of course you believe.

CONSTANTINE. No no – I do not – I must not, I believe only my little true watchdog who gave me life when she was a child.

He is appealing to her now with an unashamed attempt at sexual seduction.

Shall you sit with me, so: just the same after all these years, once again my two large arms to encompass your ungrown breasts, and no one shall ever know what truth you will be telling me . . .?

FAUSTA (*by no means averse to sexuality, but determined it shall be realistic*). Husband, my breasts are grown and they have already fed five children . . . Truth of a woman, not of a girl . . . if that is what you want . . .?

CONSTANTINE (*breaking away from her: he cannot accept this*). Whether I want it or not, don't you see I must not have it! Fausta, just one moment . . . when my father was still alive, and I was, you might say, a cadet officer on his staff –

FAUSTA (*prepared to be playful still*). Apprentice Emperor, that's what you were.

CONSTANTINE (*nothing playful about his memory*). He found out I had been taken by my friends, to – they called it a 'singsong house'. They thought I was being too – too carefully educated . . . D'you know what he said?

FAUSTA. I can guess. He said, 'Don't give yourself. Those women are there to give themselves to you, and you pay them with money, not with your life.'

CONSTANTINE (*in distress*). So why could I not say to him, he took my mother out of such a house? And so therefore, the mother of Crispus . . . Fausta, where do you think my first wife came from?

FAUSTA (*casually*). Why of course, I know that.

CONSTANTINE (*ignoring her answer and talking over it*). The same age as I was, a year or two older, perhaps, I had given myself to her: and he told me I was wrong. Too late: I did not believe him. I defied him, kept her with me. But when he was dead, I must make terms with your father –

FAUSTA. And your marriage to me was part of the treaty. Then was the time you did pay her with money: you gave her a pension, you sent her away, how many years too late? Which is why you believe your unhinged Colonel when he says –

CONSTANTINE (*sharply*). So you do know what he said?

FAUSTA. I can guess. It needs no witchcraft.

CONSTANTINE (*forcefully*). You mention witchcraft, not me. You have been engaged in magic, or you stood beside someone who was: and she –

FAUSTA (*scornful*). Did she cut entrails out of dead animals and observe in them the future? Because you do that in the name of god. In the name of another god wine is drunk and bread is eaten and you call it blood and flesh – and nobody's practising magic? Flesh and blood three days in the rotten grave, and out it comes alive, and still there is no magic? Oh, Constantine, husband, great big lump of a loveless boy, hesitating at the whorehouse door: you can believe anything, and they will still proclaim you Emperor! When you needed to believe, you believed even what *I* told you, a queer little girl unhinged by the brutality of her father. But when I, for my own need, Constantine, most desperate need for a magic, here, now, and outside of the magic of Christ – when I did what I did – accusation at once, witchcraft, unnatural lust, conspiracy –

CONSTANTINE (*shouting*). I did not accuse, I said nothing of conspiracy, I – (*He abruptly changes tone to a police-interrogator's harshness.*) Fausta, at command of the negro-witch Melantho, did your slave-woman come out of death alive or did she not?

FAUSTA (*quick retort*). Did Jesus or did he not?

CONSTANTINE (*ignoring the retort*). Then where is her body?

FAUSTA (*enjoying herself*). Where is his?

CONSTANTINE (*refusing to be diverted*). She is your legal property –

FAUSTA. If she died and rose again? How can she be? When her life stopped, my ownership ceased to exist.

CONSTANTINE (*losing patience*). We are Emperor of Rome, we are not an Attorney, and therefore as Emperor, we put one precise question. You will answer it 'yes' or 'no'. When the sun and the moon and the morning star all appeared in the sky together, did you hear the crowd shout for you, 'Sole Empress of Rome and Persia'?

FAUSTA. Did you hear your regiments shouting for you, when the Cross of Light was in the sky?

CONSTANTINE. Let it be recorded, the respondent refused answer. Let it therefore be recorded, her present seclusion is to continue indefinitely without access to her children.

FAUSTA (*as formal as he is*). Emperor, I have no children. I received them, enclosed them, they came forth; passed through me as oil is run through an olive-press; and then they were yours. You have said it: in your own church, begotten not made. Lord husband, I have one child, and no more than only one: her name is Helen-Fausta, she is made not begotten, and there is no man in this world or the further world to whom she is – subsequent.

CONSTANTINE *gets up, strides to the door, opens it, goes out, shuts it sharply behind him, and turns the key.*

Scene Five

Exterior: a garden, bird-song, etc. CONSTANTINE's *footfalls continuous from preceding episode.*

CONSTANTINE (*pacing about – to himself*).
> Let it be recorded, the respondent refused
> > answer.
> Let it be recorded, her husband, judge,
> > and Emperor
> Made no furious threat
> But quietly walked out
> Into his own secluded garden-yard
> Out of sight even of his own guard –

(*He calls out:*) Are you there within call?

GUARD (*from a little distance*). In call, my lord, behind the wall.

CONSTANTINE. So stay there till I call again.
(*To himself:*)
> Let it be recorded, the Emperor felt
> > no pain
> That his brave wife should have denied
> His own children to his face,
> No pain, but
> Consider the facts
> Till we know what must be done:

(*Aloud:*) You there, behind the wall – The Great King of Persia, how old is he, d'you remember?

GUARD (*from a distance*). Lord, he will be seventeen at the end of November.

CONSTANTINE (*to himself*).
> When I was seventeen, I was destined
> > already Co-Emperor's Co-Emperor –
> When I was eighteen I was commanding
> > my own war . . .

And already this boy of Persia is persecuting Christians, to provoke me in their defence, to lure my army into his deserts,
> – To utterly destroy our eastern Roman power
> As other Persian Kings have destroyed
> > it before –
> My immediate necessity, destroy him and
> > yet make
> No more endless dangerous war –

> Craft and silence to destroy him by
> > political design –
> Design of political religion – said
> > Constantine –
> Sole course of action and that action
> > shall be mine –
> Clap my hands, pace up and down –

He smacks his palms together to encourage the working of his thought.

> How can Fausta's foolish treachery contribute
> > to this plan . . . ?
> Seek and find within religion, and God
> > will give a sign.
> Why, he has already given it!
> Helen-Fausta, Semiramis, the old Palmyran
> > line
> Of Persian-born Zenobia, I have it in
> > my hand – !
> Let me think, let me think – I have expelled
> > out of the land –

since the Council of Nicaea, so many thousand heretic Christians: and in Persia the
heathen clergy of Zoroaster have reformed their own doctrine, expelled their own
heretics, creating between the Empires a vast confused mingling of refugee
dissidents, and where have most of them gone – ? The five disputed provinces,
debatable between me and Persia, giving allegiance neither to me nor him so to
whom *would* they give allegiance? Suppose, a triad of females: Fausta, of Rome and
the west. Melantho, of Babylon and the east.
Semiramis of Palmrya in between . . .

He paces more rapidly, chewing his words and ideas with gathering excitement.

> And between them they shall share
> Angel-child Helen-Fausta their anointed
> > magic Queen –
> Do not believe she will be the only heir –
> Three young sons of me and Fausta,
> Let her deny them or not –
> It is now myself, not her, manipulates
> > her subversive plot –
> I will bind my sons so tight
> From me to her, from here to there,
> That once she is in place, Persia cannot
> > pull her nearer,
> No, not by the length of her beautiful
> > hair . . .
> Yes yes, a third force and in the
> > end it will roll

complete with its new religion into the hands of me and my sons – my other son
Crispus keeps himself clear, controls the west, necessary therefore I disabuse him of
the idea he is to be made an equal Augustus with me, not yet, not just yet – we
keep his role, as it were – hidden, even from himself. Likewise, my sister
Constantia: her function to conciliate the irreconciled friends of Arius, while I deal
with the orthodox clergy, which I can, I am an Apostle . . . and my mother will
help me –

> For out of all this *she* uncovered the
> > root,
> Setting Christ upon his cross where three
> > roads met,

And yet the face of Venus she could not
 trample under foot.
If that was not God's omen
I have lost all the love of women,
Which can not be possible, for why does
 my blood so tremble
At thought of Fausta at last made obedient
 meek and humble
When she takes from my desire
So great a gift of power,
When I shall give life
To my life-giving wife . . . ?

But not until the Jubilee. Keep everything as it is until I make announcement, in
Rome, upon my Jubilee. And first of course Jaxartes must seek and find Semiramis,
Melantho – and the child. Immediate edict, immunity to all informers, someone
must know something of where they have hidden themselves . . . But where is
Jaxartes, where has *he* hidden himself, by God I can do nothing without him . . . !

This last line is a dreadful bathos: he sounds all of a sudden completely collapsed.

'PAUL OF TARSUS'. All your flank so black with blood. For kicking, kicking,
against the goad?

CONSTANTINE (*in a rage*).
 You again? The man of Tarsus?
 I thought I left you where you lodge
 Catching hold of travellers as you yourself
  were caught
 In a highwayman's ambush, haunting the
  edge
 Of the thoroughfare –
 Road to Damascus, road to Byzantium,
  and now you corner me here . . . !
 Don't you think I have not read
 Your tendentious correspondence
 To Galatians, Corinthians,
 Colossians, Thessalonians,
 Purporting the inevitable psychological
  triumph
 Of that enormous unprovable client
 For whom you so mercilessly plead?
 Let him – if he can – pretend
 That in his father's house
 There are so many mansions
 That I cannot lend
 Him but one widow's mite, the tiniest
  portion
 Of my crafty political help
 To let him fill them up,
 According to his pledged desire,
 With the maimed and the poor
 The halt and the blind – !

'PAUL OF TARSUS'. I should call to your mind
 The twist at the end of that story:
 A certain chancer came to table
 Who claimed he was not able
 To wear the white and proper garment
 For the wedding of the Lord.
 Many are called but few are chosen

To participate in glory:
Those who slide back receive the uttermost
     fury,
Weeping and gnashing of teeth,
Darkness and death.

CONSTANTINE. And who said that? He did, or you?

'PAUL OF TARSUS'   You will find it in the gospel-book,
Turn the pages, take a look,
You'll find it in Matthew, find it in Luke.

CONSTANTINE (*cunning*). No. Luke says nothing about the guest with no garment. Luke says when a man sits down in the lowest place, the ruler of the feast says, 'Friend, go up higher'. I crouched in the Council on the smallest stool in the room, and that is why they made me the Thirteenth Apostle! I and I alone can reconcile every shape and size of man-Christ and woman-Christ who so contort the truth of the world! When you made your Christ, Luke and Matthew had written nothing. I have had these books examined by the best scholars in my Empire, in every page they discover the evidence has been tortuously edited to make it fit the affidavit already presented by you, to a packed jury: and who did the packing? You did. Bed of Procrustes, if there's not enough, then add a bit in: if there's too much, then cut it out and be damned.
What is cut will not be missed:
What is not missed cannot be hissed.
Why, my teacher of rhetoric told me that when I was twelve!

Fade.

Scene Six

KYBELE (*as narrator*). Constantine's new Grand Design did indeed need Jaxartes, but the ex-Director of the Secret Service had defected, in pursuit of his own Grand Design. Where Constantine's deranged mysticism thrust him towards female power, Jaxartes was consumed by a transcendental longing for masculine divinity in the shape of Crispus, the Emperor's beautiful son. All along the German frontier he was unable to find him, until he got to Ratisbon, divisional headquarters, where a nerve-racked General Officer at last gave him definite news –

Interior: a room in a military barrack, with parade-ground noises heard at a little distance.

JAXARTES (*in some surprise*). Over the Danube?

The same German GENERAL we have met in Part One.

GENERAL. Far too far over. Five, six days' march into the Bohemian forest, and all he's taken with him is two cohorts and a screen of scouts.

JAXARTES (*worried at the prospect*). If he's moved into the forest I have no choice but to follow him.

GENERAL. You will find it a perilous journey. Are you familiar with these districts? No? In one year, Crispus Caesar has taught himself more about we Germans, friendly and hostile, than I think his distinguished father could learn in a whole lifetime. And *he*, do not forget, was the best we had had since Trajan.

JAXARTES. The Emperor will be glad you have spoken so warmly.

GENERAL (*bitterly*). Will he? If he is glad for the achievement of his son, who now faces for him such great dangers, there will be some in this army most pleasantly surprised. Colonel, I speak direct. I am a straight man. You go to Crispus: see for yourself. And then tell them, on the shores of Bosporus, in the midst of their theology.

Fade.

Scene Seven

Interior.

KYBELE (*as narrator*). Helen the Dowager-Empress believed that her holy-woman, Mary, had connived at the disappearance of Semiramis: she could get nothing out of her and turned her over to Bishop Hosius. Hosius was heavily occupied with the aftermath of the Council: he turned her over to his confidential man Eumolpus, who uncovered – to his own satisfaction – a most monstrous anti-Christian plot.

EUMOLPUS (*very excited*). All we need is her confession, Bishop, and now that the Imperial government is enabled to act on our behalf against heretics –

HOSIUS (*worried*). The Emperor does not wish to concern himself with heresy every day of the week, Eumolpus: this council has been more than sufficient to –

EUMOLPUS (*disregarding him*). She propagated heathen sorcery under the cover of Christian doctrine, she incited as her accomplice the witch-woman Melantho, to corrupt the Empress Fausta –

HOSIUS (*in great alarm*). What – ?

EUMOLPUS (*disregarding him*). – and to entice away the slave Semiramis, a Christian – from her Christian husband.

HOSIUS. I hope you can prove this, Eumolpus, because if not –

EUMOLPUS. It will be proved: by the intercourse of Mary with Melantho in the prison of Antioch: and – prior to that – by Mary having given to the Empress and interpreted for her an heretical text – here it is: 'After the seventh day, the Lady of Wisdom sent her daughter who is called Eve as an instructor to raise up Adam'.

HOSIUS. Let me see . . .

Paper passed over.

I don't believe a word of this. Have you evidence she passed this text personally?

EUMOLPUS. Once she has confessed there will of course be ample evidence. I will scourge her yet again and then –

HOSIUS (*enraged*). Scourge? You have scourged her? By whose authority did you dare to –

EUMOLPUS. By whose authority was she admitted into this palace?

HOSIUS (*disconcerted*). Why – of course – by mine: as a very holy woman who –

EUMOLPUS. – who will confess. And when she has confessed, who will be blamed for bringing her here?

HOSIUS *makes a hopeless little noise*.

EUMOLPUS (*pauses a second to let him realise his predicament*). As for scourging, if she is innocent, she cannot be more innocent than Our Lord was when he was scourged. Come: she is in the cellar.

Scene Eight

Interior: an underground room.

MARY *gives a moan*.

EUMOLPUS. The Bishop is with me today to hear whether yours or Lucifer's is the voice that this whip shall drag from your suffering flesh.

We do not hear the flogging itself, MARY'*s thoughts come against a background of her thumping heart-beats*.

MARY (*to herself*). I knew this, had had it done to me, [the heathen Romans did it in
the days before Constantine: I had withstood it then, I had strength to withstand it
now. But it had been done] often before to me by heathen men, as to Jesus by
heathen men. Whereas this time it was no punishment but an act of love, to test my
faith: [and I pledged to Eumolpus I was ready to be tested.] But why must he ask
me questions? Jesus Christ was asked no questions: [ah no, they had such mercy as
to leave him alone with his pain. And then, he was God, omnipotent God, he
would have known the answers.] Out of all the words Eumolpus threw at me as he
whipped me and whipped me and whipped, I clutched on to only one, the only one
that would help me – (*Aloud, gasping with pain*:) Mother – yes, Mother. We did
give prayers to Mother.

EUMOLPUS (*rapidly*). Mother of God or Mother of All Living –?

MARY. Why, yes, of course, yes –

A merciless follow-up of the questions.

EUMOLPUS. Or Mother the Blue Hag of Death –?

MARY (*totally confused*). Why no, I did not mean –

Her expostulations collapse as she collapses.

EUMOLPUS (*with savage condemnation*). First she says yes, then she says no: she has
convicted herself of her own false witness. And upon that, we leave her: let her
kneel in her own blood.

The two sets of feet walk out of the room and the door is slammed and bolted.

Scene Nine

Interior: Continuous from the previous scene. In the passage of the cellarage.

HOSIUS (*appalled*). Voluptuous lust from the infliction of pain. You deliberately
confused her! Between words and blows, you –

EUMOLPUS (*quite unabashed and self-satisfied*). Were she really a woman of Christ
she would have been silent as Christ. She intended to pretend that she was. And I
outwitted her. For three hours I prayed for guidance before determining this test. I
read over and over again the records of the interrogation of the Valentinian
heretics: they held every church official to be possessed by the Father of Lies, so
every form of falsehood was to them permissable truth. And yet they broke down,
and submitted. I followed the same format: behold my success.

HOSIUS. Good heavens, what success? Eumolpus, we have learned nothing.

EUMOLPUS (*patient with* HOSIUS's *obtuseness*). We have confirmed our supposition
that she is probably diabolic. Now we must discover to what precise end. She
provided Fausta with the text, it sets the Great Mother up above God the Father.
Mary's name is in the margin, it was found by Lady Helen: among Fausta's
belongings. The very day she found it, Fausta had been present at Melantho's
alleged miracle.
[Don't tell me there is no connection. What we do not know is which heretical
party extruded the text in the first place.] I think it is up to you to make the next
move. Compassion, I think, the emotion you should imply.

HOSIUS (*coldly*). Imply? I will state it: it will be true.

Scene Ten

Interior: MARY's *cell again. Fade up* HOSIUS *attending to her, gently.*

HOSIUS. Mary, here is lemon-juice, with honey and hot wine, try to drink it, my dear, it will help restore your strength. [And a blanket to cover yourself. You need ointment for your lacerations, I will see what can be done.] 'By his stripes, we are healed' . . . you will not forget the consolation of the holy prophet . . .?

MARY (*broken down*). I answered when I should not have answered, and yet when I was asked questions it would have been wrong not to answer, I allowed my pain to master me, I have fallen from grace . . . (*She is weeping.*)

HOSIUS (*weeping also*). No, no, I am to blame. Had I only known earlier, the confusion of your conscience. Let us both try, between us, to find out how we have failed. Pray for me as I pray for you, and I will ask you some – gentle – questions. (*A slight pause as he masters himself*).

MARY *tries to do the same.*

(*Quiet and easy*). How did you first come to your knowledge of the Lord Jesus?

MARY (*trying to answer it as truthfully as possible*). You know that I was a slave-child, I lost my mother, my life was my mother, I was very small, all my world one field of flowers and fruit where I would lie deep in the leaves, talking to the bees, and playing my pipe and singing. I had to keep the wild beasts away from the crops, every night my mother came out to me with fire in an earthen pot, and food: and then one night she did not come. Armed men with great booted feet, destroying the garden, pulling down my little hut. They left me there alone, until at last my mother found me, we ran weeping through the vineyards where I'd never been before – there were others on the same road, children just like me, their mothers and fathers crying and raging – till we came to a gate: and more armed men, and dogs. 'Get out of here', they shouted, 'Don't you know what's happened? Your master's left his lands, all his trade is broken down, he's no use any longer for five hundred hungry slaves, you're free to go – so long as you don't come here!.' And they let loose their dogs and we ran. I lost my mother's hand in the dark, I lost her for the rest of my life. But the people who found me, dead-alive upon the mountainside, and brought me to their house – it was those people who gave me to myself. They gave me a name – Mary. They gave me a place – Spain. They told me everything I ever knew . . .

HOSIUS. And instructed you in the teachings of Christ. What instruction?

MARY. That he had come from God to love even the slave-people: and therefore on his shoulders he was carrying our burden, our own wickedness even as he carried the cruelty of those who by their oppression had made us wicked. To prove this, he himself was hung on the cross as a wicked criminal, just because he was not wicked. All he asked in return was our love: love for him, love for his father, love for his mother. We would eat bread and remember him. And, of course, I remembered my own mother. When they told me about love, what other sort of picture of it could I make?

HOSIUS. What name did you use for the Mother of Jesus?

MARY. My own name.

HOSIUS. Of course. But there were others? The Lady of Wisdom?

MARY (*urgently*). Never the Blue Hag! He should never have said that, never!

HOSIUS. Indeed he should not. Indeed not, indeed not. But – Mother of All Living –?

MARY. She gave birth to the Living Christ. How could she not be called –?

HOSIUS (*anxious to avoid anything like an argument*). Did these good people ever speak to you about the Prince of Darkness?

MARY (*simply*). He had been bound for a thousand years, he had no power over us any more, we had a Father and a Mother now who had driven him into his den. And therefore we were not afraid.

HOSIUS (*slily*). You read that in a book?

MARY. I cannot read.

HOSIUS (*taken aback*). Not? Oh child, how can you say so? Don't you remember, the very beginning, when all this trouble first emerged, did you not tell me, in a voice of such anger, that you had been sent to bring the good news to the poor, to proclaim liberty to captives and –

MARY (*capping his quote*). – and to the blind sight, to set the downtrodden free –

HOSIUS (*severely*). Out of the pages of scripture those very exact words: not one slip of the tongue, and you say you have never read anything?

MARY. What I have heard read, if I believe it, it is fixed in my heart: whenever it is needed, I wait for the hand of God to fetch it out at my mouth.

She is recovering herself rapidly and the readiness of her answers is beginning to irk HOSIUS.

HOSIUS. And you travelled the world, with all of it inside you: and now and then you repeated this, and now and then you repeated that.

MARY. If it gave comfort to the people.

HOSIUS. Or if you thought it would make them think well of you? You were only poor and ugly, as they were poor and ugly: but you had this one gift, and it made you remarkable.

MARY. [(*seeing the catch*). No no – I did not mean –

HOSIUS (*ignoring her protest*). So remarkable indeed that you turned your crooked back on them and went to live in an Emperor's palace among princes and noblewomen.

MARY. But it was you who suggested that I live in the palace –

HOSIUS. You could have refused. Oh admit it, you were so proud that through you the Emperor's mother was kneeling at the feet of Christ.

MARY (*stung into incautious self-assertion*). But I never turned my back. Bishop Hosius, go and walk in the foul alleyways of Nicomedia, the shantytown outside the walls – and bring back to me what you see – how the blind have received their sight, the lame walk, lepers are cleansed, and the deaf hear, the dead are raised up –

HOSIUS (*shocked*). What –!

MARY (*anxious not to claim a miracle*). I am talking about dead souls. Oh yes they are raised up, and the good news has been preached to the poor! And ask them who did it? I am not proud: I never told you: the Dowager Empress did not know. I did not eat at the Emperor's great table, my place was the place of a serf, which is what I am.

HOSIUS. Which is what you chose to be. Had you asked me I could easily have upgraded your status.] Do you not know that a false humility is the greatest pride of all? And the false humility of a woman who presumes to the priesthood of a god-ordained man –

MARY (*breaking down again*). [Oh but there is pride and pride . . . How proud they must have been who were hung upon posts by Herculius, by Maximin Daza, and whipped to death in the circus: and were able – and were able – to submit in perfect silence. No: I have no pride.] Oh Bishop, I am deeply ashamed . . .

HOSIUS (*no longer denunciatory, but still severe*). So, out of your shame, tell me. You did help Semiramis?

MARY. I don't know how she escaped. But I – I – yes, I tried to help her, yes. [I sent messages into the desert to try to find the soldier Joachim: and fetch him to prove he was her one true husband.]

HOSIUS. And by so doing, you deceived Helen, let her perjure herself with the fabrication of an Imperial document?

MARY (*after a pause*). Thou sayest it.

HOSIUS (*great anger*). How dare you! You admit a crime in the very words by which Our Lord affirmed his divinity! For a woman of no books, your insistent quotations reveal only the one thing – that which plucks them through your teeth is indeed the Prince of Darkness!

MARY (*in great trouble*). Oh no – no – but yes – perhaps –

HOSIUS. Yes. Now: do you see this text? You know where it came from.

Rustle of the paper.

MARY. From Fausta. Thirteen years ago. She met me in a snowstorm and asked me to explain it.

HOSIUS. [Who told her where you were?

MARY. Semiramis.

HOSIUS. How did you know Semiramis?

MARY. The House of the True Way, in Gaul.

HOSIUS. Where you, as a serf, preached freedom to slaves, and you so worked upon one slave that she brought you to the Empress. And you said to the Empress – what?

MARY. I asked her for her jewels. Christ's poor had a need of them. And in return I interpreted the text that she told me:] Eve gave Adam life. And I said, for her reward he now treads upon her head. Has not that been true? And when Jesus reproached Martha for continuing her household submission to him, I thought that might be a sign that the cruel foot of Adam was at last to be lifted up from such indecent sovereignty. I was wrong?

HOSIUS (*with judicial gravity: and scorn for her account*). I cannot believe that Fausta would have stripped herself of jewels just to hear your mere opinion. [Such payment could only be offered for the most momentous service.] The truth is, she told you no text: but you yourself gave her one. And that is what she paid for.

MARY (*frightened, but absolutely determined*). No no, she had the text, she told it me and I told her, and now I tell you and I have no more to say.

Scene Eleven

Interior: In the passage of the cellarage outside the cell.

HOSIUS. Eumolpus, she is not lying.

EUMOLPUS.* She made the document! To entangle the Empress all her life in the web of the devil – [do not forget Fausta was but fourteen years old, the unclean monthly courses of her body were just beginning . . .] And why did she demand jewels . . .? Let me think, let me think . . . Simon the Magician, the original heretic, or rather anti-Christ, or rather, his woman was: brothel-bait from coasts of

---

* This speech was condensed for recording.

Syria, he called her Selene, he called her Helena, he called her the Queen of Troy, and by Troy he meant Rome. She is said to have worn jewels, nothing but jewels, when she danced at his orgies: and what did his orgies commemorate? Three goddesses in front of Paris, vying for the crown of beauty in fulfilment of the prophecy that Troy would be burnt to the ground, and all the heroes who burnt it would thereafter lose their kingdoms. Bringing back into our world the age of the Great Destruction, the carnal filth of women to condemn all humankind. Don't you see, don't you see, it all fits together –!

HOSIUS (*blankly*). No, I don't quite see –'

EUMOLPUS (*highly patronising and impatient*). Of course you don't, you never did. [Had it been left to you, that priest-woman in Cyprus would still have been offering the eucharist:] when it was left to you, you lost the whole of Carthage to the Donatist Schism. Do not forget when Simon the Magician set himself, in Rome, against the gospel of Peter and Paul he was destroyed by them: but now he has returned, to be once again in Rome upon the day of the Jubilee of Constantine. Anti-Christ the Prince of Darkness, and it is the woman who leads him thither . . .

HOSIUS (*in the utmost gloom*). Fausta . . .?

EUMOLPUS. Did not Tertullian tell us that the secret parts of women are in truth the gates of hell?

Fade.

Scene Twelve

KYBELE (*as narrator*). Year of the Jubilee: year of the death of Crispus: death unexplained; except by rumour, that he was disloyal, that he conspired, that he had for a long time exchanged letters with an unregenerate heathen woman, who helped him conspire . . .

Jaxartes, who had read my letters, Jaxartes who had followed him to his dangerous advanced bivouac in the unconquered German forest, sat up with him all night in his tent talking – the next day there must be a battle: but they did not talk much about that. Philosophy, poetry, love . . .

Interior: A tent in the forest. Outside the wind in the trees, night-birds, etc.. The canvas flaps at times.

CRISPUS (*highly excited, talking at great speed*). My dearest Jaxartes, if Virgil says Aeneas denied the love of Dido because of his duty and is therefore to be praised, then I deny Virgil – or at least I deny your reading of Virgil – because if love and duty do not go together, something is wrong with the duty –! My duty tomorrow to fight a horde of Germans who completely outnumber me and why do I do it? Why do I submit to the intolerable ecstasy and despair?

JAXARTES (*softly*). For the reward?

CRISPUS. To be declared Co-Augustus with my father at the Jubilee? I don't give a damn for it.

JAXARTES. But you will, if you don't get it? (*To himself:*) Dare I assert that he won't get it? Dare I assume Constantine's mind is already sufficiently poisoned by the intercepted letters? No, not assert, imply, keep it slow, keep it suggestive, wait . . .

CRISPUS. Oh I'll get it, there's no doubt of it, he's owed it me for years . . . more to the purpose, he owes it to the soldiers of my regiments, and I owe it to them not to bring more of them into this battle than I can possibly avoid, fifty-fifty we might lose it, it's a gamester's throw this fight, and after all my only loyalty is to my troops – you do realise in such a war they have no chance of profitable loot? Our commitment to the secure frontier is all that holds us together, never mind about Virgil – Jaxartes, I call that love.

The tent-flap is pulled aside.

CENTURION (*in a low voice*). Excuse me, General, the moon is down: our ambush-party now in position as per orders to outflank the enemy at first light.

CRISPUS (*also in a low voice*). Ah thank you, Centurion, excellent news: carry on.

CENTURION. Sir.

He slips out again.

JAXARTES. You said ecstasy . . . surely to risk your beloved soldiers in an ecstatic gamester's throw is to bring love and loyalty very close to the ecstasy of death . . .?

CRISPUS (*a speculative remark, not a fervent avowal*). We are told Jesus Christ, by his ecstasy, conquered death.

JAXARTES. He and he alone? Exclusively, Christ?

CRISPUS. We are told so. At least I am, perhaps not you. Do you have a religion?

JAXARTES (*self-deprecatory hesitation*). Why, my dear, I – er – (*Change of tone to apparent deep sincerity:*) I do not like exclusion. I was brought up on the Persian border among the followers of Mani. Not to accept their faith, but – I was influenced. The Manichees include all, exclude nothing. Christ, Jehovah, Mithras, Zoroaster, even Buddha from the mountain of Hindustan. They teach that all creation, men, beasts, birds, fishes, women – particularly women – have a duty against their nature, to abstain from the cycle of nature – from what you or I would call 'humanity', 'animality', anarchy', 'ecstasy' . . . thus to achieve the purity of a naked flame: essential if we are to fight in the ultimate combat of Light against Darkness. Mani, you know, like Jesus, was crucified: by the King of Persia, not by Caesar, Zoroaster being exclusive as Christ is exclusive. Now that Rome turns Christian, Christ and Zoroaster are matched in unending warfare. But which is the Dark: and which is the Light? Diocletian would have crucified Mani, if Mani had been a Roman. I wonder, would Constantine . . .?

CRISPUS. In every battle every soldier must believe he fights for the Light.

JAXARTES. And if the Light should turn out to be Darkness? If the Thirteenth Apostle of Christ should turn out to be so – exclusive – that he finds it his own duty to devote his dearly beloved son to sacrificial endless death at the hands of interminable Germans? – oh yes, you have your ecstasy, oh, yes, you have your despair, oh yes, this tent is Gethsemane . . . But what do you suppose he is doing with your stepmother?

CRISPUS (*astonished*). With Fausta? What should he be doing?

JAXARTES (*in an apparently light-hearted throw-away manner*). If you want my opinion, he should be drowning her in her bath . . . Now she is a creature that has never abstained. Nor will she, till her sons are Emperors.

CRISPUS *gives a gasp.*

JAXARTES (*pauses briefly to let him take it in*). You could stop it, if you would, you are beautiful enough to be consumed by the will for it. Whereas his will, after all these years, is totally consumed by hers. I don't even think he knows it. (*Even more of a 'throw-away':*) Why don't we go and tell him?

CRISPUS (*deceptively innocent: after another pause*). Tell him – or, kill him? You were speaking very quietly, I did not quite catch . . .

JAXARTES (*in a kind of sadness*). Oh my dear, my dear, this is indeed Gethsemane, you see the cup and you twist and turn, you sweat your blood that you shall not have to drink it . . .

CRISPUS (*meditatively*). Dearly beloved son, you said . . . sacrificial death . . .? (*With sudden cold sharpness:*) Not quite: you got it wrong. We have in fact in this forest no Christ at all – I'm not sure we can say truly there is any sort of ecstasy – we certainly possess despair. We call it our Trust; and we keep to it: as you have not kept to yours. (*He gives a quiet call*). Centurion?

CENTURION (*looking in*). Sir?

CRISPUS (*very hard and final*). Take this man, give him a sword, and put him in the ambush. If he dies, that's his finish. If he lives, he may go free: but I am never to see him again.

Scene Thirteen

Interior: A room in the palace with echoing marble floors.

EUMOLPUS (*approaching at speed*). Bishop Hosius –! She has confessed!

HOSIUS (*dully*). You have tortured her once more?

EUMOLPUS (*with a crackle of parchment*). Here is her statement, read it: she is an accredited agent of hell.

HOSIUS. Eumolpus, I must go to my diocese of Cordova. Unexpected administrative problems. I think your talents would now be better placed in the service of the Bishop of Antioch.

EUMOLPUS (*cockily*). That has already been arranged. Antioch and I are one in our zeal against the Prince of Darkness.

Feet approaching, outside: then through the door, and so across the room).

HELEN (*calling as she comes*). Well – did you find from Mary where is Semiramis, and how to get her back? That bugger of a baker is threatening a public petition!

EUMOLPUS. Lady Helen, your mind can be at rest. You were not at fault for mis-using the Imperial seal.

HELEN (*angrily*). And who said I was at fault! You and your church advice which muddled the whole business!

EUMOLPUS (*business-like*). Madam, by means of the forged text you so acutely uncovered, the devil crept into Mary the Companion, took her over, and used her to help him spirit Semiramis away. The baker has been told, he has resigned all his claim to the ownership of the slave-woman, and has declared his intention of becoming a priest.

HELEN (*bluntly*). So he should. But this damned devil of yours has made off with Imperial property. You'd better run after him and get the money quick sharp! (*She gives a burst of laughter.*)

EUMOLPUS (*angered by her crude materialism*). Your daughter-in-law, not the money, you need to catch hold of! Instead of laughing at the devil like the crackle of thorns under a pot, it is up to you and no one else to undo his present work!

He stalks out.

HELEN (*explodes in disgust*). Pooh!

HOSIUS. Dear lady, he is rough, but he is right. Fausta is secluded; you are the only one of us who can reach her . . .

Cross-fade.

Scene Fourteen

Interior: FAUSTA's *quarters, as in Scene Two.* HELEN *enters with a bevy of* ATTENDANTS, *a clatter of brushes and buckets, and an unstoppable rush of objurgation as she passes through the outer room.*

HELEN. Let me through, let me through – make way for my slaves for the annual cleaning – clean and sweep, clean and sweep – stand away from that door – no one bars the way of the Emperor's Mother when she comes to clean the quarters of the Emperor's wife –!

She enters the inner room and shuts the door behind her: though the noises of the SLAVES *at work still penetrate it at intervals.*

   Well, Madam Constantine, still abed, still sulking?

As she talks she is rearranging furniture, sweeping the floor, etc..

HELEN. That moth-eaten mother of yours, Eutropia, I am sending for her, she can't understand how you could be such a fool, she's going to tell them all at the Jubilee, tell them all you've always been a foolish vain little girl – taken in like that by the trick of a fraudulent text (*She gives a burst of laughter*). You're the one that should have been tortured, not that harmless Mary, there's no such thing as tricksters, only fools who believe in them –

FAUSTA (*reeling, but striking back*). No such thing as tricksters – only fools who believe in them –? Madam, I got the text from Diocletian's martyred wife: when I visited my sister who was married to your husband.

HELEN (*horribly shocked*). You're lying!

FAUSTA (*enjoying herself*). No I am not! Find Semiramis and she will swear it. To talk about tricksters and their dupes –! Semiramis will tell all! And I will tell all! That the vision of the Cross of the Emperor of Rome was nothing more than white paint on soldiers' helmets in the sun –

HELEN (*speechless*). Wh-what –! No – no –! What is that noise?

FAUSTA. It is a hornet –

There is the buzz of a wandering insect which has been about the room for the past few seconds. HELEN *is heard trying to hit it.*

FAUSTA. No point in trying to kill it – with your prying and probing and cleaning, you're sure to uncover the nest and they'll sting you to death . . .

HELEN *storms out.*

FAUSTA (*to herself*). At last I experience the passion of life I could only observe in Semiramis! To keep my word and save her has been worth it one hundredfold: even though it be Fausta, Empress of Rome, in the end to be stung by the hornets . . .

Fade.

Scene Fifteen

KYBELE (*as narrator*). Lady Helen in great distress took ship for Spain and came unheralded to Cordova to Bishop Hosius. She told him in strict secrecy all that Fausta had told her: and he said she must go back straightaway, to Rome; she was needed at the ceremony, Constantine must be forewarned.

Exterior: Carriage-horses clattering their feet and their harness as they wait.

HOSIUS (*as he helps* HELEN *into the carriage*). Dear lady, have faith the hands of Christ will guide, guard, your son, his true apostle. You yourself, keep safe: you are as precious to the church as was the Blessed Virgin when her son on the cross commended her to his disciple . . .

She is now in, and the door is shut. HOSIUS *has an after-thought.*

HOSIUS (*drily*). Oh, you need be concerned no longer about Mary the Companion. The Bishop of Antioch has received her again into the church: they have sent her back to Spain, to be here under my care. Without her tongue. I am told, it is a voluntary penance.

The carriage starts up.

Fade.

Scene Sixteen

Interior: CRISPUS *is defending himself to an* INTERROGATOR, *who does not speak.*

CRISPUS (*forcefully*). I am Crispus Caesar and I tell you the indictment is nonsense: treasonable conspiracy –? I deny it absolutely, why don't you ask Jaxartes, he's a man of some rank in your department, is he not? Very well, you've never heard of him . . . You won't speak a word . . . For me, to do the talking, so I will. The first thing I saw, when I came into Rome for that hyperbolic Jubilee: the children of Fausta, a carriageful of brats, why, they had their own procession, and where was the queen-brat? When she was nine and I was seven, I was informed she was my mother. Well, she was their mother now: observably kept apart from their new precocious glory. She looked as though she had been walking in the ghost-fields of the further world – unearthly beautiful she stood there, with all of the rest of us, in front of the great new church, as we waited for my father's procession . . .

Scene Seventeen

Exterior: Fade up sounds of a great open space full of people, the buzz as they wait for the ceremony. Cathedral bells booming. Distant trumpets, coming nearer.

CRISPUS (*continuing straight on with his narration*). As though she herself were the dishonest beautiful voice of that unearthly man Jaxartes reading me Virgil, dividing my mind, driving it, this way and that. Oh yes, I do admit, I was disturbed in my mind . . . (*He is now in scene, thinking his thoughts upon it.*) Next to Fausta, her mother; next to her, my aunt Constantia, innumerable uncles, half-uncles, Herculians, every man and woman cloth of gold-and-silver from nape of neck to jewelled shoes: and my grandmother Helen. (*To his interrogators:*) Oh yes, I will admit, I was aware of – certain portents . . . (*Into the scene again.*) Rome has a new Governor, Christian, and the Senate do not like it, they have been refused their heathen ceremonies, look at their faces . . . Rome has a most privileged Bishop, decrepit, and the people do not like it, look at their faces, look . . . at the far side of the square under the statue of my father, confronting both us and the other huge new statue of Peter, the Fisherman. Peter holds out his net over the heads of the royal family and hopes to drop it onto us. But no, he's too late, we're already in the basket . . .

(*Still in the scene.*)

> Catch 'em all and fry 'em up
> Lord Jesus cooking dinner
> When Constantine comes into town
> He won't get any thinner . . .

(*To* INTERROGATOR:) Oh yes, I will admit I make now and then satirical verses. How else to amuse myself while my father paraded the City, aloft on his chariot, at the head of *my* regiments? The shape of his progress a figure of the dream of his heart . . .

Scene Eighteen

Exterior: a street in the middle of the procession. Trumpets blaring, cymbals clashing, the hooves of cavalry, feet of marching MEN, *and, dominant, the grinding of the chariot-wheels on the cobble-stones.*

CONSTANTINE (*to himself*).

> Not so much a blood-stained conqueror
> As a good and faithful servant
> Rewarding my lord
> In the hope of my lord's reward
> I ride,
> I ride with the highest God
> I ride alone . . .

Scene Nineteen

Exterior: In the square again. The processional trumpets enter it, some distance away. Then the sound of chariot and ESCORT.

CRISPUS (*to himself: in the scene*). And here he comes, at last. He knows he is not God. He is the man who made God, is making God, and he also made me. Am I supposed to like it?

CRISPUS (*to* INTERROGATOR). He dismounted from his chariot, erect as his own war-horse, [ha ha among the trumpets,] he crossed himself and took three paces – most exact, no doubt he counted them in honour of the Holy Trinity . . .

CONSTANTINE (*taking his three paces, speaks to himself*). *One* for Moses, who brought the word to the Jews, *one* for Paul who converted it into the word for all humanity: bring my feet together, I encompass them all three.

CRISPUS (*to* INTERROGATOR). He turned to the Bishop of Rome – and – he went down upon his knees. So did the Bishop.

CONSTANTINE (*a loud announcement*). We both of us kneel together to the one true master of Rome.

He and the BISHOP *rise to their feet.*

CRISPUS [(*to* INTERROGATOR). Acclamations at this point were no doubt anticipated. They did not come. I alone would not project myself, applauding all on my own: they would think it was a sarcasm. In any event, sufficient choirmen, well able to fill the interlude.]

CONSTANTINE (*to himself*). Upon this hilltop Peter the Fisherman hung to his death head-first and upside down. Upon this hilltop Simon the Magician fell to his death, head-first and upside down. Peter destroyed Simon, Nero Caesar destroyed Peter: Constantine now intends to reclaim them both: so that the Father and Mother of God will include them both.

> I have taken the Man of Sorrows and led him hand and foot
> Over seven hills of Rome
> Till he stands upon Number Eight:
> 'Friend, go up higher,' *I* said that to *him*.
> And all this *I* have done.
> The creeping craft, the dream, of Constantine . . .

The lost child Helen-Fausta will fly before me now: as great a vision as the Cross of Light!

A CHOIR *launches into 'Te Deum': and there is a rhythmic marching of feet on the flatstones.*

CRISPUS. He mounted a rostrum, at the base of his own statue, the populace were shoved back by the guards. [A good deal of choreography, soldiers, clerics, Imperial eunuchs, this way and that, following the white lines chalked out for them on the pavement. Incense swinging everywhere. Once it concluded,] we presumed he would make a speech. But he stood brooding, his gaze fixed toward the church behind me.

(to INTERROGATOR). [No, he made no speech: he signed to his heralds, and the heralds called me forward –

HERALD (formal call). Lord Crispus, Caesar and General –!

CRISPUS (to INTERROGATOR). What to do? It was unrehearsed. Across the square, the Heralds met me –

We hear him walking out and being met by the HERALDS).

CRISPUS. – one on each side of me, as though I was under arrest.] The bloody flunkey at my left ear informed me I must prostrate myself. Of course I did: I deny utterly there was any hesitation.

CRISPUS prostrates himself.

CRISPUS (to himself: in the scene again). This man has made God and the god whom he made sent his son to be tortured to death. Is he to be Abraham, and I am Isaac? No: I am Crispus Caesar, and my soldiers depend on my life. Will he hold up the show for ever, staring down at me with eyes like oystershells . . .? Oh, in the name of God, Emperor, speak . . .!

CONSTANTINE (to himself). No vision, no Christ-child, no female Christ? Then Crispus alone will be my Christ upon this earth: and that shall be the portent. (A loud announcement:) Men of Rome!

A Trumpet-blast.

CONSTANTINE. This –

Another Trumpet.

CONSTANTINE. This is my beloved son, in whom I am well pleased!

An astonishingly loud and wide-spread burst of cheering: EVERYONE crying 'Crispus, Crispus, Crispus!' and clapping rhythmically.

CRISPUS (to INTERROGATOR, as the acclamations continue). He must have been about to say something more. Raise me to equal sovereignty? Dash my hopes with small preferment? Send me to exile? Which? But they cheered and cheered and he had to stop. No: I did not provoke it. Yes: it did please me. More than that, it frightened me. If I rose to my feet, it was not to encourage the crowd; rather, to calm them down . . .

He stands up: the cheering is redoubled.

CRISPUS. Believe this or not, I saw that mob as Satan in the wilderness, I was its victim brought high up the mountain-side to be dazzled by the width of the world! [Tell me, what the devil would the devil have done, had that offer been accepted . . .?]

The cheering is developing into something more aggressive.

CRISPUS. Those who started throwing stones had obviously been paid by someone. I repeat again, ask Jaxartes.

Stones landing on the pavement, etc., PEOPLE shouting, running.

CRISPUS. [We all thought they were throwing them at Constantine, he thought so, he jumped off his rostrum like a jack-rabbit, and why wouldn't I laugh? Jaxartes did.] Because I saw him, amongst the eunuchs, pressing forward to the Emperor's elbow: with the grin of a deep-sea shark.

JAXARTES (*hissing into* CONSTANTINE*'s ear*). Emperor, look at the Senate: they veil their faces with their gowns and they've all turned away from you. Look at the troops: d'you hear their slogan?

CRIES FROM THE TROOPS. Con-stan-tine of Nero's line! (*Repeated*).

CRISPUS (*to* INTERROGATOR). Extraordinary: it was not at the man they continued to throw stones, but at his statue. Bronze-and-marble had become more important than flesh?

JAXARTES. Emperor, look at your son. This has all been pre-arranged. The Army of the Rhine and Danube is calling upon him to divide the Empire: so that he can rule in Rome, new sovereign of the old religion. Emperor, I have the evidence. He could stop it, if he wanted to: but does he? Look at his face!

CRISPUS (*as the clamour of the scene in Rome fades away*). Had I at that moment put my arms out, embraced my father, I would now be his assured successor.

Scene Twenty

Interior.

CRISPUS (*continuing straight on with his statement*). But can you not see, I would also have betrayed my soldiers? You do know that three of those regiments had been ordered to the eastern frontier under command of god-knows-who? Ask him what would he have done when he was a young general? Oh he was once! Oh yes, and I'll add two things. One: there may have been riot, there was no uprising, the troops – when they were told to – went quietly back to barracks. Two: myself and the Empress Fausta had exchanged not a single word. That she and her absurd angel-child should have taken over the East, while I controlled the West, is – why, it is so incredible only Jaxartes could have thought it up! Yet you tell me there is no Jaxartes. All you have is his 'evidence'. So present it: and do your worst.

Closing music.

9
HYPOTHESIS

Scene One

Throughout this play CONSTANTINE *is speaking directly to the* radio audience; *and there is no specific location for him, except the images of his mind conjured up by his discourse. In this sequence he speaks with hard unassailable authority, the brutal facts of his imperial necessity for which he offers no apology.*

CONSTANTINE (*hard*). I killed them. In accordance with the ancient Roman law. My family was a model of Imperial rule, rebellious members must be treated like rebellious subject-nations. My son Crispus allowed himself to be called by the people Emperor of the West: my wife Fausta allowed herself to be called by the people sole Empress of Rome and Persia. God alone gives Imperial title . . .

The number of their accomplices disposed of by the security forces remains a state secret.

In accordance with law? There was no public trial. The occult imagination was allowed to work unhindered, whisperings like the wind through every crevice of the popular mind . . . In the palace at Rome, three hundred and twenty-six AD.

Scene Two

Interior: the palace corridors. Rushing of feet and frightened whispers from one COURTIER *to another.*

WHISPERS.   Crispus is dead . . . (*Repeated.*)
                       Scores of his officers dead , . .
                       Three leading senatorial families wiped out.
                       Hundreds have disappeared . . .
                       Thousands . . .
                       Psst – here comes Helen!

The feet scurry away. Two pairs of feet running together.

HELEN (*on the move, agonised*). Oh my heart, my heart, it breaks, the pain tears me –Constantia it is not true – Crispus is not conspiring – !

CONSTANTIA (*hard*). *Was* not, Helen, *was* not conspiring.

HELEN (*to herself*). Quick, quick, we run, we run faster and faster – no one is in charge – no one knows, no one says –

VOICES OF OFFICIALS (*in* HELEN*'s mind*). I'm afraid I cannot help you – we have no information – no documents available without the Emperor's signature – the Emperor is in sole charge –

HELEN (*to herself*). They smile and they smirk, I know what they are plotting – never never never – not over my son: he is the one given the power to rule on earth – (*Aloud as they run: and then slow down to a walk*:) Constantia, who is in charge?

CONSTANTIA. The Emperor does not speak, he does not hear, he lies without moving: every day the purple rash creeps over his body –

They have come out of the corridors into the open air, into –

Scene Three

Exterior: a garden, birdsong, etc.

HELEN. Rumours of mutiny, war, again again conspiracy, the Persians, the Germans: the regiments refuse orders, heretics, heathen, insubordinate slaves, terrorists – Christian people are sacrificing to the old gods in their fear: to prevent the plague

of Egypt descending upon their first-born: O Crispus, first-born of my first-born –
oh – ! Constantia, we are in danger! And the Bishops are doing nothing!

EUTROPIA's *footsteps hurrying toward them.* EUTROPIA *is a refined lady of
intellectual tastes, rather faded; and out-of-touch with court affairs, which she
carefully avoided for years.*

EUTROPIA (*aged about 60*). I want to say goodbye to my daughter Fausta and my
grandchildren: where are they today? Dreadful news from my estates, I am being
robbed by my manager, disaster if I don't return home at once –

HELEN (*savagely in control of things again*). Constantia, quick, your hand over her
mouth, get her into the chapel –

Scuffle and a squawk as they grab her and haul her out of the public eye.

Scene Four

Interior: A small echoing chapel. EUTROPIA *is hustled in and the door is slammed.*

HELEN. Eutropia, sit: and listen!

EUTROPIA *is plumped down on a bench, the hand still over her mouth.*

EUTROPIA *moans slightly.*

HELEN. The Emperor is as good as dead. Your daughter *is* dead! Don't roll your
eyes at me: Listen! I am in charge. I am the Emperor. You have a choice: your
orders from me or get the chop the same as Fausta. You and I are going to travel.
The endangered provinces on the Persian border must be shown who is in charge:
and shown there is no bad blood between Herculians and Constantians. We travel
together: twin Augustae, Mothers of the Empire, Grandmothers of all the Caesars,
God's Chosen Leaders.

CONSTANTIA. Nor is there bad blood between Arius and the church. Arius must be
brought back and the feuding among the Bishops must stop. I myself will go to
Nicomedia. I will be the rock to anchor the church.

HELEN. None of this can be done without the Emperor's signature. You and I,
Constantia, between us, are well capable of providing it, one way or the other.

Scene Five

Exterior: wind in trees. Murmur of listening PEOPLE.

KYBELE. My friends – my adopted family, clan, tribe – who have accepted me in
this island of Hibernia as a guest-friend, have told me that only by magic can I now
prove I am a true philosopher, and therefore categorised as a free person: for if not,
I am listed as un-free. So what must I do? If I were a druid-philosopher I would
know the mysterious words to turn this yellowish-white sow with her ancient
withered udders into a woman of the other-world and cause her loose the secret
knots that bind me for my trial into this wicker basket.

As she speaks this, we hear the sow grunting, and the basket creaking.

KYBELE. Such feats can be done, and are done, after years of study and practice:
Christianity also has magic and it calls itself superior to yours. But I cannot do it:
we rational philosophers discarded the art centuries ago. I was taught a different
skill.

Sow snuffles.

KYBELE. Learned travellers for generations have fled here from the deeds of Rome, merchants have traded; the hospitality you gave me was an honour to you, made you proud of your own customs – if Roman victims sought your shores, you were worthier than Rome . . . By my presence, your mind was opened; by my presence, you could see yourselves. Is not that a sort of magic? But a magic imperceptible, no formula, no secret teaching. Do you tell me it is to be feared? I learned another magic from Grimonia and Proba. Those aged women passed on to me a true compassion, a true healing, a true freedom: of their own choice they remained listed as un-free, because they understood that where only a few are free, none are free: and from their understanding I understand it too. It is nothing for me to lose my free title: to live cast out in your fields, your wild places, is to live in my own spirit uncontrolled by your rules and rituals. Under which rules and rituals did the Druid of Armagh kill Proba, kill Grimonia: and what freedom did he gain by it? What freedom was gained by Constantine when his son and his wife disappeared out of history?

Scene Six

CONSTANTINE (*his voice trembling, indicative of the disturbance of his mind*). Listen, I had a messenger, last night, to my bedside. I did not at first recognise Death. I would have thought, a towering rattling black phantom, black rags, yellow bones, all smeared with green mildew, and a stink would knock you down a mile off . . . Instead; a small white terrier-bitch barking and growling, nipping at my counterpane . . .

Fade up sounds of little dog, as described.

CONSTANTINE. She was my own little dog, Lucky, I used to call her, I had her when I was a schoolboy. Ha, I had forgotten – you perhaps would not know this – we have talked so much Greek all these years in this palace – the word for 'Lucky' in the Latin tongue is – 'Fausta'. All the more certain, therefore, the nature of the message.

We hear him getting out of bed and following the dog, as described.

CONSTANTINE. I knew at once that Lucky wanted me to get out of bed and follow her. I was uneasy on my legs, having been so ill . . . I plunged after her down the corridors, calling her – (*He calls.*) 'Lucky – 'Lucky –!' And I found myself then in a narrow lofty tunnel of a room I had never been in before.

The dog's noise fades away. There is a buzzing as of a number of PEOPLE *whispering together and bustling about.*

It was lit by flaring candles in tall lamp-standards placed here and there along the cluttered floor: the whole place was one great chaos, shelves and tables, piled up with papers, parchments, engraved tablets, thousands of words, falling about everywhere in every possible kind of alphabet. And people I had never seen before: in and out, scurrying, flurrying, busying themselves with all these documents, muttering, whispering. I had a distinct feeling my little dog had been trying to lead me away from some very immediate danger. Was this place safe? I could not stand there ignored: it was not seemly, I was, after all, that which I was – and I said so, to a bent bedraggled penpusher who was stooped over the nearest table. (*Aloud: self-assertively*:) I am that I am.

JAXARTES (*in a narrow bureaucratic tone of voice*). No you're not. You're a slave, you've been sent here on an errand, and you'll abide by the proper procedure. Sit down, please over there.

CONSTANTINE. A slave? I was wearing a collar, it had begun to hurt my neck . . .

JAXARTES. Sit still, you're disturbing the office.

CONSTANTINE. Jaxartes . . .? My own secret man . . .?

There is a pause. After a moment.

JAXARTES (*matter-of-fact*). I know what you're here for. You are looking for Crispus Caesar.

CONSTANTINE. All my life looking for someone. I had a mother, I lost her: I had a wife, I lost her: I had a god, Helios-Mithras the Unconquered Sun, and I lost him – or rather, he so changed himself I couldn't understand any more who he was or why.

JAXARTES. Name? We have his name. Age? Profession? – Yes. Can you describe him?

CONSTANTINE (*to* JAXARTES). The last time I saw him he stood and threw stones at my head.

JAXARTES. Features distorted with rage. That's not much use. Describe him in repose.

CONSTANTINE (*to* JAXARTES). He was beautiful as Lucifer, the day they threw him out.

JAXARTES. Wait a moment, we might have something . . . I don't know about Lucifer: what about Phaeton, running wild with the sun-god's chariot? Come this way . . .

His feet are heard moving off, followed by CONSTANTINE*'s.*

Scene Seven

Interior: of a carriage rolling along a road. The hooves of escorting HORSEMEN *can also be heard.*

EUTROPIA (*to herself*). So: here we are in the Imperial carriage, followed by the Imperial bullion-wagons crammed with Imperial gold.

ESCORT (*shouting*). Give room! For the Imperial Augustae, Mother of Constantine, Mother of Fausta, Grandmothers of all the Caesars, God's Chosen Leaders –!

EUTROPIA (*to herself*). We are heading for Antioch, nearly two thousand miles from Rome, where we will separate. My head spins from Helen's energy – giving me orders, taking them back, pulling out of her bag list upon list, adding and subtracting from them – will I ever remember everything I've got to do?

HELEN (*who has evidently been talking incessantly*). – you are to cover the itinerary of Abraham and Sarah: progenitors of the Chosen People, and the Chosen People are now Christ's People, if you find heathen cults exalting Sarah to a goddess, put a stop to them. This is how: look for the local Bishop, call a public meeting, announce yourself Grandmother of all the Caesars and God's Chosen Leader, tell them to prepare for salvation because the Second Coming is at hand, distribute money to build a church and money to all the poor, especially to soldiers, prisoners, orphans, widows. Here is your route –

As she talks she is shuffling papers.

HELEN. – Batnae, Edessa, Carrhae, Ur of the Chaldees, and then back by way of Hebron to Jerusalem where we meet. Now here's a list of Bishops, a list of Fairs and Festivals, a list of Trading-posts . . . (*Suddenly, yelling to the* DRIVER). Wait – stop the coach!

They grind to a halt: and we hear the excited noise of a small CROWD *outside on the road.* HELEN *gets out of the carriage, to applause.*

EUTROPIA (*to herself*). Another village market-place, we will never get to Antioch if Helen has to descend among every ragged mob we pass . . .

HELEN (*addressing the crowd outside*). We are all little children in the eyes of God, better a millstone round my neck than to harm any of these little ones –

EUTROPIA (*to herself*). Why is it always the most leprous child in the crowd who is thrust into her arms for her passionate embrace?

Cross fade to show lapse of time.

Scene Eight

Interior: The carriage lumbers on.

HELEN. Learn from me, my dear, keep your eyes and ears open, and then act – that's how we save the Empire. Make sure they know you're coming, before you reach the market-place. Arrive just before midday, ask for the 'holy man': if they say there's no holy man, only an 'illustrious Bishop', you know he's too big for his boots, so you bring him down a peg or two, the people love that, they're on your side immediately. Have a medicine-man ready bribed to find a disfigured child who is not in fact contagious. When you kiss the child, they'll think it a miracle.

EUTROPIA (*in great disgust*). I have never done anything like this in my life. I will not disgrace the memory of Diocletian. I would prefer to die rather than so dishonour myself.

HELEN (*grimly matter-of-fact*). If you don't do it, you'll get the bloody chop.

EUTROPIA. Helen, I will chop myself, I will cut my wrists, now – with this knife – and that's the end of it –!

She unsheathes a knife.

HELEN (*crying out in alarm*). No! Oh no – no – no –!

There is a struggle. HELEN *is badly upset.*

I can't bear the sight of blood –! Bandages, bandages –!

EUTROPIA (*the worm passionately turned*). No bandages! I will bleed to death! Here is my list. I want all this guaranteed and the Emperor's seal at the bottom of it!

A paper pulled out of her bag.

EUTROPIA. Recompense for loss of revenue on my estates through theft while I am away, a letter of credit to be given me at Antioch to pay off my foreclosers, and after Hebron I go straight home.

HELEN (*desperate*). No – no – oh, very well, if I must – any bloody thing to stanch her bloody blood!

Cross-fade to show lapse of time.

Scene Nine

Interior: the carriage again. It is moving once more.

EUTROPIA (*laughing*). Helen, you are soft! It is no more than a tiny scratch.

HELEN (*angrily*). Bah, you Herculians – bad-blood bitches all of you . . .

EUTROPIA (*on her dignity*). I am not a Herculian. I am Greco-Egyptian-Hibernian . . .

Cross-fade to show lapse of time.

Scene Ten

Interior: the carriage, still rolling along.

EUTROPIA (*tetchily*). My headache powder is nearly finished.

HELEN (*sulky*). You can replace it in Antioch.

EUTROPIA. I must have my own physician, from the Island of Cos.

HELEN. Oh don't be so provincial, there are perfectly good doctors in Syria.

EUTROPIA. But not from Cos.

Scene Eleven

CONSTANTINE. I went after him, through a maze of passageways: and then – a small door.

Two pairs of hurrying feet: they stop. A door is opened.

CONSTANTINE. He opened it, I went in. All manner of rubbish, shovelled up against the walls. And what appeared to be an old skin bag, huddled into a corner. He caught hold of it and dragged it out.

Sound-effect appropriate.

CONSTANTINE. Not a bag, but a withered body, red-gold fur all over it, made dim and gray with dirt: the carcase of a young lion . . . No: but the head was human. And when I brushed the faded hair out of his wide-open sightless eyes – oh . . .! (*He gives a great cry of agony.*)

JAXARTES (*casual*). You want to pull that woodwork out of the way, it's the broken yoke of a four-horse chariot, he somehow managed to get himself all tangled up with it . . .

Sound of wooden beam being pulled aside.

JAXARTES. – there.

CONSTANTINE (*anguished*). My son my son Absalom, would God I had died for thee, O Absalom my son my son . . .

A pause: then the sound of wind blowing.

CONSTANTINE. I was standing in a desert place: I held in my arms the dead lion, I was unable to run any further. (*His breath comes in heavy pants, behind his narration.*) Those who were chasing me were still behind me and they would know me: this mark upon my forehead, I felt it burning all the time, a great blotch of angry pustules from one eyebrow to the other.

A thin crying sound.

CONSTANTINE. There they were! Three – little boys – and then behind them, two more, little girls in torn frocks – barefooted on the sharp stones – oh no they weren't here to kill me. Suffer the little children to come unto me. So I did. And they gathered round me, plucking at my clothes, and pleading with me –

CHILDRENS' VOICES (*coming nearer until they are pressing in on our ears*). Oh sir, please help us find her – our Mama, we have not seen her for ever so long – oh sir, have they taken her away? Please please help us find her – please . . .!

CONSTANTINE. I was trying to console them – they took my mother away, even so I made myself the greatest man in the world . . . But they were looking at the dead lion.

CHILDREN's *voices fall silent.*

Their faces changed: their soft clutching hands changed, to the talons of eagles; they tore the dead lion out of my arms –

Bestial noises from the CHILDRENS' *throats. A sound of scuffling and tearing.*

Scattering and tossing his fragments all around them, bone, skin, dead dried meat. And then they turned to chase me. (*Panting.*)

Sound of his running feet.

But they had been delayed: and I outran them.

His feet slow down and stop.

It could not be chance that I found their lost Mamma. I was led to her surely: but I don't know who by. I can tell you this now but understand, understand, I did not know it then! If she was my wife Fausta, then those children had been *my* children . . .

The wind ceases. A strange twanging sound: as of harpstrings plucked, over and over, the same string.

All I saw was this woman, naked, spread-eagled across an outcrop of rock at the base of a rocky hill: she had been stapled to it with rings of iron, ankle and wrist. You would suppose she was in anguish, was enduring some atrocious punishment? Not at all. Why, she smiled at me, compassionate. Was she expecting me? I was meant to have congress with her. I am that I am: she was laid there as a tribute. I accepted her: and she accepted.

A pause. The harp-music continues.

CONSTANTINE. When I had finished –

FAUSTA (*quietly*). Lie still, lie still, you helpless naked fellow, I will tell you how and when you will understand the gift of life.

There is silent moment, after the harp-music stops: and then a ferocious hissing like a bundle of serpents.

CONSTANTINE. Was it me, was it me, who had transformed her by my act of lust? She had become a gorgon-creature; forked tongue like a sting-tailed insect in and out of her poison teeth. Or had she transformed me? I clapped a hand to my face: the blotch upon my brow was spreading, spreading, down my cheeks, down my neck, I could feel it like a crust underneath my shirt . . .

Scene Twelve

Interior: the carriage, rolling along.

EUTROPIA (*to herself, checking her itinerary*). From Antioch to Edessa, one hundred and fifty miles: shrine of the Apostle Thomas, obtain copy of historic letter from King Abgar to Jesus Christ: then to Carrhae, rich in the memory of Abraham . . . What luxury to be without Helen! And what a lah-de-dah in Antioch! (*She laughs.*) She sacked the bishop! She refused to kiss his ring, he called her a common barmaid. A very nice bank in Antioch, all my business transactions correctly concluded, the manager referred me to his cousin, a highly-qualified doctor from Cos . . .

Cross-fade.

Scene Thirteen

Exterior: A country garden. Birds, wind in the trees, a small group of musicians playing a sweet air.

EUTROPIA (*to herself, luxuriously: writing up her diary*). Couldn't get to Ur of the Chaldees, Abraham's birthplace, miles and miles inside the Persian border and forbidden to Roman citizens. Helen didn't mention that: and there's a lot of other things Helen didn't mention, crafty woman. At one of the trading-stations, I was hailed as the Mother of the Queen of the East, and when was my grandchild coming, the Anointed Angel, the New Messiah, to liberate them from Rome? Poof . . .! In some of the primitive villages there were even crude effigies of Fausta and the child set up ready for the occasion. And even more tricky, we only missed by a hair's-breadth driving straight into the middle of a ceremony where the Flying Angel was actually manifest, we were forewarned in time and made a detour round the oasis . . . I denied knowledge of everything, I showed them the statement Helen had supplied me – confession of forgery by Mary the Companion – I told them straight, 'God's Chosen Leaders: all else from the devil!' . . . Bitterness against Rome: they're willing to adopt anyone who shows any sympathy for them and their culture. Silly girl, Fausta, to have her head turned like that . . . I just hope that the first account of her death was the true one, cutting her wrists decently in her hot bath. Not being pinned, like Andromeda, to a rock in the desert . . . Oh I loathe the desert! The stupidity of Rome to think we can hold those eastern provinces.

A servant has arrived with a clinking tray.

SERVANT. I think it is time for Madam's special cup of herbal infusion . . . Shall I ask the musicians to leave?

EUTROPIA. Yes, please.

The music stops.

EUTROPIA (*to herself*). I wonder did Fausta take after me or Herculius? Me, I think. She did show a certain style. Could she have waited all these years to turn the tables on Constantine? His smugness was infuriating, once he had got her to chop off her own father! I must stop using that word 'chop': so plebian . . .

Scene Fourteen

CONSTANTINE. I was back again in the tunnel, the dark vault of piles of paper: those who worked so busily there took one look at the appalling lazarus-mask I had brought into their midst, even they were unable to bear it. They scuttled like beetles into every adjacent recess.

Sounds of people scuttling away.

CONSTANTINE (*calls out to them*). 'Come back, come back, I must ask you a question!' But they didn't: they ran and hid. (*He calls again:*) 'Who the devil d'you think you are, to make mock of my prerogative! If you do not come back, I – I will strip you stark naked and leave you in the desert to be devoured by the wild beasts! I can do it, you know, I did it to her!'

A pause: no sound.

CONSTANTINE (*speaks to* AUDIENCE *again*). It was true, wasn't it? My son Crispus fell from heaven: such sorrow for my son, even though he were not guilty of what had been alleged, such sorrow for crucified Jesus because Jesus too was innocent and he too consented to his death at the hands of his father, or agents of his father: they knew not what they did, and neither did I. But when it came to Fausta. I now remembered every detail of it, how we stood her in the guard-room and despoiled her of her raiment, oh ritual salacity – three or four well-trusted officers of the frontier-guard who thought they were on to a good thing with this frozen-faced degraded tart whom I put into their power. That is, until the evening, when they drank their poisoned wine-ration . . . Oh, I remember that, so it must have happened, mustn't it? If it hadn't, I would have forgotten it, is not that so? Because this was Empress Fausta, murderess of her own father, who – with her hairdresser, with a mutinous fanatic soldier, long since discharged the army – had colluded to create, out of an unattributed text and a few buckets of whitewash, the very finger of Almighty God writing his sign in the sky for the entrapment of the Emperor's life. So you see, it was not to be thought of that Fausta should be kept alive, or that anyone should be kept alive, who knew what had been done with her and what it was she said.

'PAUL OF TARSUS'. You knew what she did, you always knew, and you're alive.

CONSTANTINE (*whirling around, highly disconcerted*). Am I? Who are you? By God, that's your opinion. D'you want to change places? You never killed yourself by killing your wife in such a manner! And yet there was no other way: she had to die as she had lived, like Prometheus who played with fire in disobedience to the highest word, and therefore – as with Prometheus – only the unbounded desert would witness her last agony . . . She had a choice: she could have kept silent. The truth of Christ that includes all truth, she could have held fast to: she did not have to prove that when I said 'God said to me', all I meant to say was 'if God had said to me': she wanted to show that my Christian Empire was no more than a hypothesis! The way she chose determined the choice I made for her.

'PAUL OF TARSUS'. Determined? You had no free will?

CONSTANTINE. How could I have had free will?

> What you want you must not have
> What you love you have to leave
> Freedom of choice from the hand of God
> Allows you always, choose the 'good'.
> If you prefer to choose the 'bad'.
> Then be prepared to find your freedom fled.

All those years ago, I could have chosen not to see any vision at all: my soldiers would have murdered me. And who would be Christian now? Are you Christian, who are you, where are you, I can't see you?

Noise of his frantic searching for his INTERLOCUTOR, *opening cupboard doors, drawers, pulling things off shelves: there is a rapid scuttling sound.*

I tracked him by the noise he made, all muffled from the waste paper, ah, there was a cloud of cobweb – I caught him as you'd catch a mouse!

Sounds of the catching.

CONSTANTINE. Indeed he was no larger: a squirming tom-thumb manikin. I wedged him very carefully into an empty inkpot – there you are, stay there, and let's have a look at you!

Scene Fifteen

Exterior: on board a ship, in pleasant weather.

HELEN (*exultation: to herself*). Helen has done it, Helen has proved it, the whole world knows who is in charge! Lord Jesus Son of God, who died on the cross in Jerusalem to save mankind! Jerusalem is now ready for the Second Coming, the Church of the Holy Sepulchre, the Church at Bethlehem, the Church on the Mount of Olives. The cross has been found, the nails have been found – one of them will go into the bridle of the Emperor's horse and the prophecy of Zechariah will be fulfilled: 'In that day there shall be upon the bells of the horses, Holiness Unto The Lord!' Why is it an old ignorant woman like me should have had to do all this? Had the Bishops been stronger, they could have done it themselves, they could have torn down that Venus-temple on Golgotha, they could have found the cross! Of course the heathens and Jews crept in together to suppress historic truth and muddle everyone up. But the Lord God understands me, understands what I had to do . . . (*A brief pause.*) And he will forgive me . . . There I was in Jerusalem, working behind the bar, I had made sure that no one knew me, I was just a humble pilgrim earning my keep like many another –

Cross-fade.

Scene Sixteen

Interior: An inn. Buzz of conversation: HELEN *laughing gaily at some retort.*

HELEN (*to herself*). – everything was very happy and jolly, people were freely talking to me and telling me all the stories. I had noticed the Jew in his corner the very moment he walked in. I knew exactly what sort he was.

LANDLORD (*whispered explanation*). A Hebrew scholar, he knows everything there is to be known about the history of this city –

HEBREW SCHOLAR (*dogmatically: he is a middle-aged man*). There is nothing more ridiculous than old women who neglect their husbands and children to give heed to false lips as a liar giveth heed to a naughty tongue.

The buzz resumes this time in excitement, what will HELEN say?

HELEN (*roused*). Do you say that I lie when I tell you Jesus died, on the cross, in this city? Do you say that I heed lies when I am told that the cross is still here, in this city, and may be found by diligent search? Seek and you shall find – it is written –

HEBREW SCHOLAR (*denunciatory*). Yes – it is written – 'I am the Lord thy God, thou shalt have no other gods before me!' And whosoever writes that a crucified man in this city was another god, a second god, indeed number two of as many as three gods, I say such a blasphemy was the work of heathen power to annihilate the Chosen People. Jesus of Nazareth, illegitimate son of a Roman soldier who persecuted us, he died, and was buried, there is a cross, it can be found – so why wasn't it? Every day I see the people going in and out about their business and walking on the very spot: no thunderbolt from God to strike them dead for their impudence? [So it cannot be a god's cross, can it?]

HELEN (*to herself*). And so, on and on, continuous diatribe, but I had heard what I wanted to hear. There was a wooden cross, and he knew where it was! Why hadn't there been a thunderbolt? I gave him a thunderbolt. I made a sign to some of my people who were quietly placed at the back of the room – they fell to their knees –

HELEN's *concealed* ATTENDANTS *prostrate themselves.*

CONCEALED ATTENDANTS.
               All hail to Helen Augusta, Mother of Constantine,
               Grandmother of
               All the Caesars!

Panic-struck sensation.

HELEN (*triumphant, to the whole room*). One minute I'm a barmaid, next minute I'm an Empress, thunderbolt enough I should have thought. Put him in irons and take him to the garrison!

Scuffle as HEBREW SCHOLAR *is removed.*

HELEN. He'll tell me what I want to know.

Cross-fade.

Scene Seventeen

Exterior: on board the ship again.

HELEN (*to herself*). He tried to keep silent, but we tortured him until he talked. And when we dug under the goddess-temple, we found a tomb: and God himself guided me to find the wood of the True Cross! Why, I could touch it . . .! A dumping-ground for all the old rubbish of what had been the execution site, the best-preserved of the ancient timbers was obviously the one . . . it had to be proved, by miracle. It was proved by miracle. I found a sick woman, I found a doctor to guarantee her sickness was cured by being touched with the wood. I found a magistrate to pass a death-sentence upon the Hebrew scholar for his insult to the Mother of Jesus, his insult to religion, his insult to the Emperor. (*Her voice trembles for a moment.*) His blood upon my head, upon the heads of my children . . . It was expedient that one man should lay down his life for the truth . . .

Scene Eighteen

Exterior: the desert. A camel caravan is proceeding. The CAMEL-MASTER *walks down the line, calling out instructions.*

MELANTHO (*as narrator*). While Dowager Helen scrabbled among ruins, desperate to uncover some sign of Imperial unity, across the desert to the south two women were in flight from the fierce edge of her blood-stained shovel. Semiramis the hairdresser, and myself, Melantho, who had brought her back to life, and thereafter lost my child. I gave the child to my mother, I do not know where she is: I believed we had the protection of Fausta the Empress; Fausta has now gone out of all knowledge of everyone.

CAMEL-MASTER. Pilgrims, listen! We are about to arrive at the oasis of the pillar-saint –

MELANTHO (*to herself*). Only Semiramis knows, with the certainty of true heart's love, that Joachim her man lives somewhere in this burning solitude –

SEMIRAMIS. If not in this place, then the next, if not there then the next after that, until we come to the edge of the ocean –

CAMEL-MASTER. Those who have booked for the round trip to the Flagellators, the Fasters, the Grass-eaters, the Silent Female Anchorites, and the Marvel of the Naked Levitators on the Holy Mountain – please do not let your slaves stray! Camels will not wait . . .

Some laughter at his witticism.

CAMEL-MASTER. A caution for Roman citizens! We are now out of your jurisdiction and some of what you will hear will be seditious and punishable by death if repeated inside the Empire.

An 'ooh' of excited apprehension from PILGRIMS.

CAMEL-DRIVER (*confidential, to those on his beast*). In plain words, lords and good ladies, safer for you to leave no money or gifts here, but save all resources and curiosity for the Anchorites who do not speak . . .

1st LADY PILGRIM. Isn't it exciting? – are you going to get down? – just to say we've had a look at them – these are the malcontents and some of them are common criminals!

2ND LADY PILGRIM (*on the same camel*). Oh no, my hair – I can't be seen looking like this!

1ST LADY PILGRIM. The slave-girl is doing her mistress's hair over there – why don't we ask her to tidy up ours?

PILGRIM (*male, on another camel*). Hercules! – I mean, Lord Jesus! – that slave-girl is cutting all of her own hair off!

SEMIRAMIS (*on a third camel: calling to the* LADIES). Madam, if you want a new hair-style, take my plait and add it to your head! Freedom in Christ means freedom from slavery to every strand of hair. (*She and Melantho, who is sharing the same camel, laugh.*)

MELANTHO. Semiramis, give me the scissors: I'll cut off mine as well . . .

Cross-fade to denote passage of time.

Scene Nineteen

Exterior: the desert. The camel still proceeding. The voice of JOACHIM *in the distance, getting louder as they approach him.*

JOACHIM (*chanting over and over*). Welcome to my bride Semiramis, welcome to the Daughters of Christ . . .!

The camels come to a halt and the PILGRIMS *begin to dismount.*

SEMIRAMIS (*in great excitement*). Oh Melantho – it is Joachim – up there, look – Joachim is the Pillar Saint, look at him waving and dancing on top –!

MELANTHO (*sharing her excitement*). Run to him – run to him –

SEMIRAMIS. I can't – everyone is looking at us – everyone is staring –

MELANTHO. All of his holy companions are waving and singing at the base of his pillar-stone. Go to him – go to your beloved –

JOACHIM'*s chant has been augmented by the voices (male and female) of his* COMPANION-SAINTS.

JOACHIM (*a new chant*). Make haste my beloved and be thou like to a young doe upon the mountains of spices – many waters cannot quench love, neither can the floods drown it!

COMPANION SAINTS (*chanting*). Make haste, make haste – beloved –!

MELANTHO (*half-laughing, half-crying-out in alarm*). He's preparing to jump – oh the lunatic, he's jumping – no –!

A great shout as JOACHIM *jumps.*

SEMIRAMIS (*running towards him*). He is floating in the air and I am floating to meet him –

His running feet coming towards hers.

SEMIRAMIS (*calling out to him*). I am my beloved's and his desire is toward me –!

They meet in a great embrace.

JOACHIM. To feed in the gardens and to gather lilies, I am my beloved's and my beloved is mine!

There is applause from EVERYONE.

JOACHIM (*calls to the company*). Let everyone here give thanks to God and to the Lady of Wisdom: these women have defied the tyranny of Rome!

Some of the ROMAN PILGRIMS *catch their breath in alarm.*

GENERAL CRY. Hallelujah, Christ is risen!

Cross-fade to denote passage of time.

Scene Twenty

Exterior: the desert.

JOACHIM (*in quiet conversation*). Semiramis, Melantho, tonight I will preach. And then we dance. To keep warm – it's very cold here after sunset. Melantho – may I thank you –?

SEMIRAMIS. Joachim, we owe our love to Melantho. Melantho, do not weep.

MELANTHO. I am not staying, my mother left a message here, she has returned to Ur of the Chaldees with my daughter Helen-Fausta: there were too many police-agents at Batnae because of the visit of Eutropia, and she feared for the safety of the child. She has arranged for one of the camels to take me straight to Ur. So farewell.

> We are stretched, we three as we are here
> The three at this place in the centre of the crossroads
> We turn and look where we came from
> We are facing east west north
> What is the thread that we can weave
> What colour
> What pattern
> What cloth
> What purpose
> That we three are here –?

SEMIRAMIS.
> What purpose? Love.
> Love is the water, the heart is the well
> Drink, and you shall live
> Vomit it out and you will shrivel.
> Melantho, you gave me life: I give you my love for eternity
> In a circle that can never break
> We are enclosed within the sky and earth
> We are each and we are one like the earth and sky
> We are mother and daughter, we are the child we are the
>   adult
> Joachim is the father and the son
> He is the child and he is the adult
> We are the earth and the sky.

What follows is a kind of light ritual-round, which SEMIRAMIS *and* MELANTHO *are well familiar with, while* JOACHIM *catches its purport as they speak.*

SEMIRAMIS. We are the air we are the water.

MELANTHO. ⎫ We are the air we are the water.
SEMIRAMIS. ⎭ We are the earth we are the sea.

MELANTHO. ⎫ We are the earth we are the sea.
SEMIRAMIS. ⎭ We are the bird we are the fish.

MELANTHO. ⎫ We are the bird we are the fish.
SEMIRAMIS. ⎭ We are the tree we are the seed.

MELANTHO. ⎫   We are the tree we are the seed.
SEMIRAMIS. ⎭   We are the day we are the night.

MELANTHO. We are the day we are the night.

JOACHIM. We are the storm we are the calm.
          We are the struggle we are the peace.

MELANTHO. ⎫   We are the life and we are the death.
SEMIRAMIS. ⎭   We are the pain and we are the happiness.

MELANTHO, SEMIRAMIS, JOACHIM. We are the one and we are the all.

A pause.

SEMIRAMIS (*suddenly*). Melantho – look! Between the sun and the sand, glimmering, glittering, moving into shapes, two shapes, flickering toward us – smiling –

MELANTHO (*seeing them too*). I see the shape of Fausta, and Mary the Companion, hand-in-hand – in her other hand Mary is holding her severed tongue, and her tongueless mouth is open and smiling . . . They are huge as the sky . . . and now they have passed through us. It is a sign of peace.

Cross-fade to denote passage of time.

Scene Twenty-One

Exterior: the desert. JOACHIM *is preaching (not from his pillar) and his hearers echo his phrases with 'hallelujah!' 'Amen Amen' 'Hear him oh Lord', etcetera, at intervals.*

JOACHIM. The blind and the lame, the oppressed and the dispossessed, we are the ones who fought for the truth of Jesus, the poor shall inherit the earth, love one another . . . And yet, the Greco-Romans of Nicaea have branded us as heretics! In the words of their tyrannical languages: 'pedagogic and cultural hegemony!' They will not permit the rendering of the holy creed into our tongues, Arabic, Syriac, Hebrew, Coptic, Armenian, Persian – and why not? Because they know 'homo-ousios, homoi-ousios' is an untranslateable semantic ballocks – the difference of a letter 'i', whether to obey Rome or defy Rome, an eye for an 'I'', tooth for a tooth – Anathema upon Constantine, who brought Christ into his Empire to crucify him anew – we of the Arabian desert look neither to Rome nor to Persia, let us swear to be true to the one true God and to be true to our own people – Hallelujah, Christ is risen, there is but one God and Christ is his prophet!

Acclamation and repetition of his last phrase. During the address, the camel with MELANTHO *has been started up by its driver, and* JOACHIM's *voice recedes.*

CAMEL-DRIVER. Lady, the friend you left behind must be most extraordinary special to the saint to have got him down from aloft. There are times in his ravings I do detect a sensible meaning: 'Look neither to Rome nor to Persia'? I bring you into Persia, I have heard nothing good of King Shapur. Burdened as we are, we are the people of the desert, we need our own prophet, to open for us this heaven, yes, even for camel-drivers –

The camel is refractory and he pulls its head about.

Even for you, you brute, even for camels – ah, son of a scavenger – would you bite your own master?

MELANTHO (*as narrator*). As I rode away the shape of Fausta passed into nothing amid the stars of the desert night. But Mary was still with me, and sometimes she was the camel-driver, sometimes the camel, sometimes just the wisps of sand caught up by the camel's hooves: but always she was words of comfort for my loneliness and apprehension.

Noises of camel's progress over stony shale and gritty sand, and of the DRIVER *grunting to the animal continue intermittently.*

MARY (*speaking as it were in* MELANTHO's *mind*). When they threw you away to work your magic for the scornful and the ignorant, you knew not who you were: only your child was your life. Beyond her you had no understanding. Now you have lost her, you are yourself alone. And even when you find her, you will still be yourself. Because once they threw me away: I can remember unhappiness . . . but also the moment when I – when I – became – I:

> I: strange sound: my self:
> That I should be noticed
> I: loved and cherished, for evermore.
> Can I believe that I
> I open my mouth and
> Whisper: louder, Melantho, louder
> I am
> Shouting with happiness
> I burst with joy, am full,
> My heart – I feel – I am –
> I run and jump –

MELANTHO (*as narrator*). And the camel sped on and on until the trail to Ur of the Chaldees seemed no longer than half a league . . .

Fade.

Scene Twenty-Two

CONSTANTINE. So he sat in the inkwell, with his tiny bald head, his little sharp black eyes blinking as though he could not endure the candle-light. He smiled and began to tell me. His name was Paul of Tarsus: he and I had talked before, so he said – I didn't remember. [He was a Roman citizen, so he said: he was a Jew, so he said. None of this was provable:] but I let him twitter away. He was the only one present not afraid to take infection from me, I was glad in my self-disgust to indulge him.

'PAUL OF TARSUS'. So you knew there was nothing in the sky above Rome
> [But your own self-induced wife-induced dream
> Of policy and craft. Thereby you were led
> To the height of divine mastery, why not call it God?]
> Don't think I don't know you know: I knew it too.

CONSTANTINE. You knew it . . .? The Damascus road. Are you saying that was fraud? If indeed you are Paul –

'PAUL OF TARSUS'. Not provable at all.
> Oh make no assumption.
> But you have my assertion
> I am at least a hypothesis:
> And as such I tell you this –

You want to know did I ever meet Jesus of Nazareth? The answer is 'no'. [I was in Tarsus most of that time. And I always took good care to avoid all involvement with violence.] For whatever he might have been, a great number of his friends were very closely implicated in subversive organisations. His family totally implicated: all those brothers. Every police-list in the archive. Put your hand up, grab that dossier.

A bundle of documents being pulled open.

CONSTANTINE. A shower of mouldering papers spilt down over my lap.

He leafs them through.

'PAUL OF TARSUS'. Page after page, what have we got? [James, Joses, Jude, Simeon – sons of the carpenter Joseph – look at their associates – Simon the Zealot, Judas the Daggerman –

CONSTANTINE. Daggerman?

'PAUL OF TARSUS'. Iscariot, the Barabbas-tendency, Sicarius, a most notorious terrorist faction. Why else would the security-forces have enlisted him as an informant? He gave them the names of Barabbas and two confederates: he also gave them Jesus.] On that page – alleged reason for Barabbas's release –

CONSTANTINE. 'Identity not established'?

'PAUL OF TARSUS'. That was only Pilate's fudging to reassure the Emperor: you're an Emperor, you should know . . .

CONSTANTINE. As he talked I became aware he was gradually getting larger and larger: at least his head was. His body grew more slowly.

His voice is growing too: until it reaches the volume at which we have heard it in previous plays.

'PAUL OF TARSUS'. Barabbas as a name is ambiguous: 'son-of-the-father'. It was the name of a man, it was also the name of a very dangerous tendency. Likewise: Jesus. Jesus means 'deliverance': it was a movement before there was ever a man. It has been claimed there never was a man. But someone was crucified. And his name in fact was Jesus. Because of his name the movement thrust him forward, till he came to believe himself preternaturally set apart. Within the movement, at least four factions. First: the women. [Attainment of total liberty through infiltration of female power] – they traced it back to Lilith, first bride of the first Adam: [potent in legend, though deleted from official scripture. They accepted the masculine Jesus-title, so the Jews would not condemn them as Babylonish heathen. A floating charisma, immeasurable nothing: refusal to accept, not only the ancient law, not only the priesthood, not only the Romans, but every possible point of discipline that keeps the human race upon two legs instead of four!] You'll understand I had no time for them. But they were important. They operated the safe-houses, carried messages, provided money. And held the whole movement together. Next: the nationalist militants, including the brothers of Jesus. And then, third: the Galileans, Peter the Fisherman, his family-colleagues, an agrarian agitation [for some sort of autonomous theocratic small-farmers' republic, abolition of exorbitant taxes not only to the State but the temple-establishment.] Finally, the spiritual-pacifist crowd: links with John the Baptist and a part of the Essene community. Simon the Magician as well. Their relations with Jesus exceedingly secretive: a mystery-cult in point of fact.

CONSTANTINE. [Simon the Magician adhered to the woman-worship?

'PAUL OF TARSUS'. Worship of one woman, to catch lascivious men. Not orthodox Jewish men, but the outcaste subject-rabble, Palestinians, who'd infested the land since long before Moses. Simon's partner, Mary Magdalene, had contacts with the other women, maybe she was working to set up her own caucus.] What was it, out of all of this, put one small Jesus, almost anonymous, onto the cross: and amazingly preserved his memory? Scarcely what he said. 'Little children love one another' . . .? Nor what he did. He had his healing powers, he used them discreetly, and so did scores of others and nobody arrested them. [There was a botched attempt at a coup in Jerusalem the last week of his life. Perhaps him, perhaps Barabbas. Jesus did tell his friends to bring swords when they went out to Gethsemane: but d'you know, the bloody fools could only muster two of them? But] in truth he was condemned, not for himself, but for the vast symbolic vagueness of the numbers associated with his name – even the Greeks were getting interested. Which is why it was such a frame-up, why they couldn't risk a show-trial, why Pilate's report to Caesar was so evasive.

CONSTANTINE (*finding another document*). He told Tiberius that Jesus was a king . . .?

'PAUL OF TARSUS'. So he was: king of the beggars. But Pilate meant Tiberius to understand the Jesus-movement as a small romantic sect with an atavistic attachment to the long-lost House of David: and therefore trivial. [No proper trial, Pilate dealt with the case in private: and handled the demonstrators, pro and con, with his craftiest diplomacy. Divide-and-rule, give 'em a choice, Jesus or Barabbas? The hard men all cried for Barabbas. The clergy went along with them because they knew Barabbas hostile to the Galilean separatists, and they held Jesus responsible for a riot in the temple the previous week. So: a routine summary-conviction, to be shuffled into the Colonial Office among heaps of irrelevant paper.] But despite all Pilate's fudging, the Rebellion did come: thirty-odd years later: and after it –

CONSTANTINE. – Jesus was a king at last: a king and a god, but not a Jew. Tell me.

'PAUL OF TARSUS'. Who made him a god?

CONSTANTINE. You did?

'PAUL OF TARSUS'. Ha, in a sense . . . No: it began at Pentecost, before I reached Jerusalem. Mary Magdalene called a secret meeting in the usual safe house, and [leaders of various groups, those who had not already defected, came timidly, furtively, to see could they not, just possibly, rebuild a little something of collective Jesus. And the women, exultant, courageous, cried out to them: 'No need! He is alive, and we are him! Stay with us now or forget it for ever.' And then Mary Magdalene] broke the news: the tomb, she said, was empty. The others had not heard of it, some of them – in their shock – were muttering, 'Miracle, miracle' but Magdalene insisted she claimed no miracle: [unless it was that seven weeks ago she had been crushed with terror and now she was afraid of nothing.] But miracle had been stated: how long d'you think before Jesus-people everywhere were believing they had seen him, in a room, on a roadside, by a lake, in the mist on the Mount of Olives . . .?

CONSTANTINE. You didn't believe it?

'PAUL OF TARSUS'. I couldn't contradict it. Even if I'd wanted to. I simply observed its consequences. It should have produced unity: instead – a few days of intense hysteria, followed by total disruption. James, the brother of Jesus, demanded Jesus' place at the head of the movement, his male kinfolk to be installed as co-adjutors. He fought and intrigued for it, like Jehu, like Samuel. The women opposed him, arguing that the leadership had never been more than an emblematic token, that all of them if they chose could call themselves Jesus, and many of them had, including Barabbas himself. [The temple-riot had been led by Jesus, only in-so-far as he was in the forefront, riding on a donkey, dressed-up in his gauds and greenery. He was their carnival king because lots had been cast for the privilege. Had they foreseen such disaster for their endeavour to reclaim for true religion the ancient altar-stone of Lilith – if that is what they thought they were doing – not even the simple Jesus would have been brave enough to serve their turn. And in any case, where was James that day? If it came to that, where was Barabbas?] For months after Pentecost the quarrels got worse and worse. Why, they even began killing each other. The mysterious deaths of Ananias and Sapphira, Peter perhaps responsible. A Greek called Stephen murdered: lay that to the account of James and his Jewish bigots, his surreptitious temple-gate militia.

CONSTANTINE. Did not you, in regard to Stephen –?

'PAUL OF TARSUS' (*swiftly interrupting*). I was in Jerusalem [as a craftsman, as a student:] I had a small commission from the Governor of Syria to check subversive groups against Pilate's dodgy reports. So I had begun to infiltrate. My teacher, Rabbi Gamaliel, was himself implicated, he was a friend of James. Yes, yes, in regard to Stephen . . . I found myself caught up in the fanatical mob that lynched him. I received such a sense of – of

CONSTANTINE. Even though he was already the same size as I was, even though he was still increasing himself, what I saw resembled a furious raging insect: my own limbs vibrated for the very proximity –

'PAUL OF TARSUS'. So fatuous, so futile, his passion against their passion – and all in the name of Jesus – deliverance, salvation . . .! Was the name misconceived, or the purpose misconceived . . .? Analyse both amend both: maybe there was still a hope. But first, find out *my* purpose: what did I want to do? Oh I will be frank with you: in the heart of my heart I wanted to replace James. And when Peter and James quarrelled, to replace Peter as well. I desired to free Jerusalem, I desired to be the king that crucified Jesus could never have been! I became indispensable to James, he sent me to Damascus, to see could I purge, purify, Judify, what there was of the movement up there . . .

CONSTANTINE. Ah and so we come to it, you invented a vision –!

'PAUL OF TARSUS' (*his passion temporarily abated*). So easy . . . if I had done . . . but not quite . . . I met a man, upon the road, in a thunderstorm, he said his name was Jesus, he showed me the wounds in his hands and his feet. Oh they were real wounds. Whoever he was, he had been on a gallows-cross: and ruined by it. He could hardly talk: [I just understood him to be begging for his bread.] The coincidence of the name: the empty tomb: could it be the same man, he had come out of it alive? [Or – or – could he – was he –? (*His voice begins to shake.*)

> It would not be the first time
> A dead man had walked and talked.
> A murdered man come back to haunt
> The enemies who killed him
> The friends who let him die
> The calumniators who traduced his life.
> It was as though a waterfall
> Was running into my eye
> It was as though a basilisk
> Was grappling at my throat:
> He tried to talk to me
> And all I could do was shout –!

No no, for *my* purposes he had to be dead! I heard my servants come up running . . . and that was it. Later on they told me I had had an epileptic fit, or perhaps been struck by lightning: but the beggarman was gone, the road was quite empty. And I was stone-blind. It took me years to recover. Out into the desert: I needed to think, think, think.

Scene Twenty-Three

Exterior: An encampment. A processional hymn is being sung, with cymbals and oriental flutes etc., coming towards us from a little way off.

MELANTHO (*as narrator*). Ur of the Chaldees was all in ruins. My mother, Oenothea the Priestess seemed to be the only inhabitant – except for the scores of holy men and holy women who processed among the tumbled walls carrying images, carrying banners, singing hymns –

HYMN (*behind dialogue*).

> 'O Queen of heaven and earth, how long how long
> O Shepherdess of pale-faced men, how long how long
> How long will you tarry, O Queen of the unwearied feet

> How long will you tarry, O Lady of Battle, O Lady of Hosts?
> How long how long how long . . .'
> (*Etc. with musical variations.*)

MELANTHO (*as narrator*). – and where was my daughter? (*Aloud: as she pushes into the procession, disrupting the rhythmn of the singing somewhat:*)

> Mother: what have you done with her?
> Where is Helen Fausta?

OENOTHEA (*abruptly, pulling* MELANTHO *out of the crowd again*). Irrelevant question, to interrupt my festival. Look at them, Melantho, look who have come to me, all the leaders of the Eastern Sects, the Manichees, the Bardesanites, the Reformed Jews of the Old Exile, the Nazarenes of Christ Rejected, all here to give honour to the birthplace of Abraham and Sarah: but which of them ought I to trust? That is the only question that needs to be put today.

MELANTHO (*urgently*). I left the child with you to be returned safe into my arms: if you had kept your trust she would be standing here beside you – I ask you again, where is she?!

The hymn has now trailed to a conclusion and there is a buzz of talk among the SECT-LEADERS.

1ST SECT-LEADER (*a woman*). I say we have no choice but to accept Oenothea's plans.

3RD SECT-LEADER (*a man*). What plans? We have sung the hymns all this week and marched round and danced and made prayers in accordance with her ritual: but we have not yet made alliances.

2ND SECT-LEADER (*a woman*). She has brought us here to consolidate opposition to the bigotry of the Persian King Shapur and his priests of Zoroaster. She is the only one to understand that every free cult east of Euphrates is in an immediate danger.

3RD SECT-LEADER. We are safer here than under Constantine. Oenothea has Shapur in her pocket.

1ST SECT-LEADER. So she says: but some of these others are in the pocket of Zoroaster. I say we must make alliances.

2ND SECT-LEADER. With whom? Do you trust the Jews?

3RD SECT-LEADER. Do you trust the Armenians?

1ST SECT-LEADER. Do you trust the followers of Bardesanes?

2ND SECT-LEADER. Or the followers of Mani?

1ST SECT-LEADER. Or the followers of Oenothea? Since when was Oenothea a devotee of Father Abraham?

3RD SECT-LEADER. Since the day she found out that Abraham's wife was his mother, and that Sarah was another name for Anna her own goddess.

2ND SECT-LEADER. Which may or may not be true. But it is the only root for our unity.

The above dialogue is spoken in low tones and listened to by other SECT-LEADERS, *who make disturbed noises of agreement.* OENOTHEA *is still justifying herself to* MELANTHO, *at a little distance.*

OENOTHEA. Melantho, I sent you letters, I sent you letter after letter – Helen Fausta's life was in danger and she took her safety into her own hands, she went in caravan to China with a merchant of Hindustan –

MELANTHO (*gives an exclamation of horror*).

OENOTHEA. 'Wist ye not' – I repeat her words – Wist ye not that I must be about my Mother's business . . .?'

MELANTHO (*furious*). Liar! You sold her to the merchant!

OENOTHEA (*unabashed*). He gave me money, yes: a guarantee for her safe return.

MELANTHO. The sight and the light of my life – and you have given me nothing but desert desert desert.

Fade.

Scene Twenty-Four

'PAUL OF TARSUS'. I had been a child, I thought as a child, now I put from me childish things . . . Jesus in the flesh had been, perhaps still was, a groping inarticulate victim, [a suffering servant, buffeted between the cross-purposes of his own people, his own contradictions, to the miserable height of six feet of timber, three nails and a crown of thorns.] But Jesus beyond the flesh could be cogent past all imagining, could catch and transform the hopeless dreams of people who knew nothing about Judaea, Palestine, Abraham, Moses, or even Lilith. [What happened in his life – for the time being, forget about it. It will always be possible to establish that later, once we have certified who he is, how he is, now, today, in the further world.] The further world becomes our world, we live only in that dimension . . . Who needs to be a king? My power, I now saw, would be the unchallengeable true power which would make me [the suffering servant of the suffering servant, on the road to my own Golgotha, yes. But I would have friends, successors, loyal men to watch me die. And so I did! When I died, I was able to remember how Herod died, Tiberius died, Caligula died, Claudius, all of them in such nightmare horror for the blood of their own blood that smeared them like a leprosy: whereas I was] the Thirteenth Apostle, if it hadn't been for me there'd have been no Apostles at all!

CONSTANTINE. You the Thirteenth? *Me!*

'PAUL OF TARSUS'. In that case we are one and the same, we are part of each other? I told you I was only a hypothesis . . .

Fade.

Scene Twenty-Five

Exterior: the encampment.

MELANTHO [(*Angrily*). Mother, you have stolen and sold my child, and given me nothing but desert, a city in ruins, and a crumbling dangerous cave which you expect us all to crawl into, telling us this is Abraham's birthplace, the mother's womb of all religions, and therefore it is your womb and every priestess and priestling of the sect has a share in it – except me –

OENOTHEA. Oh, but you do have a share in it –

MELANTHO. Oh no I do not and I never did, never, since you threw me away and sold me as a child just the same way as you sell my child –]

OENOTHEA. Come quietly, come quietly, daughter, to the edge of the river, the second greatest river of the world, Euphrates, is she older than Nile?

As OENOTHEA *talks she leads* MELANTHO *away from the others and we shortly hear the run of the river and the wind in the rushes on its bank.*

I think she must be, because it is from the Nile that I am led here, and where would I be led if not to the very beginning? Let me tell you about sale and purchase. I was born near the mouths of the Nile, Alexandria, the temple of Isis, Queen of All Things, Mother of One Hundred Names. My Mother was her servant, she gave her virginity to the Goddess, and so, when my day came, did I. I was the only one of the temple maidens to be so honoured upon that day – I shared it with nobody, it was mine. They put the garland on my head, the white robe upon my body, they sat me down at the top of the steps and I looked out over the haven. I waited for him to come. He might have been anyone: he was not. He was a Prince. From Nubia, black and beautiful, tall as a tower, in a golden turban, with his slaves and his soldiers, they held over his head an umbrella of scarlet, they blew horns to proclaim his arrival. He stood in front of me in the glaring sun, he bowed his head and smiled: 'Hail Isis . . .,' he said. At that moment, I was Isis . . . And when he came the next day, did he ask again for me? He did not. He wanted only another new virgin. I said to my mother, 'This is no temple but a brothel-house, Isis has deceived me!' She answered me, yes: we had one duty, survive: and one hope, our search for the truth of the goddess. I survived, and I searched. And my darling black child brought me money for my search. In the communal riots when Jews and Christians rampaged together and the temple was burnt and all the women driven out on the streets, I should have starved had I not been able to get a price for you from an army contractor. I saved your life, I saved my own, and now Helen-Fausta is saving both of them again. [Here is her gift to us, this ancient shrine restored, this dust-choked garden newly-irrigated, this – see the vine, see the fig-tree – *I* brought the water to them. And we can bring the water everywhere, just as it was before.] When Abraham in the old story went out of this city to betray his goddess-wife and commence a cruel fierce nation all upon his own, he left behind him the –

MELANTHO. I am so sick of your stories, [I am sick of all the stories, your dream of an unspoiled goddess who has nothing to give humanity but all the same old lies we have always been hearing –]

OENOTHEA. I said, he left behind him the first civilisation the world ever knew, and that is not a story [– you in Nicomedia, eating your grapes and olives – it was here they were first produced, and that is no story, and] I am going to do it again! From the success of my festival I will be able to pay for the entire irrigation, for new hydraulic engines, for –

MELANTHO. Stop drivelling, Mother! Irrigation! What happened to the irrigation? The armies of the Medes, the armies of the Chaldeans, the armies of the Persians, the armies of Alexander – why, the first thing they did was to break the irrigation, trample all over it – do you really think that King Shapur and Constantine, marching through with their regiments in the name of religion, are going to say, 'Oenothea's little patch, we must leave her dream for Oenothea . . .?' Mother, they will leave you nothing, nothing but dry dust. With Helen-Fausta, I had a religion, I had a future, and you have ruined it. What have I got now? Except myself: and this much I know for certain – my self is not you.

OENOTHEA. No: but it is a dream. It is a dream upon two legs, and despite all your anger, I think you are aware of it.

MELANTHO. If I am, I refuse to let wicked people like you destroy it.

OENOTHEA. Melantho, I do not destroy dreams, I use them, I go and do what has to be done. [Helen-Fausta is not dead: think of her contacts, her influence, as far away as China, to help us feed the people, clothe them, look after them –] who is hungry, even here? Is it wicked to grow food? But the dangerous vain old men who have turned the dreams of the poor into immortality for themselves so that they can rule the world and leave the people to starve – that Melantho, is wickedness!

MELANTHO (*to herself*). They cut the tongue out of my friend Mary because she dared to denounce the vain old men. Must I, as my mother's daughter, carry Mary's voice in this desolate land?

MARY (*her voice seeming to come out of the wind in the bullrushes*). They shall beat

their swords into ploughshares, and their spears into pruning hooks: nation shall not
lift up sword against nation, neither shall they learn war any more . . .

Scene Twenty-Six

'PAUL OF TARSUS'. . . . Half-Jew, half-Greek, I went out to the Jews of the
Dispersion. They had evolved what was more or less a new religion, it lacked one
ingredient, Jesus: and I provided it. [My intuition was fulfilled. From every feuding
group of the original Jesus-people I found men and women just as I was, sick unto
death with the discordance. No longer necessary to argue such nonsense as who had
been where the day Jesus entered the temple – in the living Christ we had our unity
because] the living Christ, being dead, could not contradict us with his human
contradictions.

CONSTANTINE. But you were contradicted?

'PAUL OF TARSUS'. I was opposed, by meagre persons who still had hope for their
own small power. [Simon the Magician: we caught up with him in Rome, Peter and
myself, friends again after all contention, we harried him without mercy and we
cornered him at last. But] the women were the worst, because the fluidity of their
method most nearly approached my own, [they had houses-of-call everywhere from
Antioch to Corinth; if I could use them, most useful to my travellings: but they
were utterly without conception of eschatological complexity, doctrinal definition,
the essential unbridgeable abyss between carnal liberty and divine freedom –]

> In Corinth their witless hilarity
> Would have suffocated all spirituality:
> Except I came back on them through the postbag like thunder
> Scorching with my words their frail tinder
> Into flame till it burnt itself quite out.
> In Pisidia they threw stones, women said to be devout,
> Honourable, but howling me like Bacchanals through the gap
>   of the town-gate –
> And when I went to Iconium, when I went to Derbe,
> There they were again, they were lying in wait
> With the great lie in their mouths that I was the liar,
> I was the persecutor, I was the murderer, coals of fire
> And thrown stones upon the head of Paul because they said I
>   stood and cheered
> When the stones flew at the head of Stephen and the blood
>   ran down his beard –

Envying, strife, divisions, some indeed said 'I am of Paul': but others said 'I am of
Apollos' and 'I am of Peter', and some even said they were not of Paul but were of
Christ –

> How could they be Christians of Christ but not of Paul?
> [From the gloom of my gaolhouse in Rome,
> With the iron spike of my invincible pen, Oh I fell
> Upon them, Samson, Hercules, half-blind and five foot tall!
> And, Emperor, you know: because you helped me do it:
> I overwhelmed them one and all . . .!]

CONSTANTINE. He was by now a mighty rushing wind, filling and fragmenting the
whole building with his gigantic turbulence . . .

Sound as of a whirlwind. It falls silent.

CONSTANTINE. And then: the still small voice.

A child's voice, singing 'La la la . . .' most beautifully.

CONSTANTINE. A clear sky, a white cloud, like a man's hand, out of the sea . . . I pulled myself, exhausted, to the cliff-top: I was burning all over with bubbles and blisters, my very feet were rotting off, my shoes reeked with what was in them.

The CHILD's *song is continuing: now with several* CHILDRENS' *voices, and words added:*

SONG.
'La la lalala la, la la lala
Oh why does the Emperor
Look like a putrid fish?
And where's the sauce to sweeten him
If we laid him in a dish?
La la lalala la, la la lala,'
(*Etc . . .*)

CONSTANTINE. On the edge of the cliff, an altar, twelve stones and a trench, and wood for a burnt sacrifice, and a fire ready to kindle. My sister, and the mother of Fausta – they shifted, like wind over water – and the third was *my* mother. She picked up the beast of sacrifice. It was human, thin and helpless, its long black hair fell down over my mother's arms.

EUTROPIA. Helen-Fausta, angel-child, beloved of heaven, born under the stars in the falling snow, for there was no room at the Inn.

CONSTANTIA. Jesus with the face of Herod has sought all ways to have her killed: to drive out the power of the woman. She seems dead but she yet liveth.

HELEN. My son, eat and drink: she is cleft into portions to cleanse the world and to cleanse you.

A pause.

CONSTANTINE (*tones of horror*). In my mother's hand the knife, dripping red from division of sacrifice. Beside her, a silver bowl, full to the brim, dark red, purple. I had sucked, I had swallowed . . . I turned my eyes to the sea, my feet to the sea, I ran out into the water . . .

We hear his feet, running, and the waves of the sea, getting louder as he nears them.

CONSTANTINE. I waded out, swam out, scrambled up into this boat – an old battered fishing-boat.

Sounds of the sea and a MAN *scrambling into a boat.*

CONSTANTINE. He sat in the stern. Held up his hands. Nail-holes. Showed me his features, all broken by the blows of soldiers. I asked him – was it true? – how to prove it to be true –? (*His voice is agonised as he puts the question.*) I don't think he could speak, he had been so mistreated. Behind me on the cliff the women were calling –

HELEN, CONSTANTIA, EUTROPIA (*a far-off cry*). How long, how long, Constantine?

HELEN (*continuing the cry alone*). How long, Constantine, halt ye between two opinions –?

CONSTANTINE. He looked into my eyes: answered my question with his own silent question. With no more than a question . . .? A hypothesis – even yet –? I caught him by the neck and I shook him like a rat –!

Fade out noises of sea etc.

CONSTANTINE. Out of the water, into the water: the water of forgiveness, tell the Bishop now, my baptism – now! Tell him, once I wash myself and rise up out of the pool, from then until my quickly-coming death, I will wear nothing but white linen, I will be washed I will be clean, I will be clean as a naked child laid out on the altar of sacrifice . . .

Scene Twenty-Seven

Exterior: Wind in the trees. Murmur of PEOPLE.

KYBELE. The Druid of Armagh craved revenge and compensation from the Christian God for the death of his brother. His rules and rituals had lost all application, all he could do was to kill the old women of the Christian God, and horrible! They were of his own people. But his own people outside his own land, outside his own structures: and so his own structures entrapped him . . .

The sow is gently snoring.

KYBELE. As now they entrap you! Look at the sow! She's asleep in the sun, she eats neither the acorn nor the hazel. You set her to judge me in this glade of judgement, and oh-oh she declines to comment . . . And then we must ask, why does the Druid blame me? After twelve years he comes and tells you his powers are destroyed. No. Armagh is destroyed, that great northern fortress has fallen to its enemies: and the Druid is an outcast man, using mystic accusation to account for a military loss. The Irish kingdoms are divided: but they burst with frustrated energy. The Roman Empire is divided, but fallen in upon its empty-hearted self. Who now are the vultures, who will be the corpse?

[Scene Twenty-Eight

HELEN. This old woman is tired: the people are calling me Helen of the Hosts, because I have travelled more roads of Empire than any of my son's regiments. So now let Christ the Saviour gather me into his bosom. Oh Diocletian, you were a great Emperor, but a stupid old bugger in your judgement of people. Helen the barmaid that you sent away was brought back to save the Empire! And she did it through the religion that you tried so hard to destroy . . .

Scene Twenty-Nine

Exterior: wind in the trees.

KYBELE (*as narrator*). 337 AD: Constantine on his death-bed has been publicly baptised, by the Bishop of Nicomedia, an acknowledged Arian: the Council of Nicaea has settled nothing. All his intrigues and wars, to become one sole Emperor, have likewise settled nothing. For he divided his dominions between his three surviving Christian sons, naming no one of them as single successor. The end of the story: but not the end of Empire, nor of Christianity.

Music.]